Correspondence 1930–1940

GRETEL ADORNO
AND WALTER BENJAMIN

Correspondence 1930–1940

Edited by Henri Lonitz and
Christoph Gödde
Translated by Wieland Hoban

polity

First published in German as *Briefwechsel 1930-1940*

Polity Press
65 Bridge Street
Cambridge CB2 1UR, UK

Polity Press
350 Main Street
Malden, MA 02148, USA

ISBN-10: 0-7456-3669-1
ISBN-13: 978-07456-3669-6

A catalogue record for this book is available from the British Library.

Typeset in 10.5 on 12pt Sabon
by Servis Filmsetting Ltd, Manchester
Printed and bound in India by Replika Press PVT Ltd, Kundli

For further information on Polity, visit our website: www.polity.co.uk

Contents

Editors' Foreword

A reflection, albeit a fading one, of intellectual life in the Berlin of the late 1920s provides this correspondence, which begins properly only after Benjamin's emigration to France, with the framework within which the portrait of this friendship takes shape. It was Gretel Karplus who urged Benjamin to emigrate and told him about Adorno's plans and Bloch's movements, thus maintaining the connection between the old Berlin friends and acquaintances. She helped him through the most difficult times with regular money transfers, and organized financial support from the Saar region, which was initially still independent from the Third Reich. But the correspondence also shows the great importance of this personal communication to both correspondents, and thus the autonomy of their friendship. Benjamin's interest in fashion, following Baudelaire and Mallarmé, is also echoed by Gretel Karplus when she writes, in August 1935, 'I would truly love to have a conversation with Helen Grund, and not only about the fashion products of the major companies, but also about the laws according to which fashions ultimately move socially downwards in the provinces and the middle classes. I am encountering this problem almost daily in my work, but I am not interested in it purely for professional reasons; this cycle has always interested me, and I would almost go so far as to say that the closer I am to it, the more difficult it seems to find the solution, and the more questionable I find the notion of taste.' Once in New York, she attempts to entice Benjamin to America with her descriptions of the city and the new arrivals from Europe. In May 1939 she writes: 'I wish we could go for a walk together down by the Hudson and talk about everything at leisure.' Unfortunately, not all of Benjamin's letters were preserved by their addressee, so there remain a number of sensitive gaps that cannot be filled. Benjamin's letters have been reproduced in accordance with the edition *Gesammelte Briefe*, and the notes appended there have also remained mostly unchanged. Gretel Adorno's letters have all been reproduced from the original manuscripts and typescripts. The editor's have marked indecipherable words with an x in square brackets, and inserted a question mark in square brackets where they were uncertain. The original letters are in the Walter Benjamin Archiv at the Akademie der Künste in Berlin.

The following editions of works and letters are cited in abbreviated form:

Theodor W. Adorno, *Gesammelte Schriften*, ed. Rolf Tiedemann in collaboration with Gretel Adorno, Susan Buck-Morss and Klaus Schultz, vols 1–20 (Frankfurt am Main: Suhrkamp, 1970–86); abbreviation: *GS* [1–20].

Theodor W. Adorno and Walter Benjamin, *The Complete Correspondence 1928–1940*, ed. Henri Lonitz, trans. Nicholas Walker (Cambridge: Polity, 1999); abbreviation: *Adorno–Benjamin Correspondence.*

Theodor W. Adorno and Max Horkheimer, *Briefwechsel 1927–1969*, vol. 1: *1927–1937*, ed. Christoph Gödde and Henri Lonitz (Frankfurt am Main: Suhrkamp, 2003); abbreviation: Adorno–Horkheimer, *Briefwechsel I.*

Theodor W. Adorno and Max Horkheimer, *Briefwechsel 1927–1969*, vol. 2: *1938–1944*, ed. Christoph Gödde and Henri Lonitz (Frankfurt am Main: Suhrkamp, 2004); abbreviation: Adorno–Horkheimer, *Briefwechsel II.*

Theodor W. Adorno and Ernst Křenek, *Briefwechsel*, ed. Wolfgang Rogge (Frankfurt am Main: Suhrkamp, 1974); abbreviation: *Adorno–Křenek Correspondence.*

Theodor W. Adorno and Alfred Sohn-Rethel, *Briefwechsel 1936–1969*, ed. Christoph Gödde (Munich, 1991); abbreviation: *Adorno–Sohn-Rethel Correspondence.*

Walter Benjamin, *Gesammelte Schriften*, ed. Rolf Tiedemann and Hermann Schweppenhäuser, in collaboration with Theodor W. Adorno and Gershom Scholem, 7 vols (Frankfurt am Main: Suhrkamp, 1972–89); abbreviation: *GS* 1–7.

Walter Benjamin, *Gesammelte Briefe*, ed. Christoph Gödde and Henri Lonitz, vols 1–6 (Frankfurt am Main: Suhrkamp, 1995–2000); abbreviation: *GB* 1–6.

Walter Benjamin and Gershom Scholem, *Briefwechsel 1933–1940*, ed. Gershom Scholem (Frankfurt am Main: Suhrkamp, 1985); abbreviation: *Scholem Correspondence*.

Walter Benjamin 1892–1940, an exhibition of the Theodor W. Adorno Archiv, Frankfurt am Main, in collaboration with the Deutsches Literaturarchiv, Marbach am Neckar, ed. Rolf Tiedemann, Christoph Gödde and Henri Lonitz (*Marbacher Magazin 55*), 3rd edn (Marbach am Neckar, 1991); abbreviation: *Benjamin-Katalog*.

Max Horkheimer, *Gesammelte Schriften*, vol. 15: *Briefwechsel 1913–1936*, ed. Gunzelin Schmid Noerr (Frankfurt am Main: Fischer, 1995); abbreviation: Horkheimer, *Briefwechsel 1913–1936*.

Max Horkheimer, *Gesammelte Schriften*, vol. 16: *Briefwechsel 1937–1940*, ed. Gunzelin Schmid Noerr (Frankfurt am Main: Fischer, 1995); abbreviation: Horkheimer, *Briefwechsel 1937–1940*.

1 WALTER BENJAMIN TO GRETEL KARPLUS
TRONDHEIM, 25.7.1930

Dear Miss Karplus,

once one has left Berlin[1] the world becomes beautiful and spacious, and even has room aboard a 2000-ton steamer for your silently cheerful servant alongside various travelling rabble. Just now I am offering it the spectacle of a droll, moustachioed old lady sunbathing in an armchair on the ship's terrace – for it simply must be a terrace, whether on the boulevard or in the fjord – with her cup of coffee beside her, scribbling away at her handicraft. So take this simple crochet piece, then, meant for us as a manner of antimacassar for our friendship, as a sign of old kinship from the undeterred traveller, descendant of *Schelmuffsky*[2] W. B.

Original: picture postcard: Trondhjem. Elgsæter bro m/Høiskolen; stamp: Tromsø, 25.[VII] 30. Manuscript.

1 At the end of July, Benjamin had embarked upon his trip to Scandinavia from Hamburg; see his 'Reisenotizen' [Travel Notes] (*GS* 6, pp. 419–22), which then became the *Denkbild* 'Nordische See', which appeared in the *Frankfurter Zeitung* on 18 September 1930 (see *GS* 4 [1], pp. 383–7).

2 An allusion to Christian Reuter's parody of a travel novel, *Schelmuffsky*'s *Curiose und Sehr gefährliche Reisebeschreibung zu Wasser vnd Land* [Schelmuffsky's Curious and Very Dangerous Travel Report by Water and Land], first published in 1696, which Benjamin had spoken about on 28 March on Southwest German Radio. Schelmuffsky flees from Hamburg at the start of his trip and subsequently travels to Sweden (see *GS* 2 [2], pp. 648–60).

2 WALTER BENJAMIN TO GRETEL KARPLUS
SAN ANTONIO (IBIZA), *c.*MID-MAY 1932

Dear Gretel Karplus,

such is life – 12 hours after I sent my last letter off to you I received yours,[1] which has afforded me a feeling of infinite relief. Perhaps it is simply the inability to take in a series of cloudless days as they come that leads to such oppressive questions as those circulating in my last letter. For it takes a long time to adjust to so climatically alien a situation, unless a certain degree of hotel comfort acts as an intermediary between the country and ourselves. And you can see from the little picture enclosed[2] how far removed we are from that here. After weeks of work, the acquaintances who brought this little house to life again after years of disrepair have now succeeded in making it a very habitable place. The most beautiful thing is the view from the window onto the sea and a rocky island, which lets its lighthouse shine in here at night, as well as the distance between inhabitants through an astute allocation of space and walls almost a metre thick, which prevent any sound (or heat) from getting through. I am leading the sort of life centenarians tell reporters of as a secret: I get up at seven o'clock and bathe in the sea, where not a soul is to be seen on the shore far and wide, perhaps at the most a sailor on the horizon around the level of my forehead; then I sunbathe, leaning against a willing tree-trunk in the forest, and its healing powers spread to my head through the prism of a satire by Gide[3] (Paludes), and then a long day of abstinence from countless things – less because they shorten life than because they hardly exist here, or are so inferior that one is happy to dispense with them – electric light and butter, spirits and running water, flirts and newspaper-reading. For the perusal of the issues of the Frankfurter Zeitung, which appear with a week's delay, already has more of an epic character. If you consider also that all my mail goes to Wissing[4] – who has so far sent me not a single piece of writing – then you can see that I am not exaggerating. I have spent a long time focusing solely on books and jottings; it is only in the last few days that I have emancipated myself from roaming the shore and taken a number of longer hikes into the even wider, even more lonely surrounding area. Only then did I become fully conscious of being in Spain. Of all the habitable country I have seen, these parts[5] are surely the most severe and untouched. It is difficult to give you a clear idea of them, yet if I should succeed in the end, I will not keep it from you. So far I have not made many notes with this intention, but I was surprised to find myself taking up the form of representation used in One-Way Street for a number of elements connected to the most important in the book. Perhaps I can show you some of this in Berlin. Then we shall also speak about Corsica[6] I am very glad you have now seen it; there is really something very Spanish about the countryside there; but the Corsican summer does not, I think, carve quite such harsh and tremendous contours into the land. Hopefully you also stayed at the wonderfully quiet and old-fashioned Grand Hotel in Ajaccio for a few days. You must also tell me in detail how things went for Wiesengrund in Marseilles. I think I should be reaching there in the course of the next few weeks, but I can never quite decide on the specific dates. You will understand if you consider that I am living here on a mere fraction of what I need in Berlin; I am therefore drawing out my stay for as long as I possibly can, and will not be back before the start of August. But I hope very much to hear from you before then.

Well, if – encouraged by your letter, which was very pleasing to me – I may request a small gift, it would be to send me a little bag (envelope) of smoking tobacco as a 'sample without value' – All right von Eicken or some other brand. There is absolutely nothing smokable here.

I too received a letter from Daga, and one from her mother,[7] before my departure. Furthermore, I was completely immersed in Russian for two weeks: first I read Trotsky's history of the February revolution, and now I am just finishing his autobiography. I think I have not consumed anything with such breathless excitement in years. There is no question whatsoever that you must read both books. Do you know if the second volume of the history of the revolution – October – has been published yet?[8] I will return to my Gracian[9] soon and probably write something about it.

For now my best and kind wishes

Yours,

Walter Benjamin

Original: manuscript.

On the dating: Benjamin tells Gretel Karplus of completing Trotsky's volume on the February revolution, which he does not appear to have finished reading before 10 May (see *GB* 4, letter no. 734); this suggests that the letter was written around the middle of May.

1 Neither has survived.

2 No picture of the 'little house' referred to in the letter is known to the editors. It is also possible, however, that Benjamin means a photo so far dated to 1933, which shows him, Noeggerath and Selz on the 'bare' terrace of the 'little house' (see *Benjamin-Katalog*, fig. 83).

3 *Paludes* was first published in 1895.

4 Egon Wissing (1900–1984) was Walter Benjamin's maternal cousin; he had studied medicine and later worked as radiologist at the Massachusetts Memorial Hospital in Boston. His first wife was Gertrude (Gert) Frank, née Feiss (?), who died in Paris in November 1933.

5 Benjamin wrote 'Ibizenkische Folge' [Ibizan Sequence] and the second series of 'Kurze Schatten' [Short Shadows] (see *GS* 4 [1], pp. 402–9 and 425–8); see also *GB* 4, letter no. 734 and the note there).

6 Gretel Karplus and Adorno had crossed over to Corsica at the end of March and taken a trip there to Bonifacio, at the southern tip; on 3 April they stayed in Ajaccio. Benjamin had spent a week in Corsica in June 1927.

7 The formulation suggests that Gretel Karplus had met Asja Lacis and her daughter during their stay in Berlin.

8 This was only published in 1933.

9 Benjamin was thinking at the time of writing an essay on Gracian for *Die literarische Welt*, as a short list entitled 'projects' (see *GS* 6, p. 157) indicates (see also *GB* 4, letter no. 741); one year later, also in Ibiza, he considered writing a Gracian commentary (see *GB* 4, letter no. 780). No notes for this project have survived. Slightly under a year later Walter Benjamin gave Gretel Karplus a copy of the *Hand-Orakel und Kunst der Weltklugheit* [Hand Oracle and Art of Worldly Wisdom] by Balthasar Gracian (no. 423 in the *Insel-Bücherei* catalogue), 'newly edited by Otto Baron von Taube using the translation by Arthur Schopenhauer', which bore the dedication 'Walter Benjamin für Gretel Karplus 3 März 1933'; the book does not contain any notes by Benjamin.

3 GRETEL ADORNO TO WALTER BENJAMIN BERLIN, 29.3.1933

29 March 1933.

Dear Walter Benjamin,

a thousand thanks for the telegram and your kind letter.[1] Please do not let the delay in my reply prevent you from sending me further news as soon as possible; above all, I would like to know how our friend Detlef[2] is faring. I am greatly concerned about him, and, as I am sure you have spoken to him, I cannot think of anyone better to tell me how he really is and what prospects he has at the moment.

Except for having caught a decent spring cold, I am well enough. On Monday I plan to begin my trainee work; they are being very friendly and accommodating. The old company will not be sold; it is more likely that the factory will be rented out without the properties. – Teddie's plans are entirely uncertain, but at least Berlin is showing itself to him in somewhat more tempting colours now. During the last few days we have been spending a great deal of time with the Wiener Streichquartett, who are giving 3 concerts here at the moment; I believe you also know Rudi[3] personally. – I was informed by telephone that the tenant[?] Sch.[4] bought his own cupboards, so I have been spared making the acquaintance of Krumme Strasse for the time being. Karola's friend[5] wrote me a few pleasant lines from Hotel Bellevue in Graubünden. – The secretary[6] you had last year, whom you have incidentally withheld from me to this day, sounds so charming from your description that I could almost become jealous. – As I have a fair amount of free time, an acquaintance[7] has employed me to maintain his library; there are some quite interesting volumes in it. I shall send you a list as soon as I have finished sorting it.

Fond and warm regards

ever your Felicitas

Original: manuscript.

1 Not preserved.

2 Benjamin had adopted the pseudonym *Detlef Holz* for his German publications. Gretel Karplus subsequently addressed him by this name.

3 The violinist and leader of several string quartet formations Rudolf Kolisch (1896–1978), who had been a friend of Adorno since the latter's studies with Alban Berg in Vienna.

4 This presumably refers to Werner von Schoeller, who rented Benjamin's last apartment in the Prinzregentenstrasse.

5 This refers to Ernst Bloch, who had been together with Karola Piotrkowska (1905–1994) since 1927 and married her in November 1934. Gretel Karplus know both of them from their time in Berlin, and was in postal communication with Ernst Bloch; of that correspondence, unfortunately, only one letter by Gretel Adorno, from 16 November 1970, has survived.

6 Uncertain. It is likely that Benjamin had mentioned Jean Selz (1904–1997) in his letter, with whom he had close contact in Ibiza. Benjamin and Selz were planning to translate the former's *Berliner Kindheit um neunzehnhundert* (published in English as *Berlin Childhood around 1900*, trans. Howard Eiland [Cambridge, MA: Belknap Press, 2006]) into French. Five pieces from the 'Enfance berlinoise' were completed in the spring of 1933 (see *GS* 4 [2], pp. 979–86).

7 This is Benjamin, of course, who had asked Gretel Karplus to look after the books he had left behind in the Prinzregentenstrasse.

4 GRETEL KARPLUS TO WALTER BENJAMIN BERLIN, 30.3.1933

30 March 1933.

Walter Benjamin, my dear,

I received your second letter[1] just after I had sent off my reply to you yesterday, and I wish to answer it immediately so that the pictures[2] still reach you in Paris. Even if you are now no longer completely alone, which I am especially glad to hear, I would still like to keep you company in this somewhat primitive fashion. I put on the green dress for the occasion, and I am sure you will forgive me if my hairstyle is still from '31. To assist your imagination a little, I enclose a small sample of the material – for stroking.

I already knew the things you wrote about Blei[3] from Marieluise v. Motesiczky,[4] whom you once met at my place; her uncle Ernst v. Lieben is Billie's divorced husband and probably down there too, and it is certain that he financed the whole thing. Please do write a word to Piz (Mrl. V. M) if you need anything Vienna IV. Brahmsplatz 7, or I can inform her if you would prefer.

Have you found anything worth recommending in recent French literature? Your letters are the dearest and most important thing I have at the moment; happiness is still taking its time in arriving. I look forward to your next message, very warm regards your

Fe-li-ci-tas.[5]

I do wonder: are you satisfied with me?

Original: manuscript.

1 Not preserved.

2 They could not be traced.

3 Franz Blei (1871–1942) seems to have settled in Majorca in 1931 for financial reasons; his daughter had a chicken farm there. The town of Cala Ratjada was also inhabited by Friedrich Burschell (1889–1969) and Karl Otten (1889–1963).

4 Gretel Karplus was a close friend of the Vienna-born painter Marie-Louise von Motesiczky (1906–1996), who was known as 'der Piz' [translator's note: meaning unknown].

5 In her correspondence with Benjamin, Gretel Karplus adopted this name, which belonged to a figure from Wilhelm Speyer's play *Ein Mantel, ein Hut, ein Handschuh* [A Coat, a Hat, a Glove], in which Benjamin had been a collaborator.

5 GRETEL KARPLUS TO WALTER BENJAMIN BERLIN, 14.4.1933

14 April 33.

Dear Walter-D,

today just a quick message: as Teddie feels so lonely here, he will probably be moving in at the Prinzenallee[1] around the middle of next week. So I would then ask you to send the letters in duplicate, now and again perhaps also one to the following address: Georg Tengler, Dresdenerstr. 50/1. for me – we could also arrange for them to be kept poste restante* if we decided on a particular day of the week. I await your suggestions and look forward with impatience to hearing from you. Many warm regards, best wishes for your move in Ibiza, ever warmly

Your Felicitas

* S 14 Dresdenerstr. 97

I scribbled this card down quickly in the tram. Just think how strange: GT. used to have his business in the house of your friends Scho,[2] who still had their printing company back then. Please forgive the businesslike tone of the card.

F.

Original: postcard; stamp: Berlin, 15.4.33. – Manuscript.

1 Gretel Karplus lived there with her parents.

2 The parents of Benjamin's friend Gershom Scholem (1897–1982) had their printing office in the Neue Grünstrasse in Berlin-Charlottenburg.

6 WALTER BENJAMIN TO GRETEL KARPLUS
SAN ANTONIO (IBIZA), 15.4.1933

Dear Felizitas,

I would long have given you[1] news of myself and my circumstances, if only I had found any peace – discounting sleep – during the last ten days. And even now it would not really be time yet, if I did not have the courage to take it up with the most miserable illumination in the world – not candles, but rather a dim electric light attached to an unattainably high ceiling. I travelled for eight days to get here from Paris – stops in Barcelona, in Ibiza – and then practically stumbled into a house move. For the house from last year, which only this winter had played a not unimportant role in my imagination, had been rented out to someone else by the Noeggeraths[2] a few hours before my arrival. And if they had kept it, I would no longer have found any part to inhabit after the various changes that had meanwhile been made.

The ceiling with the dim light, then, is in a different house. Compared to the old one it has the advantage of being one-quarter or one-eighth more comfortable, but the disadvantages of a less convenient location and architectural banality. For it was built on the outskirts of San Antonio by the doctor there, who had to move away, and is three-quarters of an hour away from the beautiful patch of forest in which I spent the last summer. But this is no more than a miniature mirror of great public changes on the scale of my private life. For it is scarcely possible, notwithstanding some less than elegant building work, to find accommodation in San Antonio at the moment. As a result, prices have risen once again. And so the economic and demographic changes are balancing each other out. In relation to the fantastically cheap overall level, however, neither of these is all too sensitive. It is a little different with the current population increase in the area. For the isolation of last summer is more difficult to find not only through the topographical changes, but also through the appearance of 'summer guests', where one cannot always distinguish between summer season and twilight years. The only person you are likely to know of among those here would be Raoul Hausmann.[3] I have not yet been introduced to him, incidentally, and am in general avoiding contact wherever possible.

But one does not need it, as one learns more here about the background and nature of the people in days than one sometimes learns in years in Berlin. And so, when you come here in a few months,[4] I can guide you on a fairly instructive tour through the local garden of fates. Incidentally, a new centre for this or that entanglement has come about through a Frenchman – the brother of that married couple[5] I told you about – who is opening a bar in Ibiza, directly by the harbour, and the gradually emerging character of its space promises very pleasant quarters.

I received quite a lengthy letter from Max[6] in Geneva, and what I can at least gather from it is that the journal is to be continued and my collaboration is still reckoned with. It goes without saying that a sociology of French literature, which is what they are expecting from me first of all, is not so very easy to produce from here. But I at least prepared it as well as I could in Paris. It seems that I can expect some reviews later on. I am also writing these for other publications at present, without having any illusions about the uncertain editorial fate of the manuscripts. May I make a request of you in this context? While I was in Paris I asked my maid[7] to forward me the review copy of a collection of letters by Dauthendey[8] that the Frankfurter Zeitung had sent me. It has not arrived here so far, and I would like to receive it quite soon. Perhaps you could ask about it by telephone. Incidentally, I have been informed in a letter that my review of Wiesengrund's book[9] appeared in the literary supplement of the Vossische Zeitung on the 2nd or the 9th of April. I did not receive the specimen copies and would be most especially grateful to you if you could send me two here, or have the ones probably lying about in my apartment forwarded.

Naturally I hope to hear very soon about the progress of your undertakings since 1 April. Not only about them, but also about your health. And finally how Wiesengrund's projects have developed. I am almost certain that he will meanwhile be inclined to accept my last spoken suggestions.[10] You must tell him that Max asked after him with some concern in the aforementioned letter. For me, the crux of your affairs is the question of your summer trip and its goal. I would be most dejected if you were to forget about the perspectives of our long conversation in Westend. But I am sure that you will take care of everything as astutely and precisely as I have always known you to do. Give me details about that.

I have started learning Spanish seriously, and am being guided by three different systems: an old-fashioned grammar book, the Thousand Words and finally a new, very clever suggestive method. I think it should lead to something in the foreseeable future. Tomorrow is Easter – I then intend to take my first longer walk into the country. But shorter ones have also convinced me that one can find all the old beauty and solitude of the region half an hour away from the houses, and I hope that I will not have to undertake all my expeditions alone. It is incidentally very hot sometimes during the day, but at night still cool, just like last year.

Since I began this letter, the view of the new house has already cleared a little. I am accommodated very decently in a room that even has a sort of dressing-room, where one can even take a hot bath in a tub after heating the wash-boiler for a long time: for Ibiza, that is truly the stuff of fairy tales. But it is also useful, as bathing in the sea will be inconceivable for me for another four to six weeks. The room contains a bookshelf and a cupboard, furthermore, so I can place the few things I have and the little papers around me in a very orderly fashion.

Many thanks for Ernst's address. I will send him a card in the next few days. I have not heard much from the great wide world since I have been here. But I expect your next letter to compensate for that too.

For today warm regards

15 April 1933 Detlef

Ibiza (Balearic Islands)

San Antonio Fonda Miramar

Original: manuscript.

1 Translator's note: this marks the first use in the correspondence of the informal address *Du* (as opposed to the formal *Sie*). As both correspondents occasionally switch between the two in later letters, however, each subsequent use of *Sie* will be pointed out in a note.

2 The New York-born Felix Noeggerath (1885–1960), who had assumed German nationality in 1909. Benjamin first met Noeggerath in 1915 in Munich while the latter was studying philosophy, Indology and Indo-Germanic linguistics. Noeggerath lived in Ibiza with his third wife and his son Hans Jakob (Jean Jacques) (1908–1934), who studied Romance languages in Berlin.

3 The painter and poet Raoul Hausmann (1886–1971), who had co-founded the Club Dada in 1918, emigrated to Spain in 1933 and remained there until 1936. Further stops were Switzerland, Czechoslovakia, Paris and finally Limoges, where he lived until his death.

4 Gretel Karplus did not visit Benjamin in San Antonio.

5 This is Guy Selz, regarding whom no further information could be found.

6 Horkheimer's letter from 3 April 1933; see Horkheimer, *Briefwechsel 1913–1936*, pp. 99f.

7 The name of Benjamin's maidservant in Berlin was Erna Dohrmann.

8 Benjamin reviewed Max Dauthendey's *Ein Herz im Lärm der Welt: Briefe an Freunde* [A Heart amidst the Noise of the World: Letters to Friends] (Munich, 1933) on 30 April 1933 for the *Literaturblatt* [literary pages] of the *Frankfurter Zeitung* under the title 'Briefe von Max Dauthendey' (see *GS* 3, pp. 383–6).

9 Benjamin's review of Wiesengrund's *Habilitation* [post-doctoral examination] thesis on Kierkegaard had appeared on 2 April (see *GS* 3, pp. 380–3).

10 Adorno, who was forbidden from lecturing in the summer semester of 1933 – he was divested of the *venia legendi* that autumn due to the Aryan paragraph of the *Gesetz zur Wiederherstellung des Berufsbeamtentums* [Law for the Restoration of Professional Civil Service] – had gone to Berlin in January to seek authorization as a private music teacher for composition and theory. Despite favourable references, this does not seem to have been granted; he was instead advised, in February, to take a shortened examination. Even at the end of April he still spoke of taking the examination for private musical teachers in a letter to Kracauer. At the same time, Adorno made attempts to write for newspapers and journals. No information could be found regarding the 'last spoken suggestions' made to Adorno by Benjamin in Berlin.

7 WALTER BENJAMIN TO GRETEL KARPLUS
SAN ANTONIO (IBIZA), *c.*19/20.4.1933

Dear Miss Karplus,

you[1] requested a report on my situation.

Well – things have cleared up sufficiently within the last week for me to deliver it. I only wish it could have turned out a little more well rounded and pleasant than is probably the case.

Certainly – I can essentially be satisfied with a constellation that – for two months at least – guarantees a roof over my head. And over this roof the blue sky and all around a wonderful country. But it can now no longer be denied that everything lying between these two poles – the sober: accommodation, the romantic: having a paradise – is looking extremely difficult.

The house rented by the Noeggeraths, which I had approached with distrust from the start, if only for its construction, which greatly deviates from the customary style here, has proved unusable for any sort of work, in fact even for concentrated reading. A ground plan would perhaps give you some notion of the situation, but it could never give you a genuine impression of the play of the wind in these rooms, of the doors that are no more than thin planks, or of how every word reverberates in all corners. I have reached the point where I must place all my faith in that good old Brechtian maxim: overcoming an evil through an accumulation thereof.[2] So the various temporary guests that walk up and down here will soon be joined by a number of permanent guests. This will then lead me to shift my daytime position entirely away from the house to my forest from last year. And I would already have done so, had there not been such a constant strong wind during these afternoons that even my virtuoso technique would not have sufficed to hold on to sheets and bits of paper while writing.

It remains to be seen, however, what it will mean to spend a full day outdoors in this climate. Returning – for lunch, say – is as inconceivable through the distance as a change of domicile, which could only lead me to a fonda, where there would by no means be any better chance of working.

Nonetheless, I am quite sure that it was right to come here, and I think that behind the backs of all the new characters who have appeared here since last year I will still get around to my things after all. The previous year I gave myself four weeks before getting down to work. This year that is out of the question. But, even under the very difficult conditions of the last few days, I managed to send off two new manuscripts.[3] I do also have some hope in a few cafés or bars that are opening partly in San Antonio, partly also in Ibiza, and where I will perhaps find a room to work in.

If this account arouses in you sufficient clemency or consideration towards the little letters that come about amid the scenery I have described in order to imagine that scenery, then it has already served a purpose.

So I have not been able to take up all my old habits from last year again; but I have – if one could put it this way – continued one of them, by now reading the final volume – 'October' – of the massive peasant novel[4] I began here last year, in which the mastery of Kritrotz is perhaps even greater than in the first. I would very much like to take up 'Berliner Kindheit' again after a while; but only, of course, once I have found a solution for my mode of working that I can consider at least somewhat secure. En attendant there was opportunity to ride about a little on my hobby horse, Art Nouveau. This was for a review in which I had to occupy myself with the extremely interesting volumes of Dauthendey's letters that were discovered posthumously.

The next study will now be the one on the sociology of French literature which I already mentioned to you in Berlin. It is naturally extraordinarily difficult to write it from here. I had to go so far as to ask Max, in my last letter,[5] to send me – if necessary à conto of my future payment – some volumes that are indispensable. Those were naturally ones that I do not own. Unfortunately, however, it has turned out that I also cannot do without some of the latter (those which I do own). I have listed them on a bit of paper[6] enclosed here. It is almost impossible to expect you to pick out these books – among the French paperbacks – and send them to me, which could cost you half a Sunday – I know all that, but not what to do. The only thing I could perhaps ask – and even here I am not sure that you might not misunderstand me – would be whether Wiesengrund would be prepared to do me this great service. He would have the advantage of being able to go upstairs on weekday mornings when the tenant is in the office.

At any rate, I shall have Miss Dohrmann call you at the apartment around ¼ past 1. Perhaps you can then also arrange with her when she should bring you the rest of my things.

Now it is enough, more than enough. Write soon, and in detail. Give Wiesengrund my best regards. I would be pleased if he were to write to me.

Warm regards

yours,

WDetlef Holz

Original: manuscript.

On the dating: This letter with the formal address follows the request in Gretel Karplus's postcard of 14 April. It is thus highly likely that the following letter – which once more uses the intimate form of address – originally belonged to letter no. 7, as the identical folding of the two sheets indicates.

1 *Sie*.

2 This exact formulation could not be traced, though the motif frequently appears: possibly it was only transmitted orally. In his 'Kommentare zu Gedichten von Brecht', Benjamin refers to 'the overcoming of difficulties through accumulation thereof' as an 'old maxim of dialectics' (*GS* 2 [2], p. 540).

3 The Dauthendey review and probably that of Marc Aldanov's *Eine unsentimentale Reise: Begegnungen und Erlebnisse im heutigen Europa* (Munich, 1932); see *GS* 3, pp. 386–8.

4 This is the second volume of Leo Trotsky's *History of the Russian Revolution*, which describes the October revolution.

5 Not preserved.

6 This has not survived; see letter no. 10, however, where Benjamin repeats his request for the books.

8 WALTER BENJAMIN TO GRETEL KARPLUS
SAN ANTONIO (IBIZA), *c.*19/20.4.1933

Dear Felizitas,

I am lying on my bed and, as it is described in medieval chronicles, having a warm bath prepared for me. And indeed, everything is positively medieval here. The only anachronism is the enamel bathtub; but at the same time a serious compensation offered by the house for a number of other things I already mentioned to you.

But outside there is an icy wind blowing.

I received your Easter letter and also the card. For now, I can only thank you for the former by telling you how you would thus become my escort on the little excursions to Ibiza that I undertake once a week.[1] For, as modest as the 'urban' pleasures I seek there might be – essentially the café; in the cinema the air is too bad – they would otherwise lie beyond the sharp-edged boundary known as my budget.

Today, however, I shall drink your health with a second glass of anise (or even rum) in this manner. This rum, incidentally, is the finest thing one can sample on this island, and one of its sights to boot. How so? – I will not tell you yet, so that we have one little sensation more when you come here.

I will hopefully soon learn more about that, and indeed about your response to the long letter I wrote you last week. I hope the new housing regime you mentioned in your Easter letter also has its pleasant sides for you. Write to me soon about all these things

and a thousand warm regards

Detlef

Original: manuscript.

1 Benjamin visited Jean Selz, who lived in the city of Ibiza, roughly every seven to ten days, as indicated by a list dealing with the time between 9 April and 7 June, noted on the reverse of a letter from Dora Sophie Benjamin of 8 April 1933.

9 GRETEL KARPLUS TO WALTER BENJAMIN
BERLIN, 24.4.1933

24 April 1933.

Dear Walter Benjamin,

it is a great load off my mind to know that there are at least a few modest prospects for you[1] once more. I am thinking of Max, and would be glad to learn of the other possibilities. Did my Easter egg arrive, and was it the right crème? I have meanwhile enquired here at the post office and found out that one can send 10 Reichsmark = *c*.27.75 Pesetas by postal order. This is a great comfort to me in that I can thus perhaps look after little Detlev after all; I would be embarrassed if I had to leave you to take care of him all alone.

My last card was a false alarm, by the way: Teddie is staying in the guesthouse, so our dispositions are as before. His father is in favour of a trip to England, but that is not directly imminent. He is writing for the Europäische Rundschau[2] here, also making a lot of music, and I could not think of anything lovelier. As we were at home over Easter we are going to Schloss Marquardt[3] next weekend[4] – my health is in urgent need of a rest, the old migraine complaints again with all their attendant circumstances; I also plan to try out some colonic irrigation.

I am having very bad luck with your girl; I cannot reach her at all, and now I have written to her repeating your wishes, and requesting that she call me or write to me, but unfortunately still without success. I am very unhappy about it; for it could easily seem as if I am neglecting the tasks I have been entrusted with, but unfortunately I really do not have the time to go there, other than in genuine emergencies. As soon as I now have a reply from you I shall at least order the Ullstein issue with the review of the Kierkegaard book. At any rate, I enclose a list of your things[5] so that it is always evident which books on my shelves are yours. The compilation is very superficial, but I think it is sufficient for the purpose.

Would you find it very immodest of me if I asked you to tell me more precisely about your life there? How is it with your daily routine; do you have the necessary quiet to work? Is your yearning for steak very great, and do you have the gramophone with the nice new Parisian records there? Everything relating to you is extremely important to me. I would like to suggest numbering our letters; I now have four from you including the card letter, and I have also sent four with today's one and two postcards. It just occurred to me that I have not mentioned anything to Teddie regarding Max's concern about him; please write to him yourself if you consider it appropriate, Pension Fritz Unter d. Linden 62/3. In part it seemed too far away, in part I did not want to show him the letter.

Dear Walter please preserve our friendship, even if I am handicapped on all sides and cannot help you much. Please believe with me in the good foundation that even adverse conditions cannot shake, and forgive me if it seems that you must be so patient with me. As I was unable to use the short breathing space to seek greater freedom, I must now reckon with being all the more tied up for the time being. My isolation is almost complete once more, and your absence is a disaster for me, even in purely external terms. It is a great comfort for me to know that you are there, even if only very far away. You will now scold me for my sentimentality and admonish me to be strict. I will gladly concede, and remain, with my best and very warm regards,

ever your friend
Felicitas

Original: typescript.

1 *Sie*.

2 The editor of this journal between 1933 and 1938 was Joachim Moras (1902–1961); Adorno's article 'Abschied vom Jazz' [Farewell to Jazz] (see *GS* 18, pp. 795–9) was published in the May issue, and his 'Notiz über Wagner' [Note on Wagner] (see ibid., pp. 204–9) in the July issue.

3 This palace in East Havelland, near Potsdam, had been converted into a hotel in 1932. Fontane deals with Marquardt in the third volume of his *Wanderungen durch die Mark Brandenburg*.

4 *weekend*: Translator's note: in English in the original. Henceforth: EO.

5 A three-page typed list of books has survived among Benjamin's belongings. It could not be ascertained whether it is the list mentioned in the letter.

Contemporary German authors

Berthold	: Versuche (several volumes with grey binding)
	: Hauspostille
	: Eduard II
	: Im Dickicht der Städte
	: Trommeln in der Nacht
Rudolf Borchardt	: Der Durant
	: various volumes
Stefan George	: Die Fibel
	: Der Stern des Bundes
	: Shakespeare [sonnets]
	: Facsimiles of the manuscript of the Dante translation
Georg Heym	: Umbra vitae
Scheerbart	: Lesabèndio
	: various volumes
Adolf Loos	: Ins Leere gesprochen
	: Trotzdem
Morgenstern	: Palma Kunkel
	: Galgenlieder
	: Palmström
	: Horatius Travestitus
Musil	: Die Verwirrungen des Zöglings Törless

Reventlov	: Herrn Dames Aufzeichnungen
Rilke	: Geschichten vom lieben Gott
	: Sonette an Orpheus
	: Weise von Liebe und Tod
Robert Walser	: Der Gehülfe
	: Geschwister Tanner
Donald Wedekind	: Ultra Montes
Frank Wedekind	: Mina Haha

Translations

Baudelaire	: The Depraved
	: Purgatory
	: Poems translated by Kalkreuth, red leather-bound volume
	: Poems and Sketches
	: Poems and Prose Verses
Boccaccio	: Decameron (3 brown leather-bound volumes)
Cervantes	: Don Quixote
	: Novellas (2 volumes)
Dante	: Divine Comedy (translated by Bachenschwanz) (3 small octavo volumes in cardboard)
Joyce	: Ulysses
Leopardi	: Aphorisms
Lucretius	: Nature translated by Knebel
Manzoni	: The Betrothed (2 volumes)
Meleager von Gadara	: Wreath of Blossoms
Petrarch	: To Posterity
Swinburne	: Poems translated by Borchardt
Rabelais	: Gargantua translated by Regis (2 half-bound volumes)
Sterne	: Tristram Shandy (3 half-bound volumes)
	: A Sentimental Journey
Simrock	: Church hymns Latin and German
Thackeray	: Vanity Fair (3 volumes)
Gesta Romanorum	:

Illustrated works

Atget	: Photographs
Octavius Hill	: Photographs
Guttmann	: Old Photography
Recht	: Early Photography
	: The Victorian Age (photographs)
Bukovich	: Paris (photographs)
Sidorow	: Moscow (photographs)
Gröber	: Old Children's Toys
Rumpf	: Toys of the Peoples of the World (large portfolio with coloured plates)

Hobrecker	: Old Children's Books
von Boehn	: Puppets and Puppet Plays (2 volumes)
le Mercier de Neufville	: Marionette

and a large number of other illustrated works on cultural history

Collected editions

Hauptmann	: Collected Works
Ibsen	: Collected Works

Varia

Creuzer	: Picture Atlas of Mythology and symbolism (small quarto volume)
Molitor	: Philosophie der Offenbarung (Everything I could find)

10 WALTER BENJAMIN TO GRETEL KARPLUS
SAN ANTONIO (IBIZA), 30.4.1933

Dear Felizitas,

you can hardly imagine the décor surrounding me as I sit under a fig tree writing this letter: a Sunday afternoon with a completely overcast sky, neither a ray of sunshine nor the slightest breeze – which latter one finds quite pleasant, for there is such a strong wind during most hours that one can barely work outside. I have covered my feet with my coat; yet I am cold all the same. My thoughts more or less match nature's mood, but have sadly not been produced by her. The house has meanwhile become only a little habitable; a project such as retreating to a secluded mill does have its dark sides, and aside from that also has little chance of being realized. Work on various reviews is still proceeding; but I do ask myself whether it might come to an end, or whether my efforts to be entrusted with new releases now and again might ultimately show some results.

It is not so much books that I lack as someone with whom to exchange a few words. But this latter, except for my Parisian friends in Ibiza, whom I see almost once a week, is completely absent. That last winter which N. spent here – partly alone with his son – seems to have pushed itself between him and his former interests like a barricade. It does not improve matters that he – for obvious reasons – has taken on further paying guests[1] besides myself. Admittedly, such circumstances only become problematic with time; I fear that time will come, however, if time does not offer anything else.

After all this it is doubly superfluous to tell you in many words how much your messages mean. The one I received yesterday[2] – from the 24th – was written before you had received my last, long letter, which contained very warm thanks for the Easter parcel and also a request for four or five books from my library that I urgently need in order to write the essay for Max. By my reckoning, you should have received my letter by now.

It would be a shame – though most definitely no tragedy – if it had been lost. For it also contained a description of my first impressions after arriving. As far as my request for books of my own is concerned, these are to be found among the paperbacks, partly in the lower rows of shelves by the window, but mostly opposite, also in the lower rows – I am essentially thinking of three books by E. Berl: Mort de la morale bourgeoise, Mort de la pensée bourgeoise, Le bourgeois et l'amour;[3] in addition Thibaudet: La république des professeurs.[4] And finally there are still one or two Cendrars translations[5] among the books above the sofa that it would be important to me to have. And I repeat my request to forgive me for demanding this great effort of you, as well as asking whether you could not entrust Wiesengrund with the task.

I do not mind telling you that I am surprised – now that my review of 'Kierkegaard' has been printed – that he has not written me a single line about it. Admittedly I am not yet in possession of a specimen, but I think I can safely assume that it was printed faithfully. At the moment I am occupied with a review of Bennett's 'The Old Wives' Tale',[6] which I would recommend to you once again. I intend to make various fundamental points about the novel in it, and it is possible that something might come of it.

I am glad that you will be going to Schloss Marquardt for a few days; it saddens me, however, that you are in need of it. You should already start thinking about how you could do something useful for yourself in the summer, and take great note of the suggestions in my last letter and write to me about them. As you are already so empathetic as to ask about my yearning for steak, am glad to report – to speak in the style of the Goethe–Zelter correspondence[7] – that, so far, more elevated inclinations have been making themselves known within my interior, especially the need to cast an occasional glance at periodicals. So, should you or Wiesengrund ever stumble on a 'Europäische Revue' or 'Neue Rundschau' or suchlike, I would be pleased if you could send it off to me once it had served its purpose.

Let us then continue to build the curved bridge between our two rather isolated positions, and I am perfectly happy to follow your suggestion and number its pillars, so I shall inscribe this letter with a highly visible three.[8]

My warm thanks for all the goodness in and between your lines and my best, kindest regards.

30 April 1933 Detlef
Ibiza (Balearic Islands)
San Antonio Fonda Miramar

PS Do you know anything about Ernst in Frankfurt? he writes just as rarely as the other Ernst.[9] And I had almost forgotten to thank you for the *exceptionally valuable* book list!

Original: manuscript.

1 *paying guests*: EO.

2 Gretel Karplus's letter of 24 April, which Benjamin had received on the 29th, i.e., 'yesterday'.

3 The first two of these had been published in book form in 1929 and 1930 respectively, the third in 1931; Benjamin cited from *Mort de la pensée bourgeoise* in his essay 'Zum gegenwärtigen gesellschaftlichen Standort des französischen Schriftstellers' [On the Current Social Position of the French Author], as he had already done three years previously in his 'Pariser Tagebuch' [Parisian Diary].

4 See Albert Thibaudet, *La république des professeurs*, Paris, 1927.

5 For his essay, Benjamin used only Blaise Cendrars' *Moravagine* (Paris, 1926), which had been published in Lissy Radermacher's translation in Munich in 1928. He had a further German translation: Blaise Cendrars, *Gold: Die fabelhafte Geschichte des Generals Johann August Suter* [Gold: The Fabulous Tale of General Johann August Suter], trans. Yvan Goll (Basel, 1925).

6 Arnold Bennett's *The Old Wives' Tale* had been published in 1908. Benjamin's review, 'Am Kamin: Zum 25jährigen Jubiläum eines Romans' [By the Fireplace: On the 25th Anniversary of a Novel], was published on 23 May 1933 in the *Frankfurter Zeitung* (see *GS* 3, pp. 388–92). Translator's note: the German edition, to which Benjamin is referring, bore the title *Konstanze und Sophie, oder Die alten Damen* [Konstanze and Sophie, or The Old Ladies].

7 I.e., adopting the elision of the pronoun 'I' used frequently there.

8 Benjamin is counting the letters sent to Gretel Karplus from Ibiza, taking nos. 7 and 8 as one letter.

9 These are firstly Ernst Schoen (1894–1960), whom Benjamin had known since his youth and who, as programme director of the Sudwestdeutscher Rundfunk, was able to create many opportunities for him in the late 1930s, and secondly Ernst Bloch (1885–1977).

11 GRETEL KARPLUS TO WALTER BENJAMIN
BERLIN, 6.5.1933

6 May 1933.

(5.)

My dear Detlef,

my conscience is weighing upon me so strongly that I must quickly give up my nap and now answer your second letter. I hope you[1] have meanwhile received my card[2] of 1 May and your books; if you had included it in your recent list, I would have been able to send you 'le bourgeois et l'amour' too – I kept picking it up while searching in vain for the other volume. I have still not received your archive, despite the definite arrangement; I will try my luck on the telephone again on Monday morning.

Please do not be angry that Teddie has not written to you yet about the review; he is feeling very nervous and down. It was a great joy to see 'die Mummerehlen'[3] in print yesterday evening. What else of yours is the Voss going to publish in the near future, and what other sort of arrangements have you made? I would be exceedingly grateful if you could divulge a little of your calculations to me, for I am better versed in business matters than you, and can perhaps help or advise you on occasion. The tone of the very last letter generally made me a little sad; it is so distant, as if you no longer wished to count me among your intimate friends. Did I do something wrong, express myself badly or behave unpleasantly? I am really not aware of any mistake, but perhaps there was something after all; at any rate, nothing could be further from my intentions, and you should know that better than anyone.

As far as my health is concerned, I am being treated by my professor again and having gastric irrigation on a daily basis, otherwise I am well. After my first month at work I can say that I could hardly have found anything better; the people and the boss are charming, I have a great deal to do, am learning the ropes well, and I think people are also satisfied with me. I told you about my sister's engagement – the marriage has had to be put off, as my brother-in-law[4] lost his job a few weeks ago and also had a serious accident at work whose full consequences are not yet clear. I will also send periodicals, and Teddie will talk to Dr Moras of the Europ. Revue regarding you. – Karola has moved once again Pension Oberholzer, Fedleggstr. 69., I am sure he is very cross with me, as I have not replied to him in ages.

I do not know anything about Ernst from Frft. As a curiosity, I must tell you that the husband of Sybill Carl[5] is probably becoming a sort of right-hand man for the films, has quite some influence and has already found engagements for several people; it sounds like a fairy tale.

Dear Detlef, I worry that you are in danger of island psychosis. Please keep in mind everything I have already said and which one should not really say, then perhaps you will know better what I want from you. But it is better for you to be cross with me for a moment than for me to set unfathomable riddles for you. Never forget, then, that since the first months of this year I have been so deeply indebted to you that it would make me infinitely happy if I were able to make your life a little easier. Please trust me and make use of me, in so far as one can say that at such a distance. I will be glad if I hear from you once every week – remember the motto that you wrote in the Gracian for me.

In honest friendship, more warmly than ever

your Felicitas

Original: typescript.

1 *Sie*.

2 Not preserved.

3 This excerpt from *Berliner Kindheit* had been published in the entertainment section of the *Vossische Zeitung* on 5 May.

4 Liselotte Karplus (b. 1909) had studied dentistry; at the time she was engaged to Ernst Schachtel (1903–1975), who worked as a lawyer before training as a psychoanalyst. He had emigrated to England in 1933, then to Switzerland in 1934. From 1935 onwards he worked for the Institute for Social Research in New York.

5 This is the Frankfurt-born Carl Dreyfuss (1898–1969), who had occasionally worked for the Institute for Social Research. In 1933 he published the study *Beruf und Ideologie des Angestellten* [Profession and Ideology of the White-Collar Worker], in which he was able to draw on his experience as a leading industrial manager. Aside from his stay in Stockholm in 1933, he worked in Berlin until at least 1935. Under the name of Ludwig Carls he worked for the Berlin film industry, mainly as dramatic adviser. Nothing is known about his first wife, Sybil.

12 WALTER BENJAMIN TO GRETEL KARPLUS SAN ANTONIO (IBIZA), 16.5.1933

Dear Felicitas,

today I have transferred my writing activity to the café for a change of scenery. It has few advantages over my forest hiding-places. But sometimes one simply needs the sight of a glass of coffee in front of one as the representative of a civilization that is otherwise sufficiently remote. This year one is even having it with milk. And neither the screaming children nor the nearby Ibizan discourses shall disturb us. I think it is right for me finally to write to you in a good moment; perhaps my last letter seemed, and was, a little clouded. Sometimes there can indeed be clouds that gather and cast shadows upon the flowerbed of my writing. But now I feel heartened by a little package of books[1] I have just received from Max in Geneva, and with whose help I can now – relying on your parcel – finally begin the study in the hope of lending its impoverished shape some scanty adornment. For such an attempt can only be a poor one, even with a wealth of technical means, because there is next to no existing groundwork. My first thoughts about it came while reading Céline's book 'Voyage au bout de la nuit',[2] which you have naturally heard of. As I am still very far from the end of that extensive tome, however, I would like to keep these thoughts to myself for today. I now have two weeks until the delivery of this manuscript, and these days must be made use of from morning till evening.

So they will, at least in this respect, be like yours. Admittedly we would both prefer the latter without gastric irrigation. I fear that it is an ordeal for you,[3] to say nothing of the time lost. Will you have to keep it up for long? hopefully it will help very soon and disappear. – As you can see, I received your letter of the sixth. And not only that, but also, to my great joy, the Rundschau issue[4] just arrived. I confirmed the book delivery with a card[5] as soon as it had arrived. But, as the only thing I can do is to thank you, you will have to put up with hearing it twice. That was, if I may say so, often a silent question for me: whether there might not be someone who answers my questions in letters without my having to repeat them five times, or who could fulfil requests – ones that are all the more onerous for relating to small matters. You have answered this silent question, and can rest assured that I know what that means. And I will not have peace of mind until I know that the rest of the journals with things of mine, which I might require at any moment during my work, are in your hands. But this should not make you fear that you will often be pestered with requests for deliveries. There seems to be a possibility, rather, of having an acquaintance of mine who is coming here send me the things. If that works out, I would ask you to hand the messenger who collects them the things you listed for me as well as the journals, which my girl will hopefully soon bring you. His proof of identity will consist in the other half of my signature, one of which I enclose.[6] This assumes, of course, that you have already received everything, for it is a favour, and I cannot very well send my acquaintance to two different places. Admittedly I will no longer be able to use the material for my essay on French literature. But after that I am planning one on Bennett. I wrote recently about 'Konstanze und Sophie', his most famous novel. Today the Rheinverlag agreed to make another major work of his available to me.[7]

I am very happy that your job has proved a good choice. But hopefully you still have a little time for leisure. I am sorry to hear that Teddie is so unwell. But through his tenacious activity he will, I think, soon find something new to concentrate upon. I should not hold it against him if that is not a letter to me. If he is to remain silent about my review, however, I would at least like to have a look at it. Firstly for my archives, and secondly also to make sure that it was printed faithfully. It would give me great joy if you could perhaps send me one (or even two) specimens of that review and of Die Mummerehlen. Otherwise I have no specimen copies.

As you can see, some little request always finds its way into my letters.

So that you might forget that a little, I shall now tell you my daily routine with the manifold thoughts and projects that float along with it on the surface. So I get up at half past six, sometimes at six, and at seven I go to a hillside where I find my hidden deckchair. Then, at eight, I unstop my thermos flask like some bricklayer's apprentice or stonemason and begin my breakfast. After that I work and read until one o'clock. The only project worth mentioning is a detective novel,[8] which I shall only write, however, if I can be sure that it will turn out well. For now, I can imagine one only with great reservations, and can do no more than take down scenes, motifs and tricks on little bits of paper for later consideration. Sometimes, when I am taking a little walk in the forest around twelve o'clock, Paris comes to mind. It is not only imagining the bleakness of winter that would await me here, but also the thought of this or that necessity which a return there can offer, at least for a short time. All that together is a rather burdensome chain of thought, however, as there is so far not the slightest notion of how to leave the island. So then I return to my chair, my mood slightly darkened, and perhaps get started on another page of 'Berliner Kindheit'. I think of 'waking up at night';[9] and one or two other things. But my current activities are still pushing that into the background.

Unfortunately even the most urgent requests for review copies have not been acknowledged by any of the parties concerned. As these in fact constitute the most binding sorts of assignments, however, it would be of infinite help to me if Wiesengrund could indeed obtain some of those – or others – for me from the

'Europäische Revue'.[10] At the moment, *faced with editors who do not know me*, I prefer the subaltern form of the book presentation, firstly because it expands my reference library, and secondly because it is binding for both parties.

Those are my literary prospects. At two o'clock there is a meal at a long table, where I do my best to 'behave'. It has not yet become so hot that one has to sleep afterwards. I normally sit under a fig tree in front of the house and read or scribble. Regrettably, attempts to sweeten the later afternoon with the help of a chess partner have so far been unsuccessful. I myself would be content with sixty-six or dominoes; but the people here, as they mostly have nothing sensible to do, are too serious for that. Sometimes there is a little conversation in the café in which I began this letter, but also interrupted it through the appearance of a guest who exchanged a few words with me. I am now continuing it in my room, which I share with three hundred flies.

At nine, half past nine at the latest, I go to bed, and treat myself to some sort of luxury reading by the fairylike light of a few candles. It is also thanks to this reading that I made the acquaintance of Georges Simenon,[11] an author of quite especially notable detective novels. Incidentally, the continuous work of the last two weeks has had a rather unexpected consequence: I have become more sensitive to my isolation. After reading so much and writing a certain amount during the day, I feel a need in the evening – not always, but certainly after a while – to speak a few sensible words, or even better to have a few meet my own ears. But then I quickly reach the limits that are set here. The last winter in San Antonio left seemingly indelible traces of nature's sadness on Noeggerath. He can almost always be ruled out from a serious conversation. There are a few young people among the new arrivals whom one could talk to; but one never hears from them. Thus it can happen now and again that the day gone by is deprived of its best part, which only the evening would have brought forth. This is unlikely to change much. And so I occasionally toy with the idea of going over to Mallorca, where Blei is residing in Cala Ratjada; he would certainly have been a moderate attraction in Berlin, but the library he is said to have here makes him gain prestige quite considerably. Naturally it is inconceivable at the moment; but how much easier and more homely such thoughts become before going to sleep, after a greeting from you has come gliding in without any commotion. Then one dares to dream a little once more; and you cannot have wished for anything sweeter.

I am concluding these lines in Ibiza, on a high terrace. The town lies beneath me; the noise from a smithy or a building site reaches me like breaths of the land beginning almost at the foot of my bastion – that is how narrow this strip of town is. To the right of the houses I look upon the sea, and behind them the island starts to rise very gently before sinking towards the sea once more behind a row of hills that patiently accompanies the horizon. You can feel what 'an island' means, and let this greeting of mine glide into your hands like a small model of it.

As ever
yours,
Detlef

16 May 1933
Ibiza (Balearic Islands)
San Antonio
Fonda Miramar

Original: manuscript.

1 No further details are known about the book delivery from Max Horkheimer.

2 Published in Paris in 1932.

3 *Sie*.

4 It could not be ascertained which issue of the *Neue Rundschau* Gretel Karplus had sent; an examination of those published before the writing of the letter did not provide any indications that the issue had been sent on account of an article that particularly interested Benjamin.

5 Not preserved.

6 Unknown. The note with the one half of the signature has not survived.

7 The novels *Clayhanger* and *Hilda Lessways*, published in 1910 and 1911 respectively, which had both appeared in Daisy Bródy's translation in 1930. Benjamin read the novels, but did not write about them.

8 See the sketches in *GS* 7 [2], pp. 846–50; it is likely that the document entitled 'Materialien zu einem Kriminalroman' [Materials for a Detective Novel] (ibid., pp. 846f.) was written around that time (see also letter no. 34, note 11).

9 This thought gave rise, in mid-August 1933, to 'Der Mond' [The Moon] (see *GS* 4 [1], pp. 300–2, and *GS* 7 [1], pp. 426–8).

10 Adorno's conversation on Benjamin's behalf with Joachim Moras, which Gretel Karplus had mentioned in advance in her letter of 6 May, appears to have been without result.

11 During his time in Ibiza, Benjamin read *Le Relais d'Alsace*, *Les Treize coupables*, *Monsieur Gallet*, *Le Pendu de Saint-Pholien* and *Le Port des brumes*.

13 GRETEL KARPLUS TO WALTER BENJAMIN
BERLIN, 25.5.1933

25 May 1933.

(6.)

My dear Detlef,

I was very glad to receive your lengthy last letter; you cannot imagine how much you reassure me with your messages.

Your archive[1] has meanwhile landed in the Prinzenallee, Miss Dohrmann apologized for the delay – she moved house, and her male friend and brother had to help her with the new apartment. With your things here it feels as if I had a part of you with me, and I am almost sad that I have to hand them over again so quickly. I actually do not know if it would not be more practical to have those scripts collected that are most important to you; the valuable books are perhaps in better hands with me, and the many duplicates might only be a burden to you. Please do not think me entirely useless, but I cannot with the best will in the world find the identity proof for your friend; I know it was the first name with a little piece of the H., and I do not think there could be any mistake, but if you want to be entirely safe then please renew this passport. I sent off the two specimens from the Voss as printed matter today, I am afraid that is how long it took to obtain them. – Teddie is now on the staff of the Revue and has given your address to Dr Moras, who will contact you. There is only one catch to the matter, namely the publisher's shortage of money. I would be very grateful if you could always tell me where your articles are published so that I can get hold of them; I would, for example, like to see the review of the book by Bennett.

Dear Detlef, I am very worried that you will be struck with island psychosis; I fear that in the long run you will not be able to bear your life of isolation, so it is at least a small comfort to me that you have been considering Mallorca and Paris for the winter. I ask you most sincerely once again to let me know in good time what I can do for you, perhaps even against your current inhibitions and reservations; for I would never forgive myself if anything happened to you, and I will be able to help you as long as it is humanly possible. Here I am, uttering such grand words, and now I must already let you down and disappoint you: the doctor has ordered me to take a period of recovery after I had another ghastly migraine attack on Saturday, and so I am going to the Baltic Sea for three weeks, to Rügen. Binz is my childhood summer resort, but I still find it marvellous today, quite aside from the memories – especially in June, when no one is there yet. Teddie will accompany me in July and then probably go to Frankfurt for a meeting. Dear, please do not be cross with me for destroying your plans, our plans, with a single word; I still have a week of holidays left over, perhaps we can arrange a meeting[2] then. I hope you will send me a line or two in Binz very soon: Binz Rügen Villa Aegir c/o Gips. Today is Ascension Day, the men's outings here are being rained off most dutifully, I wish you a pleasant Whitsun, my fond and warmest regards, ever your Felicitas.

1 Benjamin's collection of his own manuscripts, typescripts and printed essays.

2 *meeting*: EO.

14 WALTER BENJAMIN TO GRETEL KARPLUS
IBIZA (IBIZA), *c.*26.5.1933

To begin with a manner of confession, dear Felizitas – with these lines, you[1] are receiving something like the primeurs of the day, an hour matured to a particular degree and under special circumstances, which hopefully – pressed into this letter – will not lose its entire fragrance and colour. As far as the contour is concerned, I think I can paint a reasonably enduring picture of it. But all I can do is to send you this rare shrub, as the others that have passed my hours these last few days mostly withered. And, as you have a share in their withering, it is only fitting that you also have a share in what I am dedicating to you with these words: that is to say, a round, ripe fruit of the hour swaying in the morning breeze.

For why have you not written to me? my last days have been more successful, though admittedly the one beginning now is not so comforting. And now, before I speak more kindly to you, I will shame you one last time by confiding in you that this comfort does not, sadly, stem from any message of yours, which I awaited in vain once more today. It is actually not so difficult to deduce its origin if you immerse yourself in the description of the room that I will conjure up before you, and do not forget various wiles in which, on occasions, I already sought refuge years ago – indeed I had promised to take them together with you. But I will now interrupt this to transport you to the room of the friends I have already mentioned to you, and whose arts, if I am not greatly mistaken, I already intimated to you once in conversation.

Meanwhile I have learnt well from my friends, and there are almost no clouds rising to the ceiling, for I now know how to guide them down deep into my inner regions through the long bamboo tube. In telling you of this, I am almost finding it difficult to part with the French in which my voice conversed all night as a gentle wind does with the fire in a hearth. When evening came I felt very sad. But

I sensed that rare state in which internal and external constrictions balance each other out very accurately, leading to that mood in which alone, perhaps, one can truly be comforted. That almost seemed like a hint to us, and after taking care of the long, informed and precise arrangements that need to be made so that no one has to lift a finger in the course of the night, we set to work around two o'clock. Even if it was not the first time chronologically speaking, it was in terms of its success. We shared the various handing back and forth, which demands great care, in such a way that each of us was both servant and served, and the conversation mingled with the handing like threads in a tapestry that colour the heavens or interweave with the battle depicted in the foreground.

I can hardly give you an idea of where or along what lines the conversation progressed. If, however, the notes[2] that I will take on such hours in future reach a certain degree of precision and I gather them all together in a dossier[3] that you are familiar with, then the day will come for me to delight in reading you one or two excerpts from it. Today I achieved considerable results in the exploration of curtains[4] – for there was a curtain separating us from the balcony that leads out to the town and the sea. Before then, however, you might receive some of the new ideas I have found regarding the art of storytelling – my old theme, which occupies me ever more, and which I approached more closely than ever before with an attempt to let an extended story structure itself,[5] interrupted by reveries and technical incumbencies.

Let me conclude the page[6] with the seemingly – but only seemingly – base and profane information that I am thus learning French in such a fashion that I will soon be able to write not entirely perfectly, but without hesitation.

That page stands out more brightly than you realize from the background of others that I was most prudent not to write you in the last few days. The house I am in felt flea-ridden from the conversations of two ghastly commune women[7] who had been taken up there and whom I had to bear until today. The atmosphere was excruciating. The broodings that are stimulated by such an atmosphere were joined by broodings on the essay that is finally almost finished, and which kept me from other work that means infinitely more to me. In particular a number of new chapters for the children's book.

The next days promise to be much quieter. Perhaps I will even have a chance to dictate a few things. And then I will begin a new novel by Bennett that I have been sent here. Do not think me indelicately reticent, dear Felizitas, for asking you only now about everything concerning you: your mood, your health, your daily work, your problem child.[8] Please do not make me wait so long again. Understand that I intended this letter more as a gift than a document, and do not hear in it merely a hesitant farewell, but also the morning sound of 'good day' from Detlef.

Original: manuscript.
On the dating: By his own account, Benjamin stayed in the town of Ibiza from 25 until 31 May; the opium-smoking described in the letter can therefore not have taken place any earlier than the night between the 25th and the 26th. In a letter to Scholem of 31 May (see *GB* 4, letter no. 788), Benjamin writes that he dictated his 'finally almost finished' essay – as he terms it above – 'Zum gegenwärtigen gesellschaftlichen Standort des französischen Schriftstellers'.

1 *Sie*.

2 These are Benjamin's 'Crocknotizen' (see *GS* 6, pp. 603–7), which can thus be dated to the end of May 1933, not 1932.

3 This is 'Protokolle zu Drogenversuchen' [Protocols of Drug Experiments], which Benjamin had compiled for his planned book on hashish (see *GB* 4, letter no. 744 and the respective note).

4 See also *GS* 6, pp. 604f.

5 Presumably Benjamin had either read out or improvised a story; no further information could be found.

6 Originally in the middle of the second page.

7 Presumably Felix Noeggerath's third wife, Marietta (see Gershom Scholem, *Walter Benjamin und sein Engel*, ed. Rolf Tiedemann, 2nd edn [Frankfurt am Main: Suhrkamp, 1992]), and his daughter-in-law, whose name is unknown.

8 This refers to Adorno.

15 GRETEL KARPLUS TO WALTER BENJAMIN BERLIN, 4.6.1933

Whit Sunday 1933.

(7.)

My very dear Detlef,
a thousand thanks for your last letter, this little present that only you[1] could have thought up especially for me. I keep reading it again and again, and am so infinitely sorry that we cannot experience all those things together. I am most disturbed by your urging for letters from me, for I reply fairly regularly, normally within five days of receiving your messages; could it be that some have been

lost? Have you found out whether one can cash in postal orders? Then I could at least imagine that I am taking part in your nocturnal undertakings.

Your words about the possibility of being able to write in French suggested a quiet hope to me, and as I do not know when else I should have the chance to see them, I would, if possible, be a most grateful recipient of any typewritten manuscripts.

Ernst Frankfurter[2] is supposedly in London, his wife at home, and I have not heard from the other one in Küsnacht. Since 1 June I have been responsible, until the final decision, for the shop with whose pretty bear-paw brand you are now familiar. Please do not tell anyone, but I am a little afraid in big Berlin all by myself, when one cannot even make a telephone call to hear a few kind words. But I am a terrible egotist to tell you of my little pains, which cannot at all be compared with your isolation.

My problem child left on Friday – I ask for your discretion regarding the examination[3] –, and I am very curious as to whether he will soon return to Berlin full of plans and possibilities. After being together for almost three months, it all seems quite simple to me, but now I am expecting complications. It is quite conceivable that harsh reality has an important function for him, that it can make up for a few things; for now I am still in the dark.

Dear, as I know about it, you need not be embarrassed, please tell me how I could make you truly happy on your birthday?; at this great distance I must ask you in good time, even though it is still five weeks away. On the same day two years ago I was at your place with Ernst and that roughneck son of a poet[4] and his wife. Please do not spare me too much and write to me not only about the pleasing but also about the gloomy things weighing upon you, perhaps we can find a better way out together. – It is already late, I wish you a good night with sweet dreams and think sometimes of

your little
Felicitas

My name
Essays
Advocacy of French literature
Apolitical
Berlin Childhood Around 1900
Names of the most important essays: Goethe's Elective Affinities

Keller	Hebel
Proust	Kraus
Green	Surrealism
Gide	

Jewish Encyclopaedia
Lichtenberg bibliography

Original: typescript with keywords handwritten by Benjamin on the reverse.

1 *Sie*.

2 This is Ernst Schoen.

3 Adorno was considering taking an examination for private music tutors.

4 Unknown.

16 WALTER BENJAMIN TO GRETEL KARPLUS SAN ANTONIO (IBIZA), c.10.6.1933

Dear Felizitas,

I am letting a little wind music sway the top of the pine tree under which I am sitting, and drawing a four-page token of gratitude at its feet. You[1] may pick this token for your last letter. I would sooner have wished you a few dry, spiky stalks from Baltic Sea dunes for Whitsun. Yes, I am sad that, rather than submerging your head in the waves, you have to hide it under the bear's paw. Let me know soon when you can show it once more.

It is reassuring, however, that the responsibility for the bear cub has joined that for the problem child. As long as you do not entirely lose the responsibility you should have for yourself. Write to me about the more decisive things: does the gastric irrigation have to continue and is it unpleasant? has the migraine passed? What can you do from time to time to cheer yourself up, and whom are you seeing now that the problem child has disappeared? Speaking of whom, let me thank you warmly for the specimen copies of the Kierkegaard; and add that the editors had removed an important paragraph towards the end of the review. I have not yet heard anything from 'Die Europäische Revue'.

I have been diligent and written an essay of forty typed pages about 'the current social position of the French writer'. For that, I had to rely on the hospitality I was shown in the town of Ibiza. For here in San Antonio, all the topographical adversities that had long been on the horizon have taken effect in such a way that my move to the town is a certainty. The expenses there will inevitably exceed the ones I have here. But after exploring, not without inventiveness, all the technical possibilities for at least somewhat undisturbed work here, without a single one of them paying off, I am forced to make this decision. I am already looking forward to describing the physiology of this house to you one day in conversation, as well as the secrets of the settler atmosphere that has gradually developed in San Antonio.

I find it absolutely hateful, and have therefore been using any excuse to get away for some time now. That recently gave me the opportunity to discover one of the most beautiful and secluded parts of the island. For I had just finished preparing for a solitary moonlit walk to the island's summit, the Atalaya de San José,[2] when there appeared a distant acquaintance of the people here, a Scandinavian lad who appears only rarely in areas inhabited by strangers and lives in a hidden mountain village. He is incidentally a grandson of the painter Paul Gauguin,[3] and has exactly the same name as his grandfather. The next day I became more closely acquainted with this figure, and found him every bit as fascinating as his mountain village, where he is the only outsider. Early in the morning, at five, we went out to sea with a crayfish-catcher and first of all sailed about for three hours, becoming thoroughly acquainted with crayfish-catching. It was, admittedly, a largely melancholy spectacle, in that sixty traps yielded a total of only three creatures. Albeit giant ones, and often many more on other days. We were then dropped off in a hidden bay. And there we found a scene of such unshakeable perfection that something strange, though not incomprehensible, happened inside of me: for I did not really see it; it was inconspicuous to me; its perfection placed it on the edge of invisibility.

The beach does not have any buildings; there is a stone hut off in the background. Four or five fishing-boats had moved high up the beach. Next to these boats, however, cloaked in black, with only their stern, rigid faces unconcealed, stood a few women. It was as if the wonder of their presence and the unusual nature of their dress balanced each other out, so that the needle stood still, so to speak, and I did not notice anything. I think Gauguin was in the picture; one of his peculiarities, however, is that he hardly speaks at all. And so we had already been ascending in almost complete silence for over an hour when we encountered a man carrying a tiny white child's coffin under his arm. A child had died down in the stone hut. The black-cloaked women had been mourners, who, however, in spite of their duties, had not wanted to miss so extraordinary a spectacle as the arrival of a motorboat on that beach. In short: to find this scene conspicuous, one had first of all to understand it. Otherwise one would gaze upon it as sluggishly and thoughtlessly as a picture by Feuerbach,[4] where one assumes, only really from a distance, that tragic figures by the rocky shore must fit in somehow.

Inside the mountains one finds some of the island's most highly cultivated, fertile terrain. The ground is cut by deep canals, but they are so narrow that they often run invisibly beneath the tall grass, which is the deepest shade of green, for long stretches. The roaring of these waterways almost resembles the sound of sucking. There are carob trees, almonds, olive trees and conifers along the slope, and the bottom of the valley is covered with maize and bean plants. There are blossoming oleander bushes up against the rocks everywhere. It is a landscape like the one I used to love in 'Das Jahr der Seele';[5] today the pure, fleeting taste of the green almonds I stole from the trees at six o'clock the next morning entered my senses more familiarly. We could not expect any breakfast; it was a place removed from all civilization. My companion was the most perfect one you could imagine for such an area. Equally uncivilized, equally highly cultivated. He reminded me of one of the Heinle brothers,[6] who died so young, and has a gait that often makes him look as if he were on the point of immediate disappearance. I would not so readily have believed someone else who declared he was fighting against the influence of Gauguin's painting; but in the case of this young man I understood exactly what he meant.

Something completely different: for the last three weeks, a book has been appearing in instalments in *Die Züricher Illustrierte* in which a certain Tex Harding[7] deals with Fawcett, a colonel who disappeared in the Brazilian jungle in 1925. I read the beginning and think that the tramp and cowboy who supposedly wrote this book – and probably did indeed write it – is a very important and exceptionally talented author. If you have read the first chapter, which must have appeared in one of the first May or last April issues, you will know what I am talking about. Perhaps you can procure the respective issues of the *Züricher Illustrierte*, read this series with breathless suspense, and then send them to me. Yes?

In return you will receive an offprint of the Bennett review as soon as I am in possession of duplicates.

Yet again I must thank you for one of your money orders, which are paid out punctually and at the relatively decent rate of 2.7. Every one of them is a little model of a secure existence for me, and perhaps with you it is as with the little model houses fashioned by architects, which are often much more charming to look at than to live in once they have actually been built. And now you already want to think about my birthday. I have given it a great deal of thought, and only desire to share my greatest wish with you. Now, Mac Orlan[8] says that, for a man of forty, there can really be no greater celebration than putting on a new suit. That is all very well – but I shall now be turning forty-one, and at that age one is in greater need of consolation than celebrations. Yes, I would like to let some blue smoke rise up and out of my chimney on that day. But it has not curled itself above my roof for a long time, and the pictures I enclosed in my previous letter were the last that were formed by it. If you could place a few fine logs on my hearth you would be with me in my happiest hours, and on the fifteenth my smoke trail above the house would drift all the way over to you.

Dear Felizitas, I shall close for today. Naturally my books should remain with you. I would only ask you to deliver the scripts; complete, for the sake of simplicity. Unless you happen to place great value on one particular piece. But that would insult the other pieces, and I can therefore hardly accept it. – My writing-paper is finished and I cannot find the envelope of which I – and you, I hope – have grown so fond. Please receive these lines, which find their way into your hands more awkwardly, with kindness.

As ever

yours Detlef

PS A cordial letter from the Europäische Revue[9] arrived just this moment.

Original: manuscript.
On the dating: Benjamin is responding to Gretel Karplus's letter of Whit Sunday, 14 June, which would have reached him around 10 June. The details he gives in the letter regarding the start and duration of the Tex Harding instalment series in the *Züricher Illustrierte* appear to be incorrect.

1 *Sie*.

2 The Atalaya de San José, located to the south of San Antonio, is the highest hill on the island of Ibiza, with a height of 476 m.

3 The Danish engraver Paul-René Gaugin (1911–1976).

4 Benjamin was presumably thinking of the paintings *Iphigenie* (1862/1871) and *Medea* (1870) by Anselm Feuerbach.

5 Translator's note: A collection of poems [The Year of the Soul] published by Stefan George (1868–1933) in 1897.

6 Christoph Friedrich Heinle (1894–1914), whom Benjamin had first met in 1913 in Freiburg, and Wolf Heinle, who is presumably meant here.

7 The book by Tex Harding (real name: Harry Brown) was entitled *Missing: In the Footsteps of Colonel Fawcett* and was published in 1933; nothing is known about the instalments in the *Züricher Illustrierte*.

8 Towards the end of the story 'Docks', he writes: 'Today I am thinking once again that, for a man who has not passed forty years of age, the sweetest of pleasures is to put on a suit that pleases him. A fresh suit brings with it a new life, one equally fresh, a life filled with immediate interest and satisfactions that are at the same time literary, new, anecdotal, social and personal' (see Pierre Mac Orlan, *Sous la lumière froide* [Paris: Gallimard, collection folio, 1979], p. 162).

9 Not preserved among Benjamin's belongings.

17 GRETEL KARPLUS TO WALTER BENJAMIN
BERLIN, 17.6.1933

17 June 1933.

(8.)

Dear Detlef,

I was so worried about you yesterday that I sent a telegram,[1] though it caused considerable problems at the post office and I am not sure that it actually arrived. – I am very proud of your letters; I preserve them all, and they form a very small substitute for our evenings. As you can see, I am getting carried away today; but I long for you, and then I even stop worrying about censorship.

My present state of health is not bad; I stopped the gastric irrigation after no. 5, and am now taking tablets and sunbathing in the canoe on Sundays. I do not have a single free evening this week, but the names are hardly worth mentioning: Carlchen, Alfred from Positano,[2] a student of Teddie's[3] and an ardent admirer of Benjamin literature; it was only the other day that I had the luck to meet – at the house of an acquaintance of whom I would really not have expected it – Elisabeth,[4] Bert's lady friend, whom I previously knew only by sight. He recently moved to Paris, and I rather liked her; I hope I shall see her now and again, and perhaps she will also introduce me to your bank manager,[5] whom I do not wish to call without any reason.

Now that I know they will arrive, I will often send you some pink notes;[6] perhaps in this way I can make things a little easier for you down there. I am content for you to view it as a birthday present, though I would have done it in any case, and was thinking more of something that you cannot get and which I could easily obtain for you here. It is only a shame that I am handicapped myself, and do not have the same means at my disposal as I used to, but you know that and will no doubt take my good will into account. You are making me very happy through this, for now I know once more why I have to earn money; I am adopting you in place of the child that I shall never have anyway. – Are you receiving regular news from Stefan,[7] is everything all right there?

The letter has become a little subdued, not as jolly as I would like to keep my messages to you; perhaps that mirrors my constant efforts not to let things get me down. – I am glad that you are thinking of me, goodbye, sleep well, sweet dreams and write to me often

ever

your

Felicitas

Original: typescript.

1 Not preserved.

2 Alfred Sohn-Rethel (1899–1990) and Benjamin had first met in Heidelberg in 1921.

3 Unknown.

4 The writer Elisabeth Hauptmann (1897–1973), who sometimes worked as Brecht's dramatic assistant.

5 The Vienna-born Gustav Glück (1902–1973) was director of the foreign department of the Reichskreditgesellschaft [State Credit Society] in Berlin. He emigrated to Argentina via England in 1938.

6 This refers to the postal orders.

7 Stefan Rafael Benjamin (1918–1972), Benjamin's son from his marriage to Dora Sophie, née Keller (1890–1964).

18 WALTER BENJAMIN TO GRETEL KARPLUS SAN ANTONIO (IBIZA), *c.*25.6.1933

Dear Felizitas,

I have now carried out the regrouping that I had planned for so long, but postponed until I could manage to avoid incurring additional expenses. I would be happy if I could hope that the new arrangement I have reached since yesterday could continue for at least as long as the old one. That is very questionable. But at least for now I am accommodated as well here as I possibly could be. I am living on the old shore from last year, which I so often visited in my dreams during the winter. It is no longer quite so deserted, admittedly; and I no longer see the lighthouse of Canighora[1] – the island on which Hannibal was born – through my window at night. But the sea is a mere twenty paces from my room once again; there is a little beach here. And in the neighbourhood there is the little house in which that very sympathetic boy[2] who owns it, and works as my secretary on the side, lives with a few guests. But I am quartered in a new building very close by. Though only one room is finished in this house, and there is heavy building work going on all around me. So one cannot stay there during the day; one has to keep to the woods, which are very close and quite secluded. But I am having my meals in the aforementioned neighbouring house, at least for now.

I would have liked to have made all these arrangements much earlier, so that I could have combined them with the hope of a longer duration; but the quarters in question were only sorted out a very few days ago. Now I hope I shall soon be able to say the same for my next pieces of work; in particular new parts of 'Berliner Kindheit'. But it will certainly take a few days until I am sufficiently adjusted to have some ideas once more. I am having little difficulty making these days easier with a novel by Bennett, which is very lengthy and very much worth reading, even if it is no match for 'Konstanze und Sophie'. It is called 'Die Familie Clayhanger'.

If it were my authorial business to write family novels, I could motivate myself to produce a few stately volumes by documenting the occurrences and events I have been following in a number of remarkable families in the foreign colony here. In particular, the 'decline of a family' studied by Thomas Mann in 'Buddenbrooks' seems mild compared to that of the Noeggerath family, with whom I had quite a lot of social, albeit not intellectual, contact last year.

I carved another figurine out of the green wood[3] the other day: I think you will have laid eyes on it by now. In reality it is nothing new, simply a reworking of a piece that you definitely once heard me read in Berlin. There is another one that should yet be awaiting you, but which, in the state you will perhaps see it in, is not new enough. I mean the 'Knabenbücher',[4] of which I shall send you a corrected copy should it be published. For I substantially revised the piece after sending it off. The next few days are not reserved for these things, I should add, but rather for the comparative editing of two essays[5] twenty years apart. I have procured a copy of my first language study, 'Über Sprache überhaupt und über die Sprache des Menschen', and want to see how it compares to the thoughts I recorded at the start of this year. These are being awaited with great suspense in Jerusalem, and I am therefore feeling somewhat uneasy.

I have not heard from Berthold,[6] though occasionally from Elisabeth. I am very glad to hear that you saw her. I have not heard a single word from the two Ernsts.[7] As you can see, my correspondence is a meagre one, and I do not even know if it seems meaningful to you that you play first fiddle in it. You should then honour this orchestra more according to the attention of its only listener than to the number of its members. But alongside you, Gerhard[8] definitely has the leading part. The letters from Jerusalem are especially interesting at the moment,[9] as you can imagine, and I can expect them fairly reliably once every fortnight.

I am very happy that the gastric irrigation is over. And hopefully your Sundays in the boat are having a cheering effect. Admittedly, I hear from people who are still corresponding with relatives, and thus hear about the weather, that it is quite rainy in Germany at the moment. The summer here is different to the last, at any rate, when storms and rains were a rarity. But I love murky days, whether in the South or the North.

Sometimes, dear Felicitas, I wonder whether your children are not a burden to you? A problem child and an adoptive child. Do you not sometimes long for an adult? I could certainly take on that role if you were present; but as things are, I suppose my outline shrinks with the distance. I at least try to make it a little more pronounced through my letters, and perhaps a very slight silhouette becomes visible at times. If its core is of a deep black, however, that does not always correspond to the original; sometimes, however, this technical procedure does lead to an unsettling degree of truthfulness. I am not leaving the realm of colour symbolism if I thank you once again for a 'little pink note'. Now and again it stands out so reassuringly against said black background. And how else can I give you a confirmatory response than with this little watercolour sketch that interprets Baudelaire's 'charme inattendu d'un bijou rose et noir'[10] so shrewdly.

Write to me soon about what you are doing, thinking and reading. As I was born in Berlin, and therefore believe I have a certain power over bears, I shall speak to Georg Tengler's and recommend warmly that he extend you his softest paw.

Here is the little ribbon[11] which you should use to tie up the many little greetings you have no doubt discerned between the lines.

Yours,

Detlef

Original: manuscript.

1 The small island of Conejera, which, according to one Ibizan tradition, was the birthplace of Hannibal.

2 Perhaps Maximilian Verspohl from Hamburg (see *GB* 4, letter no. 754, and the note there).

3 'Zwei Rätselbilder' [Two Picture-Riddles] from *Berliner Kindheit*, which had appeared in the *Vossische Zeitung* on 16 June 1933 (see *GS* 4 [1], pp. 254f., and *GS* 7 [1], pp. 400f.); the version of the 'Felicitas copy' that Benjamin would most likely have read to Gretel Karplus bears the title 'Herr Knoche und Fräulein Pufahl'; before this, the section about these two teachers of Benjamin's can be found even earlier, in his *Berliner Chronik* (see *GS* 6, pp. 503–5).

4 This piece was published in the *Vossische Zeitung* under the title 'Schmöker' [Light Reading] on 17 September 1933; going on this part of the letter, it is highly questionable whether the title of the first edition was Benjamin's own; see *GS* 4 [1], pp. 274f. (the title of the first edition there), and *GS* 7 [1], pp. 396f.

5 'Lehre vom Ähnlichen' [The Doctrine of Similarity], written at the start of the year, and his first language study, written in 1916. The result of this 'editing' was 'Über das mimetische Vermögen' [On the Mimetic Capacity].

6 Bertolt Brecht.

7 Ernst Schoen and Ernst Bloch.

8 Gershom Scholem.

9 Due to the reports on the state of Zionism in Palestine and the great number of refugees from Germany; see in particular Scholem's letter of 15 June (*Scholem Correspondence*, pp. 74–6).

10 This is the fourth and final line of 'Lola de Valence', based on Edouard Manet's portrait of the Spanish dancer; the poem is one of the 'Épigraphes' from *Épaves*.

11 Benjamin had led into the 'H' of 'Hier' with a widely swung line.

19 GRETEL KARPLUS TO WALTER BENJAMIN BERLIN, 27.6.1933

27 June 1933.

Dear Detlef,

today just a few lines, to confirm to you[1] with this yellow bit of paper that I delivered my foster children as arranged; I hope they will get through their journey in good shape.

Do you know that a part of the F. Z. is gradually accumulating at the Voss? Welter[2] with partner, since 1 June also Gubler,[3] is that any use to you? In response to the little article,[4] which I enclose, there was recently a telephone call from a man who asked for the address of Herr Holz, saying that he had something important to tell him. For the little girl[5] named L. v. Landau had not died at all, but was living happily married in England.

Thank you for your reassuring response to my telegram;[6] I have meanwhile received and answered the letter. I await your next message with impatience. Forgive my haste

Your Felicitas

who is really waiting for you

Original: manuscript.

1 *Sie*.

2 Erich Welter returned to the *Frankfurter Zeitung* in March 1934 following the dissolution of the *Vossische Zeitung*.

3 The Swiss journalist Friedrich T. Gubler had been features editor of the *Frankfurter Zeitung*; he had started work at the *Vossische Zeitung* shortly after 1 June.

4 'Zwei Rätselbilder', which appeared in the *Vossische Zeitung* on 16 June 1933; see *GS* 4 [1], pp. 254f.

5 'Her name was Luise von Landau, and the name had soon cast its spell on me. It has remained alive in my memory to this day, though not for that reason. Rather, it was the first among those my age that I heard touched by the accent of death' (ibid., p. 254). Nothing more is known about Luise von Landau.

6 Not preserved.

20 GRETEL KARPLUS TO WALTER BENJAMIN BERLIN, 6.7.1933

6 July 1933.

Dear Detlef,

you unfortunately failed to tell me your new address in your last letter, and I am not quite sure whether the pink notes still arrived at the old one. So please forgive the interruption and tell me as soon as you can where I should send them from now on.

Unfortunately I cannot fulfil your wish for me to send you the Züricher Illustrierte, as I cannot obtain the paper here in Berlin; perhaps Ernst can get it for you directly: Küsnacht, 12 Schiedhaldensteig.

On the surface, my life has changed little in comparison to before: as far as my health is concerned, I often feel very exhausted, but it is at least more bearable than last year. I am hearing little from Frankfurt, as usual, which is starting to make me think that the examination I had mentioned to you is currently under way; but perhaps I am wrong. My parents[1] have been in Gastein for the last five weeks, and are returning on Saturday; the time I spent here alone was pleasant, though tempered by my brother-in-law's illness, for which there is still no end in sight. It was a quiet month for business, though the liquidation of the old firm and filling in as a holiday replacement at the new one offered some variety. I have been closely involved in the creation of two new winter models, which I would love to show you. I would like to ask you something as an old fashion-lover: why does one always think one looks awful in the old dresses and hats at the start of a new season, even if one has not got any fatter or thinner or changed one's hairstyle? Does fashion truly change us, to the extent that we have a different impression of ourselves?

Well and now I must congratulate you on your birthday, and I thought that we should always stick to 'Du' in our private letters, if that is all right with you. I would also like to have added officially and forever, but I do not know if that is really what we want. I, at least, love a trace of secrecy, and I find it marvellous to hide in the names reserved almost only for us. And I certainly did not mean to offend you with my suggestion of adoption, I really only meant that you should feel a little at home with me and know where you belong. Otherwise you are quite right, I am just a little girl in great need of an adult, and I am overjoyed that you wish to take that part in my life. I would not even have dared to ask you, for fear that you would condemn it as too intrusive, but your little Felicitas feels very safe with you and sends you a thousand thanks for this rare little bouquet.

I have so far spoken only about myself in my congratulations. My wish for you is that you might settle down in the not-too-distant future, without this constant tormenting worry about your bare existence, with a few pleasant friends nearby, who could certainly include me, and the true success and recognition of your work. Perhaps this plan strikes you as a little too much in one go, but my imagination has so much freedom at the moment that it easily veers off into the distance, and I cannot make enough wishes for you. My dear great friend, I have only told you a fraction of what there is to say, but your powers of decipherment will yet find one or two other things between the lines. I lean trustingly on the rod of green wood and swing myself over to you

your

Felicitas

Original: typescript.

1 Amalie and Joseph Albert Karplus.

21 WALTER BENJAMIN TO GRETEL KARPLUS SAN ANTONIO (IBIZA), *c.*8.–10.7.1933

Dear Felizitas,

it is not so very long ago that I last wrote to you.[1] But in the end it always takes weeks, before writing and replying combine to form some sort of whole that one can cling to. That is why I cannot exactly say how much you actually know about the realization of my intention, frequently hinted at, of changing my domicile. I have your letter of the 27th, but I am sure that it crossed a fairly long one of mine that probably already contains what there is to say about my new housing.

In short, I am now finally living on the other shore again, finally alone, finally close to the seashore and close to the forest, where I can work undisturbed. It is, incidentally, certainly an unusual abode that I have found – a single room in a new building of which almost nothing else has been built; a room that was completed to lodge not me, but rather its owner's furniture. And it is with them that I share mine. Nor are there any windowpanes yet, the well by the house does not yet exist. But those are all entirely bearable disadvantages compared to those of an inapposite housing community and a domicile in a loud village. My address remains unchanged.

Do you remember, dear Felizitas, the first piece in 'Berliner Kindheit' – 'Die Mummerehlen'? In it I mention a childhood picture of myself, which I once showed you in its original state.[2] I am standing beside a palm tree in a little sequinned outfit. On the picture enclosed you also see me – thirty-five years later – in front of a palm tree. And even if it is not a house palm, the photo on which you now see it was taken for no less external reasons than the masquerade of the childhood picture, for it is a passport photo[3] that I had taken in Mallorca. It is not a bad one; it has not yet reached its destination, however, as I am still waiting for a response from Berlin. This time I took the opportunity to explore Mallorca a little better; the only place I knew from last year was Palma. And this year I became acquainted with a stretch of the Mallorcan high mountains: Deya, where the lemon and orange groves are in bloom; Valldemossa, where the romance between Georges Sand and Chopin took place in a Carthusian monastery;[4] castles perched on the rocks in which, forty years ago, an Austrian archduke sat and wrote very extensive but amazingly unfounded books about the local history of Mallorca.[5] The island's countryside bears no resemblance to that of Ibiza. And certainly Ibiza is richer and less open. I also went to Cala Ratjada, where there is a German colony, and spent a few hours visiting Friedrich Burschell, who will soon be here for a return visit, together with Fritta Brod.[6]

In any case, I shall be staying here until at least the first of September; then, however, I shall go to Paris if it is at all possible, and there it will, I very much hope, only be a question of days or weeks at the most until we see each other. Meanwhile, I daresay your paddling Sundays on the Havel will continue in the most undisturbed fashion; interrupted only, I hope, by a forthcoming holiday. Where and how will you spend it? Your last letter contained no mention of your health. Can I read that favourably?

I have meanwhile heard about the transfer of the archive documents.[7] I only hope that it will not take place all too slowly, and once more send you a thousand thanks for all the effort you have gone to. I heard about Gubler's new position from Burschell while your letter was probably arriving in Ibiza. This complicates matters for me – for reasons it would be too long-winded to expound – to such an extent that I do not know, and cannot assess, whether this new combination will ultimately be advantageous or disadvantageous for me.[8]

Keep your chin up. Bear in mind that I am very well, if that is of use to you; and bear in mind that I am sometimes not well at all – for that too can be comforting. And in both cases you will be right.

As ever

yours Detlef

Original: manuscript.
On the dating: Benjamin had travelled to Palma de Mallorca on 1 July, but returned to San Antonio before the issue of his passport, which took place on 10 July.

1 *Sie*.

2 Only the first version, which was printed in the *Vossische Zeitung* on 5 May (see *GS* 4 [1], pp. 260–3), contains the passage about a childhood picture; Benjamin later removed it – presumably when he wrote the essay on Franz Kafka, introducing the section 'Ein Kinderbild' with a variation on the passage from 'Die Mummerehlen' – from *Berliner Kindheit*. The original picture of Benjamin has not survived; its description resembles the photo of Kafka (see fig. 20 in the *Benjamin-Katalog*, p. 247) so closely, however, that the latter somehow seems to represent the former.

3 According to Benjamin's description, this can only be a photograph also reproduced as a picture postcard by the Deutsche Schillergesellschaft, Marbach am Neckar (see the reproduction in Hans Puttnies and Gary Smith, *Benjaminiana* [Giessen, 1991], p. 82), which was previously dated with the indication 'Ibiza, 1932'. The passport for which the photograph was taken has not survived.

4 See the third part of the report *A Winter in Mallorca* by George Sand.

5 The seven-volume account *Die Balearen in Wort und Bild* [The Balearic Islands in Words and Images] by Ludwig Salvator, Archduke of Austria and Tuscany (1847–1915), which was published between 1869 and 1891; there is a two-volume edition dating from 1897. He lived mainly on the Balearic Islands from 1860 to 1913.

6 Burschell had, like Benjamin, gone to Spain from Paris with his later second wife, the actress Fritta Brod (1896–1988), following their emigration in mid-March. Fritta Brod lived in Mallorca for a year.

7 This refers to the handing over of Benjamin's collection of his own manuscripts to an unnamed acquaintance of his, who was supposed to transport them to Paris.

8 Benjamin is here alluding to his difficult relationship with Gubler.

22 GRETEL KARPLUS TO WALTER BENJAMIN
BERLIN, 15.7.1933

15 July 1933.

My dear Detlef,

I just received your picture today, on your birthday. I simply cannot tell you how happy it made me. I do not know if I ever actually expressed my wish to receive one of you; it almost seems more likely that you read my mind once again. You write that you will probably still remain there until the first of September and then go to Paris. With that sentence you not only made me very happy, as I know that you will be in good hands, although I would ask you most sincerely to write to me in detail about how you imagine your life in France. Please let me continue to be your little adviser, as here on Sunday afternoons ...., but you also voiced delicately what I can never bring myself to say, namely that our meeting in Ibiza will not happen. (The dots are simply to indicate that I have not forgotten the beginning of the sentence despite the long interruption.) Even though I have imagined my arrival and the stay there so often that I still cannot believe that it will come to nothing, and yet perhaps we both knew it from the start. But I will definitely not be denied the chance to go to Paris, even if I cannot make any plans for the winter yet. On 9 August I plan to go to Binz Rügen Villa Aegir with Teddie, perhaps he will already be coming to Berlin before that for a few days, and the question of living in the Prinzenallee will also be aired once again. September – October – November are my main working months and then? But Paris is also easier to turn into as a place for fashion matters and investigations. And even if it were only a few days, I would be prepared to forgo everything except for walks with you, of which I almost had a foretaste after our afternoon out in the Westend. But what will my problem child say about that, and what if he wants to come too? As you can see, I must still be well enough if I can seriously give myself headaches over such lovely, distant matters.

It is so sweet of you always to ask after my precious health; I am often very tired and very much ready for a holiday, many headaches. I shall even bore you with a weather report, on Sunday it rained almost all day, the rest of the time mostly humid, interrupted by downpours. I hardly have any time for reading, as I go to bed very early now I am on voyage au bout de la nuit. You have not written anything to me about it since you finished reading it.

On Tuesday I shall probably be seeing Elisabeth, but good fortune continues to avoid me (just for your friendly information). Many thanks once again for the picture. If I always enjoy receiving gifts, then especially from you; for you have such wonderful ideas, and there are still truly great surprises ahead. For our letters it would be extremely practical to have some farewell ritual, so that we could then always remind each other of it. As ever

your

Felicitas

Original: typescript.

23 GRETEL KARPLUS TO WALTER BENJAMIN
BERLIN, 5.8.1933

5 Aug. 1933.

Dear Detlef,

today I am stealing an hour at work so that I can still write to you before I leave. There are so many sweet things in your two letters[1] for me to respond to that I really do not know where to start. But first of all: how are you, how is the leg-wound? Have there not been any complications, can you walk about again[?] Please write me a quick line in Binz, Rügen, Villa Aegir, otherwise I shall have no peace of mind for the whole three weeks.

I immediately took care of the assignments you gave me: your Kaktushecke[2] should meanwhile have arrived, I wrote to Kiepenheuer, asking him to send me the manuscript, stamp-addressed envelope enclosed, I have still not had any reply; has he perhaps got in touch with you? To speed things up I also wrote that I would be sending you something directly by courier next week. The F. Z. then promptly sent me the document enclosed.[3] When I hear sometimes how badly Friedel[4] is faring it makes me mortally afraid that something could happen to you, and I am so infinitely happy that you have proven your trust in me once again. I had 140 Ps written in my passport for you and have already sent them off. I tried to send you your remaining 10 Marks by postal cheque, if it does not work they will still follow. I hope the tailor there is at least vaguely decent, so that you will not regret it afterwards. Please do not laugh at me, I truly feel responsible for ensuring that you make it through your time there and I cannot ask you urgently enough always to come to me with your troubles. Before you raise the objection that I also have to limit myself at the moment, I must tell you that I feel so relieved after the liquidation, even if I have lost everything, so glad that I no longer have to look after the 3 partners[?], and now no longer expect much of an inheritance. The constant fear of loss would drive me insane, and this way I can appreciate what I have today. This security is also excellent with regard to Teddie; I am always prepared to accept everything and then dress very elegantly too, but I have become more aware and modest in my way of life, without minding it at all. I cannot have a clear conscience buying all sorts of unnecessary things just for myself when I know that you are in much greater need; please forgive my sentimentality and do not reject me.

On Monday T. will read Tom,[5] which has now much improved, to a small group of people, it is a great shame that you cannot be there. Elisabeth is also coming – we spent last night with her. She is one of the few women with whom I, as a woman, would like to have a real friendship, but perhaps I do not have the time for it, and I also do not know whether she has any desire for it. She is strangely naïve, incidentally: she thinks from your letters that you are very well over there, for example; but I can imagine that she would not be so prolific otherwise. She told us about a delightful little story[6] you sent to Glück, do you remember what it was? I did not receive the piece you promised to enclose about 'George',[7] and I would ask you urgently to send the most important piece from Berliner Kindheit.[8] Loggien[9] seems to be related to 'Das Fieber', where the carpet-beater stood in place of the real trees in the yard.

I will remind Dr Moras once more of the request for a few sample copies; he has a sweet little wife, incidentally, who worked for Bébé Goldschmidt-Rothschild as a nanny for a while. – I am spared nothing: Paulus[10] is in Rügen at the moment, in Sassnitz, and will naturally visit us, that is simply fate. – My sister left for Zoppot today, are there any particular sights there that I could recommend to her?

I am thinking of you a great deal and wishing us both good things.

Ever your

Felicitas.

Original: manuscript.

1 One of these appears not to have survived.

2 In his lost letter, Benjamin had requested the manuscript of this story [The Cactus Hedge], as the first printing in the *Vossische Zeitung* was incomplete. He wanted to look up various passages in it for 'Der Mond' [The Moon] from *Berliner Kindheit*. The manuscript has not been found.

3 This is the copy of 'Die Schränke' [The Cupboards] from the *Frankfurter Zeitung* of 14 July, for which Rudolf Geck had selected the pseudonym C. Conrad (see *GS* 4, pp. 283–7).

4 Siegfried Kracauer (1889–1966) had emigrated to Paris with his wife Elisabeth in early March, and his novel *Ginster* appeared there in the French translation by Clara Malraux in August. In late August 1933 he was dismissed by the *Frankfurter Zeitung*, where he had worked for eleven years, and he subsequently lived in poverty.

5 Between November 1932 and early August 1933, Adorno had written the text of his planned lyrical drama *Der Schatz des Indianer-Joe* [The Treasure of Indian Joe], of which he subsequently sent a copy to Benjamin; see Adorno, *Der Schatz des Indianer-Joe*, edited with an introduction by Rolf Tiedemann (Frankfurt am Main: Suhrkamp, 1979). The only music Adorno composed for it was *Two Songs With Orchestra* (see Adorno, *Kompositionen*, ed. Heinz-Klaus Metzger and Rainer Riehn, vol. 2 [Munich, 1984], pp. 63–72). The typescript that Adorno sent Benjamin bears the dedication: 'For Walter Benjamin / as a greeting / from island to island / Binz/Rügen, August 33. /Teddie Wiesengrund.' (typescript copy in the Moscow state archive).

6 This is 'Die Warnung' [The Warning] (see *GS* 4 [2], pp. 757f.), which had appeared in the *Kölnische Zeitung* on 22 July under the title 'Chinoiserie'.

7 Benjamin's 'Rückblick auf Stefan George' [Looking Back at Stefan George] had been published in the *Frankfurter Zeitung* on 12 July 1933 under the pseudonym K. A. Stempflinger (see *GS* 3, pp. 392–9).

8 This presumably refers to 'Die Mummerehlen'; see letter no. 21, note 2.

9 'Loggien' [Loggias] had appeared in the entertainment section of the *Vossische Zeitung* on 1 August 1933, 'Das Fieber' [The Fever] in the same place on 17 March.

10 Paul Tillich (1886–1965), who taught philosophy and sociology at Frankfurt University from 1929 to 1933. Tillich left for America in the course of that summer. Translator's note: *Paulus* is also the German name for St Paul.

24 WALTER BENJAMIN TO GRETEL KARPLUS
SAN ANTONIO (IBIZA), *c.*12.8.1933

Dear Felizitas,

I sent off an envelope with a few printed documents to Rügen yesterday. You should above all become acquainted with 'Rückblick auf Stefan George'; I am so sorry that I must even supplement this slim package with the constraining request that you send 'Rückblick' back again; I do not yet have a duplicate.

You know that I have so many things to thank you for that I could barely have started this letter if I had begun it with thanks. The aforementioned package is certainly not a token thereof. Rather, I entertain the hope of ambushing you with it when you are sitting somewhere in a remote Parisian bistro and least expecting it. I will then make sure that I am not wearing the suit you will send me, and which would sooner give me the freedom for many other things than this show of thanks. For now, however, please accept it in the weatherproof packaging of these few words.

I am glad you have some days off, and only hope that they will be fine ones. Regarding Paulus, it is entirely futile for you to wait for my sympathy; though I would once have had an inexhaustible supply in such a case, I think that in this one – which is so very different through its background – envy would be more appropriate. The pleasure of interrogating him now strikes me as being not the worst of holiday activities. At any rate – I hope there will be better ones, the reading of 'Tom' among them. I would naturally be very happy if I could have a look at the manuscript here. Not that I am short of reading material here, but I am greatly interested in it.

Regarding said 'reading material', however, my appetite for it is sometimes inversely proportional to its urgency. I received a commission from Frankfurt to write the commemorative article[1] for Wieland's 200th birthday, and had to have a substantial number of his works published by Reklam sent here. I did not know any of them previously, and it will be a matter more of luck than of skill if I manage in this short time – and of course in this shortest of spaces – to write anything decent on the matter. Before I disappear entirely in this reading, however, I hope to complete a further part of 'Berliner Kindheit' entitled 'Der Mond'.[2] The similarity you observed between 'Loggien' and 'Fieber' is naturally there. The two pieces are of very different personal importance to me, however; I am much closer to the former, which strikes me as a manner of self-portrait. I will probably place it at the start of the book instead of the photographic self-portrait in 'Die Mummerehlen'. The French translation is proceeding slowly, but very reliably.

My warmest thanks for the efforts through which you succeeded in procuring me duplicates for some of the 'Briefe'.[3] I am glad at least to have these. There is a complete collection of the entire series – together with 'Berliner Kindheit' with Kiepenheuer, whose unscrupulousness in the treatment of these things is beyond compare. If you think you see any chance at all of intervening, the most decisive form should be just about sufficient. Thanks to you the 'cactus hedge' has closed once more, to my great joy. I have not yet received any journals from Moras.

Let me close with a word on the small delivery that preceded these lines. 'Chinoiserie' is the same small story Elisabeth mentioned to you. Though I well knew that it would merit a different title, I nonetheless gave it the one under which it was printed. Things are more complicated and unsatisfactory in the case of 'Die Schränke'; the name of its author – Rudolf – was chosen arbitrarily, and it was only very late on that I laid eyes on the text. If I did not know – all the more so as time passes – just how isolated such efforts as 'Berliner Kindheit' will remain, now of all times, the publishing fate of the letters would intermittently drive me to despair. Now, however, that fate only strengthens my belief in the seclusion that is necessary to develop such things, and this conviction once more helps me resist, for now, the temptation to complete it. The remarkable thing is that the pieces I am adding are not long-planned texts, but rather mostly ones that came to mind only shortly before I set to writing them down.

After receiving a letter yesterday regarding my quarters in Paris,[4] I am hardly likely to leave here before 15 September. As you can imagine, I will travel there without any illusions. So far the intellectual situation there does not contain many elements that would be conducive to an understanding of my writings. What perhaps makes the case of Krac[5] – which I admittedly know about only from hearsay – so especially difficult are precisely those deep-seated illusions that are particular to him, and which I have occasionally discussed with you in the past.

I would like to hear from you again quite soon. And I hope that the holidays will bring you such well-balanced days as those I sometimes spend in my hidden workplace in the bush.

Very warm regards

yours Detlef

Original: manuscript.
On the dating: At the time of writing, Benjamin must already have been in possession of the letter from Gretel Karplus of 5 August.

1 Benjamin's text 'Christoph Martin Wieland: Zum zweihundertsten Jahrestag seiner Geburt' [On the 200th Anniversary of his Birth] was published in the *Frankfurter Zeitung* on 5 September 1933 under the pseudonym 'Conrad'; see *GS* 2 [1], pp. 395–406.

2 'Der Mond' [The Moon] appeared on 8 September 1933 in the *Vossische Zeitung*.

3 This refers to the letters printed in the *Frankfurter Zeitung* with commentaries by Benjamin, which he later published under the title *Deutsche Menschen* [German People]. Published in English as 'German Men and Women' in Walter Benjamin, *Selected Writings, Volume 3, 1935–1938* (Cambridge, MA: Belknap Press, 1999).

4 Not preserved.

5 Siegfried Kracauer.

25 GRETEL KARPLUS TO WALTER BENJAMIN
BINZ AUF RÜGEN, 31.8.1933

My dear Detlef,

thank you for your letter. These holidays are without doubt the most restful and peaceful I have had in years, with constant sunshine.

You did not write any more to me about your condition, but the stamp was from Mallorca; is your leg injury still causing you pain?

You may be pleased to hear that Ernst has asked for your address; you are sure to hear from him soon. We were very glad to hear of your desire to read Tom – the letter had gone out to you only the day before.

I find Kiepenheuer's behaviour indescribable. From what Elisabeth tells me I gather that she is on good terms with him, do you not want to try to recover your manuscripts through her[?] As he did not dignify my letter with any response, I hardly think that he would receive me in person.

Have you really used up all your lovely yellow writing paper? If you were not coming to Paris so soon I would send you some from B., but as it is I shall buy myself some like it as a consolation. – My holiday reading is Musil's 'The Man Without Qualities', what do you think of it?

This autumn will probably bring all sorts of decisions for us that will certainly be decisive now, and possibly also later. There is so much for me to wish for, but above all being together with you as in the last hours in the old Westend in Berlin, so close to me at this moment and yet so distant from all daily routine.

Be sure to fare well and give me your new address soon. I wonder if you will still find the peace to write to me amid the initial commotion? All my fond, best wishes ever

most warmly

your

Felicitas.

31./8.1933. Where was 'Der Mond' published?

Original: manuscript.

26 GRETEL KARPLUS TO WALTER BENJAMIN
BERLIN, 13.9.1933

13 Sept. 1933.

Dear Detlef,

I daresay this will be the last time I write to you in Ibiza. A thousand thanks for your sweet letter[1] with the account of your Ulyssean journey. How are you now? Is your foot usable once more and has your angina been chased away?

I have meanwhile read 'Der Mond' and utterly love it. I hope you will also be able to send me a few samples of the French translation from Paris.

Teddie has now been turned down for good by the university[2], and things are not looking so rosy for him in other respects either. He might spend some time in Berlin again in October, perhaps the matter will be settled in some other way. Under the circumstances it is now very difficult for me to tie myself to a new business contract, even though I am still very interested in working in the new company.

I am very curious to read your latest accounts, and of course it is simply a comforting thought that the distance is now no longer quite so great. In the next few days it will be half a year since you left Berlin. Reading through the letter, I have just noticed that the word 'now' appears suspiciously often. There was one remark in your letter that I was unable to understand regarding Conrad and the cookbooks.

I hope to hear from you soon, and at length. I wish you the greatest possible number of pleasant surprises and no unpleasant ones whatsoever for the autumn, which has started quite decidedly here

Your Felicitas,

according to a newspaper announcement, I will soon also be performed in New York.[3] How I am already looking forward to the premiere!

Original: unstamped postcard. Manuscript.

1 Not preserved.

2 Adorno's teaching licence had been withdrawn, as he was informed in a letter of 8 September.

3 That is to say: Speyer's play.

27 WALTER BENJAMIN TO GRETEL KARPLUS IBIZA (IBIZA), *c.*19.9.1933

Dear Felizitas,

I received your letter of the 13th – and now it has turned out that I would have wished for at least one further one. It is no longer my health that is responsible for the further delay in my departure, however, but rather the unknown disposition – in both cause and effect – of the Paris location I had hoped to make my quarters. It has now indeed been far more than eight days since I was telegraphed from there not to leave before I had received a letter.[1] That letter has not arrived to this day, and I do not know what information it will hold for me when it arrives.

I had to give up my lodgings in San Antonio, as I would otherwise have had to enter a new long-term commitment and defy the instructions of the doctor, who did not reckon with any quick recovery in San Antonio. And indeed there was already a noticeable improvement only two or three days after my move. Now I can walk, albeit carefully.

A thousand thanks for the picture from Rügen.[2] It is friendly and contemplative, and I think that in Berlin too you will not be entirely without such moments. At least, I took your very kind words about 'Der Mond' as a message from such a one. And it made me very glad. I have lost two weeks of working time, and probably more, through my pains. Now I have dared for the first time to make a serious start on one piece from 'Berliner Kindheit' that conveys the school atmosphere.[3] This work and the change of location – this latter to no lesser extent, regrettably – are absorbing me entirely, and I must confess that I have not yet read Wiesengrund's opera. But I shall do that soon.

Where? Most probably in Paris; I think that, even if I do not initially receive word from there, I shall set off in about eight days to explore the possibilities there for myself. I have tried, through a number of official papers, to keep the option of a withdrawal to my asylum here – which is becoming increasingly difficult for Germans to enter – open at all costs.

Conrad's cookbooks[4] constitute, as you can imagine, his entire archive. He is and remains a fool.

You must have received at least one further new letter after the one you confirmed. And I have meanwhile gained possession of your last delivery.[5] Many thanks for all that. Please think about Paris with highly concrete perspectives. Even in the worst case, I do not think I shall leave there without having seen you.

What better reading have you taken on after the Musil? I am reading the Princesse de Clèves[6] by Mme de Lafayette, who inhabited the seventeenth century, and as long as I am still in Ibiza I shall be furthering the translation of 'Berliner Kindheit'. I completed a fairly successful translation of 'Loggien' just this minute.

Ernst has not written, of course, and Moras has naturally not sent any issues of the 'Europäische Revue'. Ça ne fait rien.

Let me know how you are. Do write to me soon; I shall have it forwarded.

Very fond regards

yours Detlef

Original: manuscript.
On the dating: Benjamin, who was in possession of Gretel Karplus's letter of 13 September, wrote this letter roughly eight days before his departure from Ibiza, which took place on 25 or 26 September.

1 The Baroness Goldschmidt-Rothschild. – No telegraphed message from either the Baroness or a third person has survived among Benjamin's belongings.

2 See fig. 1 on p. 59.

3 The only surviving text that can be considered complete and fits this description – 'Schülerbibliothek' [School Library], which remained unpublished during Benjamin's lifetime and which he did not include in his 'Handexemplar komplett' [complete hand-copy] of 1938, but was mentioned with the note 'still to be revised' in a handwritten list enclosed there (see *GS* 7 [2], p. 695 – would seem to have been written much earlier; it was already in the 'Stefan-Exemplar' (see *GS* 7 [2], p. 700), which the editors dated to late 1932. It is also possible that Benjamin is here thinking of the second version of 'Schülerbibliothek' in the 'Felicitas-Exemplar' (see *GS* 4 [1], pp. 276–8). Benjamin may also have intended, however, to revise the two and a half pages about the Kaiser-Friedrich-Schule in 'Berliner Chronik' (see *GS* 6, pp. 473–5), though there are no documents to support this.

4 Meaning unclear. Benjamin's 'Die Schränke' was published under the name C. Conrad, which had been chosen by Rudolf Geck. The fact that Benjamin refers to this pseudonym suggests a veiled request for Gretel Karplus to procure the manuscript of 'Berliner Kindheit' as well as the proofs of his recent publications, all of which were in the possession of Kiepenheuer, and which constituted – especially the parts of 'Berliner Kindheit' written in exile – the only authentic texts.

5 Unknown; possibly a lost letter with enclosures or a money order.

6 The novel by Marie-Madeleine Pioche de la Vergne, Comtesse de La Fayette (1634–1693), was first published in 1678.

28 GRETEL KARPLUS TO WALTER BENJAMIN BERLIN, 24.9.1933

24 September 1933.

My dear Detlef,

I was most distressed to read your last letter; for it is extremely worrying to think that you are alone, abandoned and sick in Ibiza. Boils in particular can take so long to heal, and even here the methods of treatment are not very advanced; some doctors use yeast, some cut them out. But what is the use of this bungling long-distance diagnosis – please write to me at once whether I can perhaps send you some medication that could help you a little. I sent out a little red note immediately in my helplessness, in order at least to intervene where it is needed most.

What is the basic state of your negotiations with Paris – is your place being kept vacant, so that you can at least go there as soon as you have recovered?

I am a little concerned that you do not write a word about Tom, all the more so because I remember that you did not much like the plan Teddie showed you. I almost take that as a bad omen, but I ask nonetheless that you tell me your sincere opinion of it at all costs; in fact, I even think that Teddie would be grateful to you for some criticism.

I spoke briefly to Elisabeth on the telephone, she enjoyed herself tremendously staying with our friends in Denmark.[1] They have bought themselves a little house near the sea with the advance for the new novel;[2] she said the inhabitants were charming, only that one was not allowed to mention God.

Following your request, Teddie received the invitation from Willy Ha. to collaborate on his newly founded magazine,[3] and I sent the latter your address post haste yesterday, as I am sure he would have many assignments for you, and perhaps even a slightly guilty conscience.

I do not know if I already wrote that Ernst is thinking of going to Spain, as Karola may be getting a commission there. The first volume of his book[4] is to be published soon, and he is working on the second. Going by the letters, he is completely unchanged, untroubled and will no doubt come through somehow; it is a small comfort that at least somebody is not letting things get him down. As I write this, I am realizing that it is not true – after all, I mentioned Denmark before. Teddie is unfortunately very troubled, does not feel at all happy in Frankfurt, does not really know what to do and is very nervous, when he could really be taking an example from you.

I assume from your words that Hessel[5] is in Berlin. Though I only saw him a few times at your place, I would like to help him if I were at all able; perhaps you could write to him that he should call me some time, as I do not even know if he still remembers me. And I would also like to spend time with him without any specific reason, if only because he has known you far longer than I have and could still tell me about you and your rambles through Paris and Berlin together.

Paulus is in Berlin at the moment, and I should be seeing him next week; he is agonizing over the origin of the theoretical human being, and is probably going to America after all, incidentally, despite already having turned down various things there.

Please forgive me that the paper is so crumpled; it got caught in the typewriter.

Do you need any sleeping tablets that you cannot get there? Please write to me as soon as possible what you need and how you are, even if it is only a card.

I wish you a good recovery, with fond regards
ever your
Felicitas

Original: typescript.

1 Brecht and Helene Weigel lived in Svendborg, on the coast of Denmark.

2 In August 1933, Brecht had signed a contract with the Amsterdam publisher Allert de Lange for his *Dreigroschenroman* [Three-Penny Novel], which was published in November 1934.

3 Willy Haas (1891–1973), who was editor until 1933 of the journal *Die literarische Welt* [The Literary World], published by the Rowohlt Verlag, founded in Prague and co-edited with Otto Pick, *Die Welt im Wort* [The World in the Word]. The first issue appeared on 5 October 1933, containing Benjamin's 'Erfahrung und Armut' [Experience and Poverty] and 'J. P. Hebels Schatzkästlein des rheinischen Hausfreundes' [J. P. Hebel's Little Treasure Box of the Rhenish Family Friend]. The last issue of the weekly journal appeared on 11 January 1934.

4 This refers to Ernst Bloch's *Erbschaft dieser Zeit* [Legacy of our Times], printed by the Zurich publisher Emil Oprecht in late 1934. Bloch was also working on a book that was later given the title *Das Materialismusproblem, seine Geschichte und Substanz* [The Problem of Materialism, its History and Substance].

5 Franz Hessel (1880–1941), who was a publisher's reader at Rowohlt from 1919 to 1933. Benjamin had intended to write an essay about the arcades with Hessel.

29 GRETEL KARPLUS TO WALTER BENJAMIN BERLIN, 6.10.1933

6 Oct. 1933.

Dear Detlef, where should I seek you now in my thoughts? Perhaps it is of some use to you if I give you Hans Bruck's[1] address in Paris, you must still remember him: VIII., Hotel Friedland, 35 avenue Friedland.

You often mention Conradt with his cookbooks, but the name is truly a mystery to me. It is Walter Benjamin that I have read most in the last few days. It was probably in that context that I was struck once more by the significance of our self-chosen names, as if we had become different people through them, but genuinely so, not playfully as with pet names. There is great longing captured within them, and often precisely the opposite of real existence, which I nonetheless do not wish to deny, even if it is forcing me, especially now, to sit diligently in the office from morning until evening and preferably stay put there. – Have you heard from Willy H yet? I hope to hear from you soon, and wish to hear much good news. Please forgive me for writing across the page, but I have nothing else to hand and do not want to be disloyal to the yellow.

Fond regards Your

Felicitas.

Original: unstamped postcard. Manuscript.

1 No further information could be found regarding this conductor.

30 GRETEL KARPLUS TO WALTER BENJAMIN
BERLIN, 10.10.1933

10 Oct. 1933.

My dear Detlef,

what terrible nonsense have you been getting up to, I am glad at least to know that you are in Paris under medical supervision. I would ask you most urgently to look after your health a little better, for there is only one Detlef Holz, and he still has great tasks ahead of him, so please take care of yourself as far as possible, if only for my sake. Going by your description, it sounds to me like an attack of flu; at least, that is how it has been turning up here, and this time the after-effects are particularly nasty.

My telegram[1] and the little pink note are simply to show you how much I am thinking of you, and I am sure you can also use them to fortify yourself. All the more so because my visit is also more than doubtful at the moment; as well as the private reasons, which could ultimately be cleared away if necessary, there is the current visa restriction for us, at least as far as I have heard. This is no cause for concern regarding me, however, but it is simply a shame that I can be of so little help or comfort to you. Please write to me quite soon how you are faring and what things from here you could use. I wish you a very speedy recovery, my dear, with fond regards

ever

your

Felicitas.

I sent you the address of Hans Bruck a few days ago, he has meanwhile received an appointment in Amsterdam.

Original: manuscript.

1 Not preserved.

31 GRETEL KARPLUS TO WALTER BENJAMIN BERLIN, 12.10.1933

12 Oct. 1933.

Cardboard boxes
Instructions regarding books: send Ray/
~~Jezower/Argonauten~~
Treatment of the library
End of the play
Cleaning the library
What other people think

Dear Detlef,

I assume from your last letter that you received my last one only very late, probably through your move; in the last, I asked for precise instructions regarding the books, have you meanwhile received it? – There are supposed to be 2 large heavy unopenable cases on the floor, are they yours and could the cardboard box you are looking for be inside them?

'Das bucklicht Männlein'[1] has become even finer with time; I was very happy when I read it. You asked so kindly how I am. And the only sincere answer I can give is: pitiful, in a great cage, without the slightest hope of ever being able to escape. The pressure of isolation that also affected my life in the past – albeit more as with Adrienne Mesurat,[2] though the family has long stopped being a strain factor for me – is becoming more unbearable by the day, there is no one with whom I can have a decent exchange; at work it is all very pleasant, but horribly petty bourgeois and only ever with gloves on. There is nothing wrong with it as an occupation, but my 'private life' is also completely unfulfilled. It wears me down so completely that I do not feeling like doing anything in the evenings, most of all just sleeping, to forget everything, or cinema, anything but thinking. I am squandering my life and am glad when another week, another month has passed. I have learned to be modest, but if there is nothing to look forward to any more. And then at the back of my mind always haunted by the thought that it can still get much worse, that I still have work, that I am still allowed to write letters, that seeing you again is actually still possible. As you can see, I am in need of our meeting at least as much as you so that you can give me a good talking to again. Please do not worry about whether it will be Christmas, the Wiesengrundian taboo, or later; I must above all see how my Nansen passport adjusts to the circumstances, the reform is already due this November. More on that when we speak.

Is it really entirely out of the question that we could meet in Berlin or somewhere in Germany? Please, please do not be cross that everything is not working out immediately, it will happen in the end, I am so terribly looking forward to seeing you.

I am still expecting Teddie here in the next few days; I do not know how long he plans to stay or what plans he has for now and for later.

I think I am jealous of Paris because it always has you.

I am already waiting for your dear old yellow paper, do send me a sheet soon. My own yellow one sends you many greetings and whatever fond things you would like to hear.

ever

your Felicitas

Original: manuscript with handwritten keywords by Benjamin. See fig. 2 on p. 60.

1 It had appeared in the *Frankfurter Zeitung* on 12 August; see *GS* 4 [1], pp. 302–4.

2 An allusion to the novel by Julien Green, which had been published in Paris in 1927; the first German translation, by Irene Kafka, appeared a year later.

32 GRETEL KARPLUS TO WALTER BENJAMIN BERLIN, 25.10.1933

25 Oct. 1933.

My very dear Detlef,

how very differently I had imagined this evening. The moment I heard of your vicious malaria there was only one possibility for me, namely to go and stay with you immediately for one or two days. In my mind I had already written the letter asking whether I could be of use to you and where I could live, and then my health, of which I have often complained (and not without reason), completely upset my plans; I would in fact never survive a drastic cure like that. Aside from that I cannot leave Berlin now, as for various reasons – Papa has just gone to a health resort in Merano – I have to stand in for the family here in Berlin. My dear I have so much to tell you that I even have to write it, and I only ask you not to lose patience with me. I know very

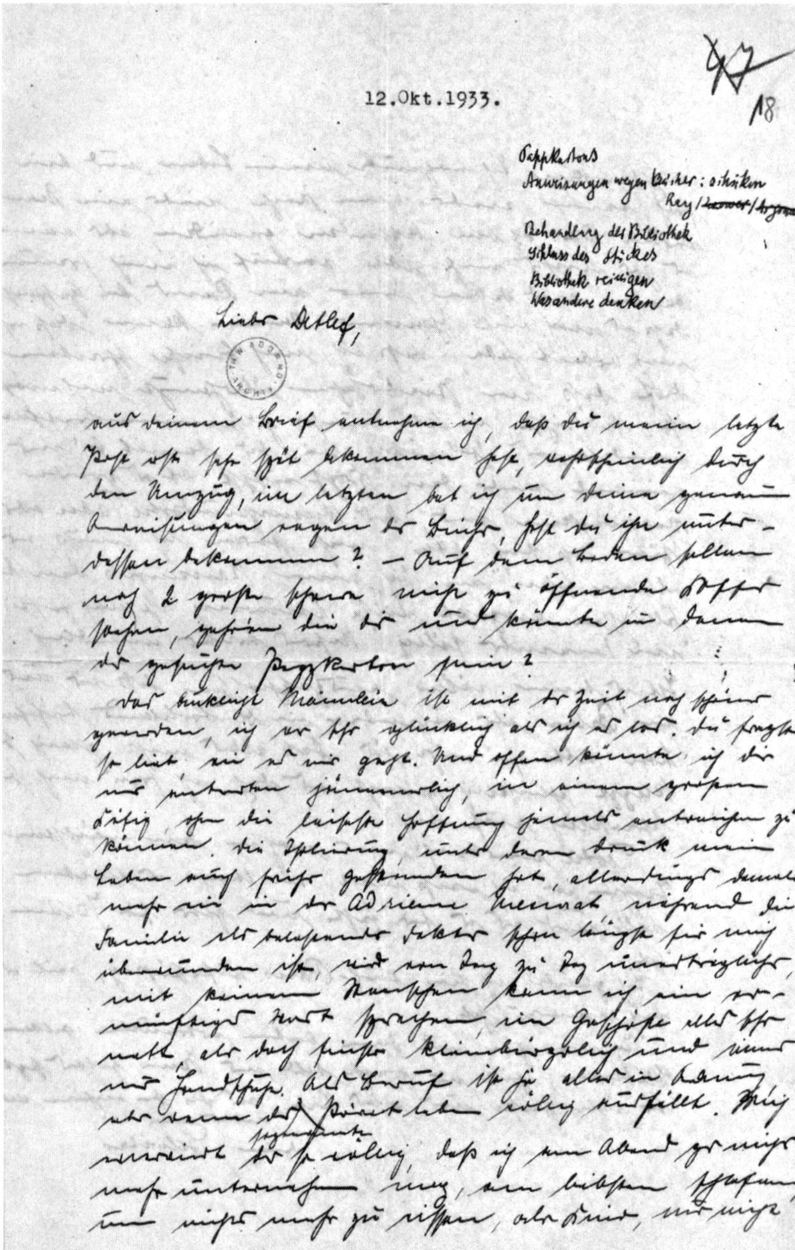

12.Okt.1933.

Pappkartons
Anweisungen wegen Bücher: [illegible]
Rey/[illegible]/[illegible]
Behandlung der Bibliothek
Schluss des Stückes
Bibliothek reinigen
Was andere denken

Lieber Detlef,

aus deinem Brief entnehme ich, dass du meine letzte Post erst sehr spät bekommen hast, wahrscheinlich durch den Umzug, im letzten bat ich um deine genauen Anweisungen wegen der Bücher, hast du sie unterdessen bekommen? – Auf deinem Boden sollen noch 2 grosse schwer nicht zu öffnende Koffer stehen, gehören die dir und könnte in denen der gesuchte Pappkarton sein?

Das bucklige Männlein ist mit der Zeit noch schöner geworden, ich war sehr glücklich als ich es las. Du fragtest lieb wie es mir geht. Nur offen könnte ich dir nur antworten jämmerlich, in einem grossen Käfig ohne die leiseste Hoffnung jemals entweichen zu können. Die Spannung unter deren Druck mein Leben auch früher gestanden hat, allerdings damals mehr wie in der Adrienne Mesurat während die Familie als belastender Faktor schon längst für mich überwunden ist, wird von Tag zu Tag unerträglicher, mit keinem Menschen kann ich ein vernünftiges Wort sprechen, im Geschäft alles sehr matt, als doch früher [illegible] und immer nur [illegible]. Als Beruf ist [illegible] aber wenn der [illegible] völlig ausfällt. Mich verwirrt der [illegible] so völlig, dass ich am Abend zu nichts mehr unternehmen mag, am liebsten schlafen um nichts mehr zu wissen, oder Kino, und mich [illegible]

well that I would have had to speak to you now at all costs, and that certain things cannot be put off indefinitely; precisely during the phase of convalescence my place would have been beside you. And now I am not coming after all. How on earth can I explain it to you, it would require an almost inhuman amount of trust, and I really do not know why I would deserve it. I must even draw a very stupid parallel, because you happen to know about that fact, namely my reluctance to meet with Ernst that time two years ago. Please, do not make this comparison for one minute, for what was a game then, even if it was a pleasant one, is a necessity with us. Not a soul knows about Detlef and Felicitas, I myself have only an inkling of our relationship, so how could I tell anyone about it. In my life, despite its invisibility, it is perhaps the most solid thing I have, the only thing I wish to rely on without always having to be fearful and on my guard. Forgive me for telling you so much today; I would suffocate otherwise. – As the short time together is almost impossible in the midst of my work, I am hoping for a week around Christmas or in January when we both have less of a load on our shoulders, and when I in particular am also free from private obstacles. –

Admittedly I have no idea what will actually become of me in the end, where I will end up one day, but in my imagination I always have the notion that you will live near us; what I would like most is to arrange all that together, but I do not know what you think about it, nor have I ever spoken to T. about it. I am sitting here in Berlin and feeling somewhat gloomy, under the illusion of being able to help you a little bit after all, so tell me quickly how I can put that into practice. – I have meanwhile received your second letter.[1] I shall do my best to get in touch with your maid, whose name and address I unfortunately no longer have, only that of your apartment, so that she can send me the things you requested. The journals and books are still with me, of course, and I think it should be possible to send them to Paris as a registered parcel. – This has worked well in the past with Ernst's manuscripts. – Should I try to find out Krac's address for you from Gub.? –

I have much to do and also a great deal of running around, as I have to sign my business contract quickly for certain reasons, but I have left myself a little mouse-hole I can slip out of. I feel very lonely and trapped in big Berlin without my friends, and I long so much to see you. I wonder if you feel what I am saying, though for that it has to be late in the evening, with me lying on a couch and you sitting in a cosy armchair not far away. I have the feeling I see you differently than other people do, but you do not fare any the worse for it, as I still know everything they do, but unlike them it does not scare me off and prevent me from exploring other parts of you.

At the moment I have no idea where Teddie is; perhaps he is visiting Max, or perhaps he is coming to you, he does not know about our 'DU'. And we spoke only briefly about how he sees our relationship; for your orientation I will simply say that on my side everything is fine, but I wish at all costs to avoid anything bothering you. Should you find yourself objecting to anything about me, I would ask you for the same open criticism that you would have given me – and indeed did – at any time here.

Detlef, please do send me some of your new things, I have not even seen 'Das bucklicht Männlein' in print, nor any of the translation of 'Kindheit', and I hunger for your words. Good night my piece of wood,[2] sleep well for me and return to health soon. I await your reply with baited breath

your
Felicitas

Essay for Haas	Archive
Marat printing house	Krac
Speyer's play	Sell books
Berthold	

Original: typescript with handwritten keywords by Benjamin.

1 Not preserved.

2 Translator's note: the second name of Detlef Holz means 'wood'.

33 GRETEL KARPLUS TO WALTER BENJAMIN BERLIN, 4.11.1933

4 Nov. 1933.

Dear Detlef,

your last lines sound terribly sad and remote, and at this distance I cannot even find out what causes lie beneath the surface. Teddie's trip is no more than a plan at the moment, I do not know any more than that myself. Even I have got wind of the rumour that Krenek[?] is going to help various people, are you in contact with him?

On Thursday I sent you 300 fr. I could not send any more than that, as I have to note them down in the passport and encounter a degree of resistance to that. Nor have I sold any of your books yet, but used my own money for now, as I would prefer to speak to you first and not rush anything in such a delicate matter. I am very inexperienced in these things, my bookshop is still the one at the Potsdam bridge, which has now also become much smaller, and I do not know if they buy second-hand books. Can you think of anyone who might be interested in your precious tomes? I do not think you already intend to give up the Berlin apartment for good, but I shall definitely await your precisest instructions. Perhaps you would like me to take something especially dear to you in exchange, then at least you would know it is not lost and the next birthday presents would be taken care of. This letter sounds a little businesslike, but I think that this is the best tone for factual matters.

As far as my health is concerned, my discomfort has finally vented itself in a fairly strong cold, which I hope will soon be over.

Many warm greetings, do let me hear from you soon

Your Felicitas.

Original: manuscript.

34 WALTER BENJAMIN TO GRETEL KARPLUS
PARIS, 8.11.1933

Dear Felizitas,

it was a great joy to read your card,[1] which showed me that everything is in order. I only hope that Miss Dohrmann[2] will reappear quite soon, as I see her as a manner of guardian spirit. That should not impair your highly justified self-esteem, as your much rarer appearance in these parts indicates a higher rank on the spirit scale.

I daresay a few things will have changed there; you can tell me about them when we speak. I would naturally be very happy if I could have the photos and the books with my articles here soon.

And now your postal order also arrived here yesterday, and freed me from the unease that had paralysed my activities, despite a maximum of willpower. Tell me from time to time what has been sold and accept a thousand thanks for your intervention.

It is late in the evening, and half an hour ago I was informed by a man on the telephone that Gert Wissing, whom you probably saw once or twice at my place, died today.[3] She will be the first one we bury here in Paris, but hardly the last. I am writing these lines with her especially beautiful, in fact precious fountain pen; the relic of a great romance with a chamberlain of the Pope.[4]

I do not know how to give you an idea of the many different steps I have taken since I have started going out again. Many of them will be futile and hardly worth the effort of reporting. A visit to the Proust biographer Léon Pierre-Quint[5] turned out a little more pleasantly than I had expected and could one day perhaps become significant in the long term. I saw Fuchs;[6] there is something admirable about his vitality. Berthold, whom I see everyday, often at length, is endeavouring to establish publishing connections for me. Yesterday Lotte suddenly turned up at his place with her husband. But I do not think they are planning any joint activities at the moment.[7]

The Frankfurt people have accepted a new contribution of mine.[8] Haas is also publishing something soon.[9] There would be no shortage of commissions from him. Whether the payment will even cover my expenses, however, remains to be seen. – I am sending 'Das bucklichte Männlein' off to you today.

Write to me about how you are faring; what you are reading; what you are thinking of; what your plans are. I hope and assume that you are reserving Christmas for us. For my part, I am reading Lionardo on the side[10] and will have some amazing finds to show you. I have been speaking to Berthold about the theory of the detective novel, and perhaps these reflections will be followed by an experimental project at some point.[11]

It is after midnight. This much, then, for today and yesterday. I hope you will receive this letter in a quiet moment, or find one for it.

Very warm regards

Yours Detlef

8 November 1933
Paris VI
2 Rue Du Four
Palace Hotel

Original: manuscript.

1 The last postcard Benjamin had received from Gretel Karplus dates from 6 October, but, going on what he writes about it, this can hardly be what he means; the references would sooner fit Gretel's letter of 25 October. It is unclear whether a card was perhaps lost later on or Benjamin was mistaken.

2 Erna Dohrmann was ill until mid-December, and therefore unable to take care of Benjamin's apartment.

3 She seems to have died from an attack of double pneumonia; see Klaus Mann, *Tagebücher 1931 bis 1933*, ed. Joachim Heimannsberg, Peter Laemmle and Wilfried E. Schneller (Munich, 1989), p. 179 (6. XI.).

4 Unknown.

5 The writer Léon Pierre-Quint (1895–1958) had published a major study entitled *Marcel Proust, sa vie, son œuvres* in 1925; see also pages 572 and 585 of Benjamin's *Pariser Tagebuch*, in *GS* 4 [1].

6 The writer, collector and cultural critic Eduard Fuchs (1870–1940), who became a member of the SPD [German Social Democratic Party] in 1886 and

was imprisoned on account of his political activities in 1888 and 1889, lived in Berlin as an author from 1900 onwards. Fuchs was a friend of Franz Mehring, and was in charge of the administration of his estate after Mehring's death. He became known primarily for his three-volume work *Illustrierte Sittengeschichte vom Mittelalter bis zur Gegenwart* [Illustrated History of Morals from the Middle Ages to the Present]. In 1933 Fuchs emigrated to Paris, where he lived until his death. In the summer of 1933 his address was the Hôtel de Beaujolais in the street of the same name in the 1st arrondissement.

7 Lotte Lenya and Kurt Weill, who had been in Paris since 23 March. Brecht and Weill had collaborated in the spring of 1933 on the ballet *Die sieben Todsünden der Kleinbürger* [The Seven Deadly Sins of the Petty Bourgeoisie], which was premiered on 7 June 1933 at the Théâtre des Champs Elysées. Lotte Lenya was one of the two actresses portraying Anna; the musical director was Weill's student Maurice Abravanel, the choreographer was Georges Balanchine, and the stage set was made by Caspar Neher. This was the last collaboration by Weill and Brecht.

8 Benjamin is probably thinking of his 'Denkbilder', published in the *Frankfurter Zeitung* on 15 November (see *GS* 4 [1], pp. 428–33); earlier – on 12 November – the same newspaper had printed Benjamin's review 'Deutsch in Norwegen' [German in Norway] (see *GS* 3, pp. 404–7).

9 'Erfahrung und Armut' [Experience and Poverty] (see *GS* 2 [1], pp. 213–19) and 'J. P. Hebels Schatzkästlein des rheinischen Hausfreundes' [J. P. Hebel's Little Treasure Box of the Rhenish Family Friend] (*Die Welt im Wort* of 14 November 1933; see *GS* 2 [2], p. 628).

10 No further information.

11 Brecht and Benjamin were planning to write a detective novel or a series of them. The notes and sketches towards a series of detective novels found after Brecht's death and published under the title *Tatsachenreihe* [Series of Facts] (see Brecht, *Werke*, vol. 17: *Prosa 2: Romanfragente und Romanentwürfe* [Berlin and Frankfurt am Main, 1989], pp. 443–55) contain two longer episodes from a novel (see ibid., pp. 447–55), for which a scheme of chapters was found written in Benjamin's hand (see *GS* 7 [2], pp. 847f.). This scheme and the following list of motifs (see ibid., pp. 848–50) were probably written in Paris in the autumn of 1933.

35 GRETEL KARPLUS TO WALTER BENJAMIN BERLIN, 21.11.1933

21 Nov. 1933.

Dear Detlef,

please forgive me for misunderstanding your request for books and photographs; it was only after reading your last lines[1] that I knew for certain that you wanted to have them sent immediately. The registered parcel was sent off on the 17th, and has hopefully already reached you.

Regarding the sale of the books, [I] would still like to receive more precise instructions from you as to what you absolutely want to keep, and it would also be important for me to know how much money you would expect to get and how one should send it, as regular monthly payments are no longer allowed. Could you not write from there to the people you mentioned in your last letter? As an unmarried woman holds no great authority – it is different in my job, as I have the company name behind me there – it would perhaps be advisable for Herr Glück to contact the interested parties; through his bank he also has greater possibilities in terms of foreign currencies, and he can also access the apartment at any time. Please do not misunderstand me, it is not that I want to pass the job on to someone else; I simply want to arrange it for you in the best possible way.

I saw in the newspaper that your play is being performed in the Renaissance Theater;[2] I would like to go there in the next few days with Teddie, whom I am expecting tonight. I was most amazed that Felicitas returns to her husband; had that already been decided on back then? I would approve, despite my predilection for older gentlemen, if Forster were to play the lawyer.

Have you meanwhile found the time to read Tom?

Have you ever been interested in knowing what other people think of you? It is often a peculiar displacement in which one no longer recognizes oneself.

Please do not be cross with me because of the last letter; I can well imagine that I got on your nerves with it. I hope to hear from you soon, warmest regards ever

your Felicitas

Original: manuscript.

1 Unknown.

2 Rudolf Forster (1884–1968) was not listed among the cast, and it was directed by the new director of the theatre, Alfred Bernau. According to the preview, the role of Felicitas was played by Hilde Koerber. The premiere seems to have taken place on 19 November.

36 GRETEL KARPLUS TO WALTER BENJAMIN
BERLIN, 14.12.1933

14 Dec. 1933.

My dear Detlef,

your last letter[1] made me a little sad; you should know that disloyalty is really not one of my faults, and it is for purely external reasons that I have not yet visited you in Paris. I too am not free to do as I please, but must rather wait for a very long time until something works out, and everyone is so busy with their own basic needs that there is little time left for anything else. There is nothing I guard more closely than our relationship, and I do not want to talk to anyone about it; for it is only that small remainder of secrecy that at all seems to guarantee its authenticity. My dear, I would like to spend Christmas with you, but it is not possible, Teddie would never forgive me, and you know that in spite of everything I am still very attached to Frft.

I will sell the books, and send you the Rm 25. through my business partner at the start of next week, as I first have to apply for my new passport, and this is where you should look for a part of my problems, which are incidentally based only on stupid coincidences and have so far been less threatening than unpleasant; for now you do not have to worry for me within my four walls in Germany. I hardly dare to wish you a merry Christmas; I am sure I shall write to you again at New Year's.

Please have a little faith in me, warmest regards ever

your

Felicitas

Original: manuscript.

1 Not preserved.

37 WALTER BENJAMIN TO GRETEL KARPLUS
BERLIN, 30.12.1933

Dear Felizitas,

these greetings should reach you – if not in time for the new year – then definitely at the moment of your return to Berlin. For I believe you will still be in Frankfurt for New Year. Once again I have a great deal to thank you for – also for the reminder from Frankfurt,[1] not to mention other more important matters. With regard to these, I had already taken certain steps[2] beforehand. I have still not received any reply, and have every reason to suppose that they were in vain, which was to be expected from the outset. Naturally, the fact that I predicted this does not make the consequences any easier to bear.

And so it cannot be denied that I am not only at the old year's but also my wits' end. Certainly: I recently – as I believe I wrote[3] – secured my first commission here – an essay about the Seine prefect Haussmann,[4] who remodelled Paris under Napoleon III. There are also one or two other things to do. But that is not enough to counteract the grey prospects and the even greyer solitude that already surrounds me now. The decision for which I would above all have to pluck up the courage would be to leave here. I still have a few things to wait for here, I am still waiting – first and foremost – for your visit, and as yet I am dreading the Danish winter, the dependence on another person I will have there, which can very easily become a different form of solitude, and an entirely unfamiliar language that is a great burden if one has to take care of all daily business oneself.

The new education act[5] makes me worry about Stefan.

At the moment my work offers me almost no affirmation, as I cannot afford to pursue that to which I am drawn most – the continuation of 'Berliner Kindheit'.

I will comment on 'Tom' next time. I enjoyed reading 'Four Hands'.[6] As bizarre as it may sound, I should also take the plunge and write down some similar memories one day. I have also conducted some studies towards it, but nothing is ready yet.[7]

I hope you have been well during the holidays and also freer from the usual headaches. Write to me as soon as you can. And take my very warm thoughts with you into the new year.

30 December 1933 Yours Detlef

Original: manuscript.

1 Gretel Karplus had repeated her request for a comment from Benjamin on Adorno's lyrical drama (see letter no. 42) on a postcard from Frankfurt. Benjamin wrote to Adorno on 29 January (*GB* 4, letter no. 831), thus resuming the correspondence after a year's interruption.

2 Unknown.

3 In a lost letter from late November or early December.

4 The essay, which had probably been requested by Alfred Kurella for the weekly newspaper *Monde*, was never written; following Kurella's departure in January 1934, the commission was evidently no longer supported by the editorial staff. See, however, Benjamin's notes on 'Haussmannization' in his *Passagen-Werk* (*GS* 5 [1], pp. 179–210) and his review of the book by Georges Laronze (Paris, 1932) for the *Zeitschrift für Sozialforschung* (issue

3, 1934; *GS* 3, pp. 435f.). Haussmann also features in the plan for the *Passagen-Werk* drawn up in March 1934, which was then entitled 'Paris: Capitale du XIXe siècle' (see *GS* 5 [2], pp. 1220f.).

5 In the *Frankfurter Zeitung* of 29 December, Benjamin could read that in 1934, following the 'ordinance for the implementation of the law against the overcrowding of German schools and universities', the number of schoolchildren who would be allowed to graduate from secondary school in Prussia would be limited to 8981. The criteria applied were 'mental and physical maturity, character value and national reliability'.

6 Adorno's memoir 'Vierhändig, noch einmal' [Four Hands, Once Again] had been published in the *Vossische Zeitung* on 19 December (see *GS* 17, pp. 303–6).

7 Benjamin thus did not consider that *Berliner Kindheit* and the pieces in that book contained such memories. The 'studies' could then only have been the things he wrote down in *Berliner Chronik* and were not included in *Kindheit* in an altered form. See also his 'Materialien zu einem Selbstportrait' [Material for a Self-Portrait], *GS* 6, p. 532.

38 GRETEL KARPLUS TO WALTER BENJAMIN
BERLIN, 4.1.1934

4 Jan. 1934.

My dear Detlef,

I really cannot tell you how much I constantly worry about you, and your last letters have shown me that I am not wrong in doing so. Sadly what I can do for you is so very little; I cannot even promise you with certainty that I will come, as I still have no passport, and it is no great consolation that Denmark is closer to Berlin. A certain inhibition has prevented me from ever speaking to you about your friend who now lives there, but I am sure we would agree at once on that matter too, and I can understand your reservations only too well. Under these circumstances, I hope you will not hold it against me that I have attempted to bring your case to the attention of rich friends[1] (more Teddie's than mine*), and I would rejoice with all my heart if it were successful, and otherwise I ask you to forgive me for taking this step, but I simply had to do so.

By the way, have you now given any more thought to Palestine, I remember you had possible plans to go there in the past, and as far as I know Gerhard now holds an important position there. Please do not

* You know them, but as I am still rather unsure about them, I would prefer not to divulge their names.

misunderstand, I certainly do not mean to pre-empt your own decisions, but I am absolutely sure that something has to happen with you, and perhaps I can set the ball rolling there.

My work in Berlin continues; I have been the junior partner since 1 January – it is still hard to say whether to my joy or my discomfort – everything still up in the air with Teddie, and France, Holland and England even more uncertain than Istanbul.

Your recommendation of the 'Allerhandmann' [?][2] (vol. 3 August) was a good one. – A little pink note for a bit of alcohol should at least give you a little physical fortification for the moment.

Please continue the good habit of letting me hear from you every 8–10 days in the new year too, warmest regards

ever your
Felicitas

Original: manuscript.

1 Gabrielle Oppenheim-Errera, from Brussels, and her husband Paul Oppenheim (1885–1977), who lived in Frankfurt until 1933 and – as Adorno later recalled – 'had the main intellectual salon in Frankfurt, the meeting-place for anyone who could more or less hold a fountain pen' (Adorno's recollections of Paul Tillich, in *Werk und Wirken Paul Tillichs: Ein Gedenkbuch* [The Work and Influence of Paul Tillich] [Stuttgart, 1967], p. 24). Paul Oppenheim had studied chemistry in Giessen, and held a directorial position in the company N. M. Oppenheimer Nachfolger from 1908 to 1926, after which he worked for I. G. Farben. From 1927 he also worked at Frankfurt University as an outside lecturer. His field of interest was the philosophy of science. The Oppenheims moved to Brussels in 1933, then to the USA in 1939.

2 Both the writing and the meaning are unclear.

39 WALTER BENJAMIN TO GRETEL KARPLUS PARIS, AFTER 4.1.1934

Dear Felizitas,

so now you are back in Berlin. I hope that Frankfurt – despite the uncertainty affecting Wiesengrund's future – offered you a number of good days. You can discern from the brief interval separating this letter from my last that I do not intend to neglect that very narrow sector of your wishes which it is within my powers to fulfil.

It admittedly detracts from my achievement that there is constantly an occasion in the form of the thanks I must give you. And I am afraid that the repetitions thereof will become as monotonous to you as their various occasions are invigorating to me. So I thank you for the little note, and will gladly gaze a little more deeply into my glass. And as for the more far-reaching advocacy in Frankfurt, it is in the nature of my circumstances – which cannot be any secret, even if I wished to make them one – that here too I can only thank you and simply wait.

I am not sure whether I told you that I am working on an essay about the préfet Haussmann at the request of a journal here. Whatever the case may be – for a few days now I have had occasion to assume that this initially solid, by no means new publication has come into difficulties. Meanwhile I have written a fairly short article[1] – my first in French; I had it read through by a Frenchman, and he found only one error – for these people. However the future of the journal might turn out – I will certainly write the article on Haussmann. Firstly, my preparatory work has already progressed too far to be abandoned, and secondly, Berthold is particularly enthusiastic about the subject. And you too will be pleased to know that this has brought me much closer once more to my study on the arcades, whose pages are now in use again after many years of dormancy. As the Bibliothèque Nationale does not loan books out, I spend most of the day in its reading room.

Now I have a small, odd request regarding those arcades pages. Since putting together the numerous study papers that are to form the study's basis, I have consistently used the same kind of paper, namely a normal writing pad of white MK paper. Now my supply thereof is exhausted and I would like to preserve the external uniformity of the extensive, meticulous manuscript. Could you perhaps have a pad of that kind sent to me? – Naturally only the pad, no envelopes. I will send you a sample page with this delivery.

I recently saw a wonderful collection, one that I am sure you would also be able to view, for the second time. I do not know if I have already told you about it. It belongs to a German who has been living in Paris for eight years, and contains primitive paintings of the present, though primarily of the nineteenth century.[2] He has arranged it in his apartment, where – as used to be the case in Hessel's room – time seems to stand still. The house is situated near the old ghetto in a wonderfully homely area.

But can you not tell me what obstacles are hindering the issuing of your passport? I have no idea whatsoever what they could be. And, as improbable as it is that I could give you any useful advice from here, it is perhaps not entirely out of the question. There is so much *en attendant* that can hardly be conveyed in writing. This also includes the long correspondence with Scholem, which naturally also involved the issue of Palestine. It would be simple enough to tell you how it ended. And one can assume that this end was an irrevocable one.

Let me hear from you very soon, and write a word or two about your health. Very warm greetings

Yours Detlef

Original: manuscript.
On the dating: Benjamin is responding to Gretel Karplus's letter of 4 January 1934. Owing to a number of ink spots, Benjamin evidently copied out the letter again and kept the blemished original as a copy. Gretel Karplus's reply of 15 January, in which she complains that Benjamin failed to enclose the promised sample of MK paper, proves that the letter reached her.

1 No French article by Benjamin is known from that time.

2 Unknown.

40 GRETEL KARPLUS TO WALTER BENJAMIN BERLIN, 15.1.1934

15 Jan. 1934.

Dear Detlef,

I would long since have answered your letter, but I was hoping daily for the sample of M-K. paper, which was unfortunately not enclosed in your last letter. I want to get it for you as quickly as possible, as this is after all the only thing I can do at the moment to support the writing of the arcades study. Hence the lines I am writing you today are supposed to form a report about how we are here. As regards my passport, we have probably been expatriated as Eastern Jews following the July regulations,[1] even though Papa has been living in the Prinzenallee for 47 years and his father was already a major industrialist in Vienna. The efforts to clarify the matter are somewhat drawn-out. – My health situation is peculiar at the moment: as my professor has gone to England, I am continuing the treatment myself in a sense; it is going well enough, but I am always tired and cannot put up with very much. The only thing that could really help me would be complete rest, i.e. giving up my work, or studying medicine; perhaps a doctor who knew me very precisely and who would be interested in the strange phenomenon of organic health in spite of the various functional disturbances, especially with the stomach and intestines.

As I immediately received a very kind reply from there, I can safely disclose to you the name of the 'mysterious lady': Gabi O, who is now living in Brussels and has very good connections in Paris. I would be happy and interested if you were to hear from her. – Do you have a duplicate of your French article that you could spare, I am sure it would be particularly intriguing to read your style in a foreign language.

Teddie is coming back to Berlin in the next few days, perhaps something can be arranged there with the musical part after all. Do you know about the sudden change, – F. T. G. is going back to Switzerland.[2] – Herr W. v. E.,[3] the best friend of Cassirer's editor T.,[4] will be the interim editor. Did Friedel not tell you anything about it?

Please do tell me whether there is a particular reason for concealing your opinion about Tom for so long; I can hardly find an explanation for your silence any more; the reason must relate to the material. I am always very glad to find a little letter from you, so do not let me wait too long for the next.

Warmest regards

ever

your Felicitas

Original: manuscript.

1 Gretel Karplus is probably thinking of the 'law on the revocation of naturalizations' and the 'removal of German citizenship' passed by the Reichskabinett on 24 July 1933.

2 The reason for Friedrich Theodor Gubler's forced departure from the editorial office was the anti-military story 'Gefreiter Nottebohm spielt hoch' [Lance Corporal Nottebohm Plays Up] by Max René Hesse (1885–1952), published in the New Year issue of the *Vossische Zeitung*, which had caused a general to protest. Gubler was summoned by Goebbels, who threatened to send him to a concentration camp if he did not return to Switzerland. (See Claudia Maurer Zenck [ed.], *Der hoffnungslose Radikalismus der Mitte* [The Hopeless Radicalism of the Mainstream]: *Briefwechsel Ernst Krenek – Friedrich T. Gubler 1928–1939* [Vienna and Cologne, 1989], p. 274, n. 441.)

3 The literary historian and translator Wolfgang von Einsiedel, who had also worked for the *Frankfurter Zeitung*, became editor for art, science and entertainment at the *Vossische Zeitung*.

4 The writer and publishing house editor Max Tau (1897–1976) was excluded from the Reichsschrifttumskammer [National Chamber of Literature] in 1935, emigrating to Norway in 1938 and to Sweden in 1942.

41 WALTER BENJAMIN TO GRETEL KARPLUS
PARIS, *c.*15.1.1934

Dear Felizitas,

it has now been a while since I heard from you, and I ask myself – and now you – whether your health is to blame. The weather here makes one wish that some – one includes oneself among them – would at least be in good spirits to welcome the spring. For here one could truly think that the winter is already coming to an end. From my room I cannot see so much of the world. But at least one of the steeples of Saint Sulpice, above and behind which the weather customarily speaks its own language.

One should be highly content if one could find the necessary equilibrium and good health to take a walk in the Luxembourg in March with the usual thoughts and observations. Has the fog bank hanging over your plans[1] still not lifted?

I am regarding the unlawful 'pl' I allowed myself to perpetrate in the previous line, and thinking about what Schermann,[2] whose acquaintance I shall be making tonight, would have to say about it. It is a pastime; and I would perhaps dispense with it if I had a better one. For it does not appear especially profitable. I have been assured, however, that he is a well-bred and very polite gentleman.

A few noteworthy books have come in. Dolf Sternberger has – amazingly enough – found a publisher for his latest work[3], which – in a whisper – settles the score with Heidegger and bears the very witty title 'Der verstandene Tod'. After having an initial glance at it I congratulated him. It seems to me that he has done everything that can be done at present on such difficult terrain. – From Palestine I received a small anthology of novellas by Agnon,[4] some of which were translated by Scholem. I will send it to you in the next few days. You will find many a beautiful passage in it.

I have been occupying myself this past week with the most recent novel by Malraux, an examination of which I had to insert into my extensive essay for Max's journal after I had initially completed it. The book, it seems to me, is highly interesting – and fascinating, though in no way beneficial. I think a translation will be coming out in the foreseeable future.[5] At any rate, you must take a look at it some time. I would like to find some opportunity to deal with the work as comprehensively as it would merit, but I know of none.

You will long since have found out that Gubler is no longer with Ullstein. There are manuscripts of mine lying about there and also elsewhere, though it hardly seems likely any more that they will be published. In the next few days I will have an audience with the Grand Rabbin de France;[6] I shall report back to you regarding its outcome.

As dubious as the position of 'Monde' may be, I was forced to accept a commission from them. But I already wrote to you about that. The piece deals with Haussmann's Paris planning. – My friend Haas is not paying at all. And as I have the opportunity for him to be sent a lawyer's letter[7] free of charge, I shall make use of this in the next few days. Speyer has withdrawn into silence since I took the liberty of speaking a little more emphatically of my situation. But I shall likewise cause him – in more or less emphatic fashion – to emerge from it.[8]

Please let me know if there is anything in the assumptions I voiced at the start of this letter. Or are you so terribly busy?

All my very warm regards

as ever

yours Detlef

Original: manuscript.
On the dating: The letter was written only a few days after that to Sternberger of 10 January (see *GB* 4, no. 826), and before the arrival of Gretel Karplus's letter of 15 January 1934.

1 The intention of visiting Benjamin in Paris.

2 The famous Kraków-born psychographologist Rafael Schermann (1874–1941?), who was said to have the gift of deducing not only a person's character traits, but also any special external features, as well as possible forms of behaviour, from their handwriting.

3 Benjamin had made Sternberger's (1907–1989) acquaintance at the house of Ernst Schoen. His dissertation 'Der verstandene Tod: Eine Untersuchung zu Martin Heideggers Existenzial-Ontologie' [Death Understood: An Examination of Martin Heidegger's Existential Ontology], with which he gained his PhD in 1932, was printed by the Leipzig publisher S. Hirzel in 1934.

4 See S. J. Agnon, *In der Gemeinschaft der Frommen: Sechs Erzählungen aus dem Hebräischen* [In the Community of the Devout: Six tales translated from Hebrew] (Berlin: Schocken Verlag, 1933) (Bücherei des Schocken Verlags, vol. 5). The small volume, which Benjamin sent to Gretel Karplus not long afterwards, bears Benjamin's inscription: 'En souvenir d'un vieil ami parisien D' [In memory of an old Parisian friend D].

5 See André Malraux, *La Condition humaine* (Paris, 1933); the first German translation by Carola Lind was published in Zurich in 1934 under the title *So lebt der Mensch* [That Is How Humans Live]. For the passage on Malraux's novel in Benjamin's essay 'Zum gegenwärtigen gesellschaftlichen Standort des französischen Schriftstellers' [On the Present Social Situation of the French Writer], see *GS* 2 [2], pp. 800f.

6 Israel Lévi (1856–1939) was head rabbi of Paris from 1919 to 1938. There is no further information regarding Benjamin's démarche.

7 This letter, assuming it was written, has so far remained unknown.

8 For his collaboration, Benjamin was expecting to receive 10 per cent of the box-office returns from the play *Ein Mantel, ein Hut, ein Handschuh* [A Coat, a Hat, a Glove]. As revealed in the lawyer's letter of 15 January preserved as a typescript duplicate, Speyer had told the lawyer (presumably

Benjamin's friend Martin Domke), in two letters of 1 December and 13 January 1934 (not preserved among Benjamin's belongings), that he was unable to make the payment at that point owing to his German tax debts. Benjamin's lawyer rejected Speyer's suggestion to transfer the payments due to him from the Dreimasken Verlag to Benjamin, and on 18 May felt he was forced to declare to Speyer, who was meanwhile residing in Switzerland, that the matter would be handed over to a Swiss lawyer. See also letter no. 45.

42 GRETEL KARPLUS TO WALTER BENJAMIN BERLIN, 20.1.1934

20 Jan. 1934.

Dear Detlef,

my last report, which dealt specifically with Berlin, seems to have crossed with your letter; that is not a bad thing, for now I can pluck up the courage to comment on my postcard.[1] I must go into somewhat greater detail and give you a precise account, so that you can properly understand the whole business and my somewhat difficult situation. Teddie sent you the manuscript of Tom last summer, and has been anxiously awaiting your judgement and a letter ever since. Now he is slightly offended that he has not heard from you, especially as you gave Dolf Sternberger an immediate and lengthy response. The book is Dolf's doctoral thesis, which arose on Teddie's suggestion, which makes matters more critical still. It would be so easy for you to settle the matter with a letter. Unfortunately your long silence will be a handicap to your opinion, but I know that you will easily find the right words. Everything can (so easily) seem different after a year's separation, and I would be disconsolate to see any trouble in your relationship. Please, my dear, help me, as you also did in January 1933. I am glad that our letters have remained alive, and I am sure that we will re-establish contact immediately. –

From Ernst B. another enquiry as to your address, perhaps you will hear from each other soon. Please let me know soon that everything between us is as it was, warmest regards

ever

your

Felicitas

Original: manuscript.

1 The card written in Frankfurt around Christmas, which contained a request for Benjamin's opinion on Adorno's lyric drama.

43 GRETEL KARPLUS TO WALTER BENJAMIN BERLIN, 10.2.1934

10 February 1934.

My dear Detlef,

your second letter[1] has just arrived, and made me profoundly ashamed, as I have still not replied to the first; but I am sure you will grant me absolution after my explanation. My former business partner gave me a terrible headache once again with the liquidation; this time he forgot himself to such a degree that the matter has now become ripe for prosecution. I know how foolish it is to take these things to heart so much, and have reproached myself for it – not least because through a stroke of luck the money is there and will be in our account again in a few months; but it is ultimately very depressing for me, and also means a loss of prestige. My body was utterly exhausted for days, and I have been recovering only slowly.

I cannot thank you enough for your tenderness and diplomacy in the Tom affair,[2] and, as far as the content is concerned, I expect Teddie will discuss that with you. What I want to avoid at all costs is either party feeling that I am standing between you; on the contrary, if I have any function, it is to balance out differences.

I am still without a passport, and it is impossible to know when that will change. Just yesterday I received a call from H. Dr Wissing to inform me about the books. He sounded clear enough on the telephone, though with the voice of an old woman. He plans to get in touch again at the start of next week once he can collect the volumes from me. So I would consider it best to give him only those explicitly requested – not all the ones of yours I still have – against receipt, and tell you at once what I have handed over to him; as I barely know him, I do not wish to set too much store by our brief encounter, nor do I know whether he will lie to me or give the genuine date of departure. He recently mentioned the end of next week. Perhaps you would prefer for me to send the books directly as a registered parcel after all?

My dear, please let me hear from you soon, and be assured (despite its lack of fruits) that our relationship has not only remained the same as before, but has in fact grown inwardly stronger despite the separation last year. Warmest regards ever

your Felicitas

Original: manuscript.

1 One letter seems to have been lost.

2 Benjamin's letter to Adorno from 29 January; see Theodor W. Adorno and Walter Benjamin, *The Complete Correspondence 1928–1940*, trans. Nicholas Walker (Cambridge: Polity, 1999), pp. 23f.

44 WALTER BENJAMIN TO GRETEL KARPLUS
PARIS, *c.*10./11.2.1934

Dear Felizitas,

in the course of today – it is now six o'clock in the morning – I hope to receive the letter you announced.[1] I am already beginning mine, after all. First of all with very warm thanks for the delivery, which arrived so precisely on time that I was able to follow up the confirmation I had given the people at the hotel. You can imagine how pleased I was. – Aside from that, I now have a serious complaint regarding my room: for it faces the courtyard, thus depriving me of the rather unusual advantages that the hotel had through its location at the centre of the unrest. This corner of the Boulevard Saint-Germain (which is met by the Rue Du Four) has indeed proved to be of particular strategic significance. I do not, incidentally, think that the current movements[2] will lead to anything concrete: but it is certainly interesting to follow them. As I am still studying an excellent Histoire de Paris[3] at present, I am located entirely within the tradition of these struggles and conflicts.

Les èxtremes se touchent: something that had only been possible while my situation was carefree – namely dealing with my arcades study – is now becoming possible once more in the most exposed of situations. The study on Haussmann I mentioned to you extends and brings up to date my collection of existing notes. Thus it has reached the point where my supply of paper for this purpose is entirely exhausted. Today I enclose a sheet of the MK paper – it is a folded one from the large writing pad – and would be very grateful if you could have me sent a pad of the same kind, and the same colour and quality.

Did you know that Wissing is in Berlin? Through a combination of several factors – the death of his wife, economic difficulties, but above all the morphine – he has reached such a desolate state that I was most reluctant – but what choice did I have? – to entrust him with some of my business. If I imagine that he might not take care of it after all, this is as much a hope as a fear. Enfin – it was his intention to return here, and as I often feel a longing for my little collection of colourfully illustrated trashy books[4] that you have at your place, I asked him – some time ago, incidentally – to request them from you and bring them along, and it is not my inclination to remind him of it. Should he pay you a visit, however, have a good look at him, and if he seems in too pitiful a state – he is drinking a great deal nowadays – it would be better not to give him the books, under whatever pretext. To be more precise: only give them to him if his date of departure is *certain*. For I am by no means sure that he will return, even though he 'essentially' wants to. But the will no longer has any real function in his case. In short – I hope, and actually assume, that he will not visit you. It is his last letters in particular, I might add, that have made his condition seem so especially threatening.

This small gap represents the day in whose course I had expected your letter. As it did not come, these lines should not lie here any longer. They are accompanied by a tiny little volume that you should accept as a present. It contains a story that I consider one of the most beautiful, and to which I have long been attached.

All my warmest regards

yours Detlef

Original: manuscript.

On the dating: The letter was evidently written following the start of the February protests on 6 February, and presumably also after the large-scale demonstrations of the united left on 9 February, but still before Benjamin had received Gretel Karplus's letter of 10 February, in which she mentions a telephone call from Egon Wissing.

1 Presumably Gretel Karplus had told Benjamin that her letter of 10 February would arrive with the money transfer for which he thanks her at the start of the letter.

2 The Daladier administration, which had been formed on 30 January, and had to be confirmed on 6 February by the Assemblée Nationale, had dismissed the right-wing police prefect of Paris, Jean Chiappe, as a concession to the socialist members of parliament. Far right organizations such as Action française, Croix-de-feu and Jeunesse Patriotes subsequently attempted to prevent the formation of the government with violent riots. Daladier's cabinet resigned on the 7th. In response to the far right's attempted coup, the socialist and communist parties, as well as the trade unions closely associated with them, united for a large-scale counter-demonstration on 9 February; this alliance formed the nucleus of the later populist government.

3 Probably the *Histoire de Paris* (Paris, 1926) by Lucien Dubech and Pierre D'Espezel, from which Benjamin quotes several times in the section on Haussmann in *Das Passagen-Werk*.

4 It could not be ascertained which books are meant here.

45 WALTER BENJAMIN TO GRETEL KARPLUS
PARIS, SECOND HALF OF FEBRUARY 1934

Dear Felizitas,

what has become of the times in which the figure of your namesake was still tied to threads of hope? Her brief career on the stage seems to be over. And she has taken my friendship with Speyer with her to her early grave.

I have sometimes thought of that friendship during these bleak days. And the smoothness with which he found – in his own complicated but by no means bad circumstances – the chance to cheat me of the slightest fraction of what is due to me forces me to concede a furious admiration.

Perhaps I shall attempt to obtain a court order against him in Switzerland. But you can imagine my chances. It would have been within his power to spare himself this shame, but also to spare me the numbing hardship from which I have been awakening only sporadically these last few days.

How are things to continue? I am not alone in asking this question. Only today I received a letter from Scholem, who is asking the same thing. And indeed he is preparing – though he has admittedly been doing so for a very long time – an undertaking.[1] Let us hope it will bear fruit for an equally long time. (It has nothing to do with the university; in fact nothing with Palestine at all.) Perhaps I can expect some relaxation in Denmark? I have not heard from Berthold in a long time; and I have learned from a third party that his wife is gravely ill. So I do not yet feel that the moment has come to leave here.

Meanwhile things are becoming ever more difficult here. Until now I had enough for the bare necessities – and now I do not. The last two weeks – after I had paid for the room again – have been a series of discouragements. Still no assurance from Le Monde of a payment date, which incidentally cannot be before 1 April in any case. Haas's journal had indeed folded, and the remuneration for my contributions was of course never to be expected.

But I do not wish to continue. Without you I could await the next weeks only with despair or apathy; I am no longer a layman in either of these. But am I allowed to cling to you?

In my situation I hardly have the strength to ask this question any more. I have been lying down for days – simply in order to need nothing and see no one – and am working as well and badly as possible.

Think about what you could do to help. I require 1000 fr. in order to take care of the urgent things and get through March. For April there is a chance of a payment from Geneva.[2] For now, however, I am at my wits' end.

I would like to write more. But I fear that such a letter would exhaust the recipient no more than the author.* And what could I add that has not already been sown between its lines as if they were furrows?

Therefore all that remains for me today is to thank you for the paper. The arcades study is currently the *tertius gaudens* between myself and fate.

I am glad that you did not give Wissing the books. The delivery as a registered parcel is not urgent.

Fond and old regards

yours Detlef

Original: manuscript.

On the dating: The letter is unlikely to have been written before 16 or 17 February, after Benjamin had received the MK paper of which he had only just enclosed a sample in his letter of *c*.10/11 February; it was probably around the end of February, if Benjamin's formulation 'Only today I received a letter from Scholem' means that the letter from 'early February' reached him with an uncommonly great delay.

1 See *Briefwechsel Scholem*, pp. 124–6. Scholem wished to 'awaken Salman Schocken's interest' in Benjamin's work (ibid., p. 125).

2 In April Benjamin received a fee of 120 Swiss francs from the Institut für Sozialforschung for his essay 'Zum gegenwärtigen gesellschaftlichen Standort des Schrifstellers', as well as for his reviews of Auguste Pinloche's book *Fourier et le socialisme* and Georges Laronzes' *Le Baron Haussmann* (see *GS* 3, pp. 427f. and pp. 435f.).

46 GRETEL KARPLUS TO WALTER BENJAMIN BERLIN, 3.3.1934

3.3.1934.

Dear Detlef,

I have so many of your letters to answer that you no doubt think me quite degenerate and disloyal, but this time I at least have the good excuse that I can report a few events of no little significance. Teddie is still in Berlin for now, but will be going to London[1] via Frankfurt in the course of the week in order to get his bearings there, as there is nothing urgent here at the moment; he may then pass through Paris on the way back. Unlike my people I still have no papers, and at present there is no possibility at all of speeding things up. It was very

* Naturally I meant to say: no less. (What a slip of the pen!)

good that your last letter still reached Teddie here, and I am sure you will forgive me for letting him read it; for this undertaking[2] has not been without consequence. Today I wish only to give you a brief intimation, and Teddie himself will report at greater length. It concerns the family H. of my former business partner, who have been very close friends of the Wiesengrunds for decades; I believe you once met Else in Frft. We have now mobilized her and possibly her brother Alfons on your behalf with the aid of Teddie's aunt Agathe, and we have been *assured* of help. For now, Teddie and I have sent off a little pink note for 1 March. You must definitely keep me informed, and should continue to view me as your last refuge.

I enclose the list of books[3] I will send off in the next few days. I would be very grateful to you for the detective novel;[4] it does not matter that it is in French. I have meanwhile read the Agnon with great delight, the two tales I like best are the one about the headscarf and the librarian; it is only a shame that we cannot speak at length about them. Which one is your favourite?

Following your insistence I went yesterday to my father's doctor, Prof. Zinn, who once again assured me – as everyone has so far – that there is no organic ailment, and is now also making an effort to strengthen my constitution; I simply have to take things slowly and be patient.

It is still your future that interests me most; did you ever think of returning to Germany? – I shall fill the lonely weeks leading up to Easter with a great deal of rest, dress matters, reading and work.

If only I could finally write *à bientôt*, a year of separation is so endlessly long. What news have you had from Berthold? Hopefully today's letter will be a small source of joy for you and cheer you up a little. Fond regards and warmest, best wishes

ever your

Felicitas

Original: manuscript.

1 Adorno, who was in contact with the Academic Assistance Council, had been invited by its members to discuss the continuation of his philosophical work. At that point he was still hoping to find a teaching possibility in England. When Adorno travelled to England in April, however, he realized that his only chance would be to go to Oxford as an 'advanced student', and this only because he did not need to request financial assistance, as his father Oscar Wiesengrund (1870–1946), who had spent a part of his youth in England, still held assets there.

2 Elfriede Herzberger (1877[?]–1962), a wealthy department store owner in the Saarland, and Adorno's aunt Agathe Calvelli-Adorno (1868–1935) had

agreed to assist Benjamin financially. In addition, Alfons Herzberger, Else's brother, who lived in Paris, was supposed to take part in helping Benjamin, and receive a dedicated copy of the arcades study in return.

3 Possibly the three pages that have survived among Benjamin's belongings; see letter 9, note 5.

4 Unknown; Benjamin evidently mentioned it in the lost letter.

47 WALTER BENJAMIN TO GRETEL KARPLUS
PARIS, 3.9.1934

Dear Felizitas,

finally I have a few more bearable days and weeks ahead of me.

And that is thanks to you. But 'thanks' – especially from so great a distance – is an inadequate expression. How long shall we still have to depend on it? – The situation from which you helped me escape was a terrible one. Your help[1] shows me that you understood it and wished to spare me any more detailed explanation.

I am now applying the new initiative I have gained through you and Teddie in two directions. Regarding one of these – the arcades study, which is now occupying me a great deal again – I shall tell you more another time. The other one concerns a – very small – art salon that is intended to be placed at my disposal for a number of lectures.[2] There I would give – in front of a French audience, and in French – a cycle of lectures on matters relating to my field of work: hence on Kafka, Kraus, Ernst Bloch and various others, organized in the form of a closed series. Naturally it is not yet certain whether it will indeed take place. I can only say that I greatly hope so and will seek to use all the connections I have here to that end.

Though the majority of experiences I have so far had with old French acquaintances by no means encourages me to renew my former connections, I must set aside my reservations in the interests of the aforementioned plan. And in the next few days I shall fall back on the oldest one I have here. I am not sure if you are familiar with the former publisher François Bernouard. Following various twists of fate, he has now come into possession of a printing house once again. He has also created a new literary situation – admittedly a more problematic one – by becoming the host of a literary club, the amis de 1914. I suppose I shall have to put in an appearance there one Tuesday; but first I must make a private visit to find out which way the wind is blowing.[3]

I recently sought out Sylvia Beach – Joyce's publisher, whom I have mentioned on occasion – for similar reasons. She has an English lending library here in my quarter. Only – at least this is what she tells me – there are no English people left in Paris. Her boutique was indeed rather quiet, and I had plenty of peace and quiet to view fine portraits and original manuscripts of Walt Whitmann [*sic*], Oskar Wilde [*sic*], Georges Moore [*sic*], James Joyce and others, which she has hung on her walls. The English milieu reminds me to wish you much fun reading Maugham's crime stories,[4] which I shall be sending you tomorrow. The other day I was by chance reading an autobiographical retrospective in the Lu by this old man, who is now in Nice, looking back upon his many successes. And this résumé sounds very melancholy. What one does learn from it is that he worked for the intelligence service, and accordingly based his Mr Ashendon [*sic*] on his own experiences.

Many thanks for the list of books you are planning to send. Just in passing: could it not be that 'Trugbilder' and one or two other books of the same category are also among the ones you have? No – I am having another look at the list – I am missing only Trugbilder (a book with amusing optical games on coloured panels).[5] It is not, I might add, especially important.

I am glad the Agnon has grown so close to your heart. Yes – my two favourite stories are the librarian and the great synagogue. The latter was supposed to be among the contributions for the first issue of my Angelus Novus (the planned journal) around 15 years ago.

Please extend my thanks – through Teddie – for kindly sending the parcel from Neunkirchen.

Wissing has still not finished his detoxification therapy. And once he has, there is a private complication[6] awaiting him that he managed to create immediately after the death of his wife. I assume it took place in a state of highly reduced willpower. But at any rate, this woman is quite insufferable, and settling the matter – whatever claims she will stake – would be preferable to any sort of arrangement. However the business turns out – because of her, I will not be asking for his help in the near future.

And so even old acquaintances are falling away, and the worth of the very few that remain is becoming ever more palpable. But now I have returned to this letter's point of departure, and all that remains for me is to close by reminding you to follow Zinn's[7] instructions quite obediently and to write to me very soon.

Old and fond regards

9 March 1934 Yours Detlef
Paris VI
1 Rue Du Four

Original: manuscript.

1 Gretel Karplus and Adorno had transferred money to Benjamin for 1 March.

2 Benjamin had arranged a series of lectures on the German literary avant-garde in a private house, the Maison de Verre [House of Glass] (31 rue Saint-Guillaume), belonging to the gynaecologist Jean Dalsace (1893–1970). Dalsace was a member of the KPF and in 1934 president of the organization that supported the Comité Thälmann. He was also a member of the Comité d'initiative for the international exhibition on fascism that opened in Paris on 9 March 1935. The cycle of lectures could not take place owing to a serious illness on Dalsace's part. Benjamin's notes 'Studien zum geplanten Vortrage bei Dalsace' [Studies towards the Planned Lecture for Dalsace] (see *GS* 6, pp. 181–4 and pp. 741–6) relate primarily to the introductory lecture, 'Les Courants politiques dans la littérature allemande' [Political Movements in German Literature], which was planned to be given on 13 April.

3 Benjamin had already become acquainted with the poet, publisher and printer François Bernouard (1883–1949) in 1926. There is no further information regarding the literary club or the private visit.

4 See W. Somerset Maugham, *Mr Ashenden, agent secret*, trans. Mme E. R. Blanchet (Paris, 1933), and 'Je suis espion par vocation', in *Lu dans la presse universelle*, 2 March 1934, p. 17.

5 Unknown. Translator's note: *Trugbilder* means 'optical illusions'.

6 Unknown.

7 Probably Prof. Dr Wilhelm Zinn (1869–1943), the internist who was treating Gretel Karplus at the time.

48 WALTER BENJAMIN TO GRETEL KARPLUS
PARIS, AFTER 18.3.1934

Dear Felizitas,

I am greatly unsettled[1] to hear how unwell you are.

What are things coming to if one can no longer think joyfully of the few people of whom one can still think at all!

I hope you are taking care of yourself as well as one can of oneself. You have proven to me on so many occasions how much better one can sometimes do so for others.

If I return to my old self one day, I shall owe it to you. And all that 'to my old self' means now is to my work. I have indeed fallen back on the arcades study with a determination of which, only recently, I would hardly have thought myself capable – and it has taken on a new guise.

Though it will hardly be its final one, I believe it is further removed from its older state than its future one. I could tell you a great deal about it; but not in writing. Only this much: in the last few days I have made a provisional division into chapters;[2] I had never come so far until now.

It is sad that the library closes at 6 o'clock and leaves me to my own devices for long evenings. For I have contact with people only in exceptional cases. This brings one into a situation where one could occasionally use a novel. And as I have found something so pleasant in Maugham, I am now reading a second book of his, 'Le fugitif'.[3]

And then a new novel by Green[4] has also come out. I hope I shall be able to obtain it and then send it to you.

You will meanwhile have learned from Teddie that I replied to him at length. Assure him from me – if you like – how grateful I am to him for the new hope he has given me. I have at least hinted to him that its impulse has done the arcades study more good than I myself could have imagined.

I have not written to Ernst, on the other hand; in part because he has not responded to my letter[5] so far; and in part because the planned lecture is by no means certain yet. It will probably only be decided shortly after Easter.

Yes, the book package arrived, and I send you my warmest thanks for it. If only you could follow close behind!

I hope very strongly that by the time you read these lines, your last attack will long have passed. Fond and lasting regards!

Yours Detlef

Original: manuscript.
On the dating: The letter was written after 18 March, the date of the letter to Adorno, and before Benjamin received that written by Gretel Karplus on 26 March.

1 Benjamin's source was either a lost letter from Gretel Karplus, a telephone conversation or a common acquaintance.

2 The arcades study had assumed the form of a book with the title *Paris, capitale du XIXe siècle*, which was planned to have six chapters (see *GS* 5 [2], pp. 1220f.).

3 See W. Somerset Maugham, *Le Fugitif*, trans. Mme E. R. Blanchet (Paris, 1933). This was the translation of the 1933 novel *The Narrow Corner*, set in the South Pacific.

4 Julien Green's *Le Visionnaire* (Paris, 1934).

5 Benjamin's letter to Ernst Bloch from January or February 1934 has not survived; Bloch's first letter to Benjamin dates from 30 April 1934 (see Bloch, *Briefe 1903–1975*, ed. Karola Bloch et al., vol. 2 [Frankfurt am Main: Suhrkamp, 1985], pp. 652f.).

49 GRETEL KARPLUS TO WALTER BENJAMIN BERLIN, 26.3.1934

When the sun shines, the birds laugh

26 March 1934.

My dear Detlef,

the fact that I have not written to you for so long, and not even thanked you for the highly interesting + amusing Maugham, is this time truly due to my condition, for I have been thinking of you so much and longing so strongly for you to be here that you should even have felt it physically. I would have been only too glad to be thoroughly selfish and discuss the complex of my ailment with you, for the matter is becoming increasingly mysterious. It has so far proved impossible to localize or clearly establish any problems of either an organic or, I think, a psychological nature. The body's harmony has been disturbed, but the cause cannot be found. Analysis? How can a person far more stupid than myself help me. My own theory? A certain revolt of my body against all I have subjected it to, an incredible resistance to the course of my life. I am ashamed to come to you with my laments now, when you have the most urgent material needs, but my faith in you will not rest easy until I have provided you with as much orientation as possible. For 1000 trifles have accumulated to create an overload, and now that the machine has fallen into a state of disorder, the repairs are proving extremely difficult. My neurologist has meanwhile been giving me intensive insulin treatment, massaging and electrifying me. Who can truly help me? Teddie sadly cannot, nor do I have any idea how to set about it properly.

I would have liked to go to Copenhagen for 3 days at Easter, but it fell through because of the passport situation; perhaps we shall still decide on Hamburg after all.

The prospect that the arcades study might be written makes me very happy, and I wish to turn all the affection and good wishes I have to that purpose. I am so close to you in my thoughts that it is almost difficult for me to write; for it seems to me as if you already know everything I could tell you; a single gesture would express much more than all these letters, perhaps tenderness is the right word.

You are mentioned with almost all your works in Karl Thieme's[1] journal 'religiöse Besinnung', which published a highly favourable review of the Kierkegaard book; the man must also be eagerly following your publications in the newspaper, Kraus. –

Have you seen any of the recent American films? We are amazed and enthusiastic about this strange new development: 'Friday Night at

Eight'[2] and the dancing dream.[3] There is a lot to be said about this; it almost seems as if film now wanted to convert to art after all.

You will have heard by now that the Voss is folding on 1 April. For Teddie, who is especially productive and on form despite all adversities, – he still plans to travel to England in mid-April – this means one possibility fewer of publishing his things. Maybe a private existence is allowed today after all?

What would you say if I decided to become Catholic? Walter Benjamin, today I must break the rule and call you by your name, the masks of Detlef and Felicitas are good, but I feel as if I knew you differently this way, better than your friends, than if I had found the proper path to you.

I send you many Easter greetings, little eggs with colourful pictures and little ribbons, with fond and urgent regards

your Felicitas.

Original: manuscript.

1 The Leipzig-born historian, theologian and publicist Karl Otto Thieme (1902–1963) taught at the Deutsche Hochschule für Politik from 1927 to 1931 and then at the Pädagogische Akademie in Elbing (East Prussia); he was first of all given leave in April, then dismissed on 5 November following a brief imprisonment. Thieme was a member of the Bund der religiösen Sozialisten [Association of Religious Socialists]. He moved to Switzerland in 1935 and became a Swiss citizen in 1943. In the last issue of the journal *Religiöse Besinnung: Vierteljahrsschrift im Dienste christlicher Vertiefung und ökumenischer Verständigung* [Religious Consciousness: Quarterly in the Service of Christian Investigation and Ecumenical Communication], Thieme had published an essay with the title 'Sören Kierkegaard und die katholische Wahrheit: Ein persönlicher Rechenschaftsbericht' [Søren Kierkegaard and Catholic Truth: A Personal Account], in which he referred to Benjamin's book on tragic drama. Thieme and Benjamin subsequently embarked on a correspondence.

2 The German title of the American film *Dinner at Eight* is *Dinner um acht*. George Cukor made the film with Jean Harlow in 1933, basing it on a Broadway play by George S. Kaufman and Edna Ferber.

3 Unknown.

50 GRETEL KARPLUS TO WALTER BENJAMIN BERLIN, 3.4.1934

Dr M. Karplus
Berlin N 20,
Prinzen Allee 60.

Berlin, 3 April 1934.

Herr
Dr Walter Benjamin,
Paris XVI
25 bis Rue Jasmin.

Dear Detlef!

hopefully you have meanwhile received my lengthy letter, which I wrote shortly before Easter.

I am most dejected, for your situation is still so uncertain. After our last effort I assumed the situation had become more stable, and Teddie will contact the respective people again so that you can reckon with a particular sum on a regular basis, and do not always bear the burden of worrying about the bare necessities. Could you name the precise sum for us?

This time I seem to have found the right doctor, for in the first week I have gained 4 pounds and feel considerably more relaxed than I did two weeks ago.

I bought the novel 'The Narrow Corner' by Somerset Maugham. Though the German translation has a different title. Is it set in the South Pacific? Main characters Captain Nichols, Fred Blake and the doctor?

Last night we entertained the former editor of the Erich Reiss Verlag,[1] who unfortunately had to give up his post because of an Aryan § (which was almost annulled) despite close friendship with Reiss himself. He will try to get Reiss interested in 'Berliner Kindheit'. Perhaps a few lines of recommendation from Gerhard would have a very favourable effect. It is possible that I will ask you for a finished manuscript for this purpose very soon.

There is a splendid house a few houses along from the factory in the Dresdener Str., the City-Hotel. A shame that I cannot show it to you now. So I do not have to go far at all to study arcades.

For today many greetings and fond regards

ever your
Felicitas

Are you in the National Chamber of Literature? This was Tau's first question with regard to 'Berliner Kindheit'?

Original: typescript with handwritten postscript.

1 Max Tau.

51 WALTER BENJAMIN TO GRETEL KARPLUS PARIS, *c*.3.4.1934

My dear Felizitas,

I read your last letter[1] with some anxiety. And this was not only because of your condition, but also for the older reason of our long separation. Certainly I cannot know whether our conversations about your well-being would find a way. Yet it is notable that I recently – I can no longer remember whether it was directly before or after the arrival of your letter – had a peculiar dream in which I had become a doctor. And it was the practice of healing through the laying on of hands[2] that I was learning.

It is inconceivable to say anything from this distance, of course. And perhaps it would not be so much myself whom my presence could animate as rather a third party. You know how limited my faith in Wissing is at present. And do not even know all the reasons for it. But: he is still a man to whom I was once very close, and to whom I will perhaps be very close again at a later point. I have a very high opinion of his medical abilities – and not only the strictly professional ones, but also those borderline functions determined by character and an advanced mind. I for my part would turn to him in any medical matter. And it would be the most logical thing for me to bring you to him if I were there with you.

As that is not the case now, however, I would like you to become accustomed to the idea of having Wissing examine you without any direct mediation on my part. He will almost certainly be coming to Berlin in the foreseeable future. I shall merely wait for your explicit consent before speaking to him about you. And I hope I shall receive it very soon.

In return I grant you my unreserved approval in becoming Catholic. And though my formulation is a laconic one, you will not therefore assume that I say it light-heartedly. This should suffice.

Now I shall mention, not without exposing you to a gentle shock, the article in 'Religiöse Besinnung'. I would be exceedingly pleased to see it, or even come into possession thereof. Could you send it to me?

And now two things: Gottfried Benn has written a programmatic text.[3] It is called: Der Dichter im neuen Staat [The Poet in the New State] – or something like that. It would be very important to me to obtain this as quickly as at all possible: for my lecture, as you can imagine. I firmly hope that it exists as an offprint. Could you have it sent to me immediately?

And a further matter: are you in possession of the folder that constitutes the archive[4] of all the reviews of my work? Not that I need the archive at the moment. But it is an unpleasant feeling to be unsure of where it is.

One of the American films you mentioned seems to be 'Dinner at eight'. I saw it a few months ago, and enjoyed it a great deal. –

How have things turned out with Hamburg? This time my Easter has been taken up by the scribblings in preparation for my conférence. There was the loveliest weather outside, and the buds on the trees stood facing the sky above the courtyard.

Now let me hear from you very soon. And start preparing yourself for recovery. As ever

Paris XVI Yours Detlef
25bis Rue Jasmin

Original: manuscript.
On the dating: The letter was written directly after Easter, which was on 1 and 2 April.

1 From 26 March.

2 See on this Benjamin's 'Erzählung und Heilung' [Narration and Healing] (*GS* 4 [1], p. 430) and the sketch on which it is based (*GS* 4 [2], pp. 1007f.).

3 Benjamin is here referring to the collection *Der neue Staat und die Intellektuellen* [The New State and the Intellectuals], published in July 1933; the eponymous speech was broadcast on 24 April 1933 by the Berliner Rundfunk and printed a day later in the *Berliner-Börsen-Zeitung* [Berlin Stock Exchange Newspaper]. The criticisms directed at Benn's positions by writers who had fled Germany, but most importantly Klaus Mann's letter to Benn of 9 May 1933, led him to write 'Antwort an die literarischen Emigranten' [Response to the Literary Emigrants], which was also first read on the radio and then printed in the *Deutsche Allgemeine Zeitung* on 25 May 1933 and included in the collection.

4 No such collection of reviews has survived.

52 WALTER BENJAMIN TO GRETEL KARPLUS PARIS, 7.4.1934

ma chère amie

thank God you are finally in the right hands.

Nonetheless, this should not automatically render my previous letter obsolete. I would still consider it a sound idea to have Wissing look at you. At the moment I do not yet know the exact date of his Berlin trip; he is away from here for a few days.

As soon as a comforting star shines in this French sky, one can expect the most eccentric coincidences: it has to disappear. Finally everything was ready for my conférence. Though I could not have expected any direct profits from it, it would have offered certain prospects. To say nothing of the significance that any objective manifestation of my work – as its possibilities are so restricted – has today.

And now I learned today that the doctor who intended to give me access to his apartment and his connections has fallen ill with pneumonia. It is a small comfort that this is true, and certainly does not constitute any sort of pretext. Nor do I doubt that the intention remains for this conférence to take place at a later date. But how much time – perhaps not precious but certainly costly time – I have lost. And now I run the risk of starting right at the edge of the season, which is ending before I have truly begun.

My preparations for this lecture have progressed too far, I might add, for me to justify breaking off my work. So I shall complete it. As soon as I have done so I will begin the piece I am planning on 'Geschichte des deutschen Buchhandels'.[1]

I had informed Herr Martin-Schwarz[2] of my change of address[3] on the telephone, and he took the opportunity to offer me the prospect of hearing from him after Easter. Unfortunately that has not yet happened. So I am doubly grateful for the question in your last letter. Regarding the sum, it was 450 fr. If I could rely on receiving that amount, it would have the very significant result that every other tiny sum I obtained as a fee would enable me to survive. If not in Paris – where it is impossible in the long term if I do not make any progress here – then at least in the country, where the living conditions would be more bearable.

I am not in the National Chamber of Literature. On closer inspection, however, this question may not have quite the significance that Tau ascribes to it. I can send you a manuscript of 'Kindheit' whenever you wish. I am not quite sure what you have in mind when you mention lines of recommendation from Gerhard. – Tell me how things stand with Teddie's travel plans.

Finally I can send you, with this same dispatch, some printed matter[4] that you will hopefully enjoy. –

Tell me what you think of 'Refugee'. The book truly helped me through the darkest of hours, and I do not think I suspended my powers of judgement while reading it.

The spring is once again tugging at all the buds like a little rascal.

My warmest

7 April 1934 yours Detlef

PS The speech by Benn is called: Die Intellektuellen und der neue Staat.

Your card[5] has just arrived. I will send you the best copy I have; but unfortunately the printing is not even. The order of the pieces is the same as in the book.

Original: manuscript.

1 Benjamin did not write about this four-volume work [History of the German Book Trade] by Friedrich Kapp and Johann Goldfriedrich, completed in 1923, which he owned.

2 There is no further information regarding Herr Schwarz or Schwartz-Martin, a Paris acquaintance of Else Herzberger's nephew Arnold Levy-Ginsberg.

3 Two or three weeks previously, Benjamin had moved in with his sister Dora, who lived in the rue Jasmin in the 16th arrondissement, for a transitional period.

4 Benjamin's review of Kommerell's book on Jean Paul; it appeared on 29 March in the *Frankfurter Zeitung* with the title 'Der eingetunkte Zauberstab' [The Dipped-in Magic Wand] (see *GS* 3, pp. 409–17).

5 Not preserved.

53 GRETEL KARPLUS TO WALTER BENJAMIN BERLIN, 9.4.1934

9 April 1934.

Dear Detlef,

now, in the spring, our correspondence is also beginning to blossom; admittedly only a poor substitute for lovely Sunday walks, but at least something. I immediately sent your last letter to Teddie in Frankfurt for the swiftest possible processing, and his letter[1] already answers your questions. – I ordered the issue of Religiöse Bestimmung and sent off the Benn today. I read some of it so that I would be able to show off, and despite some decent things I was ultimately disappointed; do you know more about him? – I do not have the reviews of your works, nor do I recall ever having seen them. – I greatly enjoyed the Maugham this time, quite unlike the things I had read in the past; he reminds me of Conrad, but that is certainly not the worst of recommendations. – I am greatly disconcerted by the friendly doctor's pneumonia; as if he could not have waited until after your lecture before getting it! And while we are on the subject of doctors, I would like to tell you a thing or two myself: after three weeks of insulin treatment by Prof. S. I am feeling quite well and lively, so that I have once and for all given up my stupid hypochondria about suffering forever. It seems that the success is due only to the consistency and dosage of the substances used. Whereas every internist considered me healthy, he knew that my condition was quite worrying and got me back in shape without any psychological treatment, only by feeding my nerves, as I would put it. In this he is almost certainly more disoriented and stuck than I am, but it has worked nonetheless. It is quite difficult to determine what exactly one demands of a doctor; ultimately that he helps one somehow, even if the method is an adventurous one.

With a few exceptions, doctors are no more than servants with A-levels anyway. This is my long preamble to the modest request to refrain from any examination by Herr Dr Wissing, as it is no longer necessary at the moment, and I do not wish to risk even the slightest threat to our relationship that could result from it. It seems to me that we should not involve the psychological element through third parties either – let us afford the psyche its delicate privilege, I am recalling our conversations back in the Meineckestr, then in the Prinz Regentenstr., and think I have understood you better with this refusal than you may remember at the moment. So please a sincere no! No!

What is the state of your plans to live in a provincial area of France? Have you decided whether you prefer the north or the south, a small town or a summer nest?

Einsiedel is going on a Palestine–Egypt trip for the FZ together with Tau. Please write to me often, for I cannot get enough of your letters. Warmest regards ever your

little Felicitas.

Original: manuscript.

1 Adorno's letter of 5 April; see *Adorno–Benjamin Correspondence*, pp. 36–40.

54 GRETEL KARPLUS TO WALTER BENJAMIN
BERLIN, 13.4.1934

Berlin, 13 April 1934.

Herr
Dr Walter Benjamin,
Paris XVI.
25 bis Rue Jasmin

Dear Detlef!

I have just sent off 'Religiöse Besinnung'. I have meanwhile learned that Karl Thieme is a famous Protestant theologian whose name has been in the newspapers a great deal lately, as he wrote a public letter to the pope and was in correspondence with the pope for a long time regarding the unification of the Catholic and Protestant churches. Perhaps you also read about it.

My enthusiasm about 'Berliner Kindheit' is growing all the time. What I would like most is to learn the individual pieces by heart, though one should really follow the method of 'One-Way Street' and copy them out in order to understand them fully.*

A thousand thanks for the review of the Kommerell. I shall see to it that I obtain the book here so that I can better appreciate how fine your review is.

My fond and warm regards

ever your
Felicitas

Original: typescript with handwritten addition.

55 GRETEL KARPLUS TO WALTER BENJAMIN
BERLIN, 19.4.1934

19 April 1934.

My dear Detlef,

I want to answer your letter immediately, albeit with the modest request that you still tell me everything there is to say, do not let it be drowned out by the hubbub of urgent daily matters.

* My medical treatment is taking place at Kurfürstenstr. 80, very near Steglitzer on the corner of Genthinerstr.

I passed on your address to the interested parties immediately, at least your sister will be sure to forward correctly the deliveries that are still on the way.

Regarding the problem of the sender, it is a lady in her mid-50s who is still very lively, her first names are Else Marianne, unmarried, but prefers to be addressed as 'Frau'.[1] – I think Teddie appealed to her very emphatically on your behalf; has the sum turned out larger, or still the agreed 400 frs? This sum is composed of three parts: Teddie, Else and Agathe. Has she written anything about regular payments?! –

I have gained more weight, and should be concluding the very strictest treatment next week, though I shall remain under medical supervision. I am so glad you understood my refusal correctly. If my condition does turn out to deteriorate once more, I would naturally have to overcome my reservations in spite of all.

Concerning your book publications in Germany, it does seem *absolutely* necessary to me that you should be in the National Chamber of Literature, otherwise the publishing houses cannot print anything of yours. If it is difficult to arrange this from there, you should very seriously consider whether you could not come to *Berlin** for a certain time (2–4 weeks) in order to sort everything out here. I am truly not saying that only because I would terribly like to see you again, but rather bringing it up for discussion as I see the situation from here. So far I have still not heard from Reiss, but if it ultimately depends only on this one factor, I am sure it could somehow be arranged monetarily, perhaps you could live here with Gl.?[2]

Please write very soon to your

Felicitas

who worries greatly and fondly about you.

Original: manuscript.

1 Translator's note: At that time it was customary for unmarried women to bear the title *Fräulein*, a diminutive of *Frau*, regardless of their age. This no longer applies today.

2 This is Gustav Glück.

* not Prinz[regentenstrasse]

56 GRETEL KARPLUS TO WALTER BENJAMIN
BERLIN, 3.5.1934

3 May 1934.

Dear Detlef,

finally your letter[1] came today. I am sending the essay[2] a little differently to how you requested. – Arnold Levy-G.[3] is a typical minor intellectual, fairly boring, but helpful and therefore to be kept on good terms with. I do not have my papers yet, otherwise I would perhaps have gone to London via Paris for a few days at Whitsun. More soon, hopefully I shall be able to give you good news then.

Warm regards ever

your Felicitas

Is it really appropriate to still keep the name after the quarrel with Speyer?

Original: manuscript on a business card of the company Georg Tengler / Lederhandschuhfabriken / Engros und Export [Leather glove factories / wholesale and export].

1 Not preserved.

2 Probably Benn's speech 'Die Intellektuellen und der Staat'.

3 The PhD art historian Arnold Levy (also known as Arnold Levy-Ginsberg) was the nephew of Else Herzberger. He and his wife Milly were among Benjamin's closest acquaintances in the last years of his life. He remained in France, changed his name to Armand Levilliers after the war, and had a second-hand bookshop.

57 WALTER BENJAMIN TO GRETEL KARPLUS
PARIS, *c.*6.5.1934

Dear Felizitas,

Yesterday I received your second card; meanwhile you have long since discovered the cause for my temporary silence.

And now, to compensate you for your anxious days as well or as badly as I can, I send you these few lines.

I am once again developing a level of activity that amazes even me. But the almost complete isolation that has become the norm for me turns even tenuous, even hopeless efforts into a way of establishing some form of contact with people.

You are familiar with 'Haschisch in Marseille'. I have had it translated. The translation,[1] connoisseurs have told me, is extremely poor.

Nonetheless, I am attempting to use my connections in order to achieve its inclusion in the Cahiers du Sud. The journal is published in Marseilles; that creates a vague chance. – But above all I have undertaken efforts to find a reliable solution to the problem of translation, which is greater in the case of my writings than even I had supposed, and there is a reasonable chance that I shall soon be put in touch with a true connoisseur of German who has the additional advantage of not being a professional translator. It is Benoist-Méchin[2] – I doubt the name means anything to you.

And then I shall try to become involved in the compilation of an extensive encyclopaedia,[3] which is being undertaken at the request of the former minister of education, de Monzie, and is still at the first preparatory stage. Naturally this could only take on genuine significance in the winter at the earliest.

I expect I have already told you that I have been in contact with the Nouvelle Revue Française regarding an article about Bachofen.[4]

The multiple translation projects[5] make me wonder if I should ask you to send me the essays of mine that have been published in journals, which are still in your hands. But I am reluctant to burden you once more with the work involved in sending a registered parcel – and as there are irreplaceable items among them, I dare not consider a normal recorded delivery.

Be that as it may – I had already asked you for the article 'Theater und Rundfunk',[6] which was published in the 'Blätter des Hessischen Landestheaters'. Hopefully it has not gone out yet and you can also enclose 'Julien Green'[7] from the 'Neue Schweizer Rundschau'. There has been particular interest in it here. – In this case a recorded delivery is naturally sufficient.

I am being sent many novels. If I receive anything decent I shall pass it on to you. What I have read so far does not merit it. I have already told you of the incredible disappointment I felt at Green's 'Visionnaire'. And – to mention something very different, but no better – Klostermann have published a text entitled 'Die ästhetische Problematik Flauberts'[8] by a certain Herr Binswanger, and the whole thing is arrogant tripe.

I now spend all my evenings in my room and read: the inkpot has defined the period of my life just as lightning defined that of Luther (in which, after all, there was also an inkpot). By day I read at the Bibliothèque Nationale: thus one must content oneself with modest contrasts.

Yes, write soon. What have you been hearing from Teddy? what of your nerves?

Before I forget – Ernst wrote. Carola has a building commission in Barcelona and they will go there later on.

The page does not look very pretty. But may it serve a good end in the shape of very fond greetings.

Yours Detlef

PS So – now a new page after all, to give you my thanks for the essay I have just received.[9] Could you now send me the one on Green too? Likewise registered. And then we shall postpone the combined delivery and the registered parcel. Because we shall not give up hope that you will one day bring it to me in person.

How nice it would have been: Whitsun!

Write at length extremely soon.

Just as your letter arrived, I was having a strange dream about Speyer that suggests we should not yet take any steps in the name matter you touch upon.

Original: manuscript.
On the dating: Benjamin's letter is a response to Gretel Karplus's card of 3 May; it also presupposes the receipt of Ernst Bloch's letter of 30 April, which mentions Karola Bloch's building commission.

1 It was by Anna Maria Blaupot ten Cate and Louis Sillier and appeared in 1935 in issue 168 of 'Les Cahiers du Sud', pp. 26–33.

2 The Paris-born Jacques Benoist-Méchin (1901–1983) had completed his military service in Germany after the First World War and become profoundly enamoured of German culture. Apart his musical and literary interests, he joined the French right early on, and was close to Doriot's PPF; after 1940 he was among the advocates of Nazi collaboration and was sentenced to death in 1947, then pardoned and released in 1954. His two-volume work *Histoire de l'armée allemande* was published between 1936 and 1938. No further information could be gained regarding the circumstances leading to Benjamin's acquaintance with Benoist-Méchin.

3 This probably refers to volumes 16 and 17 of the *Encyclopédie Française*, which dealt with 'art et litterature dans la societé contemporaine'; they were published in 1935 and 1936. A review written by Benjamin for the *Zeitschrift für Sozialforschung* remained unpublished during his lifetime. There is no documentation of Benjamin's planned collaboration; in the following letter to Gretel Karplus he writes of a forthcoming meeting with Pierre Abraham, the editor of the aforementioned volumes. What is certainly conceivable, and suggested by Benjamin's characterization of the second volume – 'The second volume of the work examines in detail the artistic production of the present and constitutes an inventory thereof' (*GS* 3, p. 585) – is that this planned collaboration contained the seeds of Benjamin's essay 'Das Kunstwerk im Zeitalter seiner technischen Reproduzierbarkeit'.

4 Benjamin received the following invitation from the writer Jean Paulhan (1884–1968) in a 'pneumatique' of 25 May: 'J'aurai plaisir à faire

votre connaissance. Vous est-il possible de venir à la N.R.F. un soir de la semaine prochaine, vers six heures (lundi et samedi exceptés)?' [I look forward to making your acquaintance. Would it be possible to come to the N. R. F. one evening next week, around six o'clock (except for Monday and Saturday)?] The French essay 'Johann Jakob Bachofen', however, was rejected by Paulhan on 8 May 1935 (see *Benjamin-Katalog*, pp. 235f.) and remained unpublished during Benjamin's lifetime (see *GS* 2 [1], pp. 219–33).

5 As well as Dora-Sophie Benjamin, Elisabeth Hauptmann and Bianca (Margaret) Mynatt attempted in vain to find publishing opportunities for Benjamin's texts in England and North America. Nothing is known about any further translation plans.

6 See *GS* 2 [2], pp. 773–6.

7 Benjamin's essay from 1929; see *GS* 2 [1], pp. 328–34.

8 Benjamin reviewed Paul Binswanger's book in the literary supplement of the *Frankfurter Zeitung* of 12 August 1934; see *GS* 3, pp. 423–5.

9 Presumably 'Theater und Rundfunk', which Benjamin seems to have requested in his lost letter.

58 WALTER BENJAMIN TO GRETEL KARPLUS
PARIS, *c.*24.5.1934

Dear Felizitas,

I think you would be satisfied with the shape I have lent your Whitsun flowers, drawn upon a pink background. They come from an invisible cup concealed in the middle of a large ring cake. The cake is called pain de Gênes here and the flowers are lilies of the valley. My great favourite among flowers has not yet appeared; it always waits for my birthday: the red poppy.

It saddens me that things are going more slowly for you again. Life is really not easy for you either. Possibly it would sometimes be a little easier if you knew in what an exotic and hardy guise you sit as a blossom in my rather bare arbour vitae.

That is all on flowers. No – one more on the grave of a small hope, on which nothing has grown so far except the most displeasing rice (erich reiss editor communis). So the bad news I heard from Palestine about him has been confirmed. Lichtenstein should be viewed with no less distrust. But naturally I do not intend to discard even the most remote possibility. Though admittedly it is possible that the lack of any Jewish orientation to my 'Kindheit' would pose a problem if he no longer has his own publishing house, and only manages that Jewish book society.[1]

You can hardly imagine how much I am missing the chance to speak to you at the moment. We are now in our second year of separation, and will not be meeting again in the foreseeable future. In addition I am leaving Paris and moving to rural Denmark. There is no longer any financial justification for continuing my stay here: there is nothing more to be done here in June. At least the next few days – I shall leave on 4 June *at the earliest* – still hold a number of important meetings: with Jean Paulhan,[2] with Charles Dubos[3] and with Paul Abraham.[4] They are essentially about three matters that have not yet been clarified: my collaboration on the encyclopaedia, my chances of finding a good translator, my Bachofen essay. If one thing does not turn out, perhaps another will. You asked about Jouhandeau and Green.[5] Those are people who could only be useful to me once I were on slightly firmer ground – and even then I could hardly say that about Green. Not only his last novels, but also their reception by the public indicate that this figure is losing significance; and with good reason. What is important is that these reasons are closely related to those which, in better times – better both for him and for me – had kept our contact within extremely narrow limits.

I read the community paper,[6] which I have always enjoyed glancing at, with doubled interest this time. Its range of subjects is naturally extremely limited; I am not sure whether one can be seen in it without being within the Jewish cultural and educational establishment. At any rate, I enclose a letter of authorization for you to carry out negotiations with Lichtenstein about 'Berliner Kindheit'. And I thank you in advance for the time and effort you are expending for that purpose. But I also ask that you greatly restrict these efforts until you have concrete signs that there is serious interest on the other side. I know from experience that publishers in particular – and second-rank ones all the more – have an irresistible tendency towards tittle-tattle.

As for the Wahlverwandtschaften study, I merely wanted to be sure that it is in your hands. There could be no safer place for it.

Have you seen Arnold? He was planning to return here in mid-May; so far I have awaited him without success. On the other hand, I would naturally like very much to see him before I go to Denmark. As I will not be leaving before 4 June, as I said, it would perhaps still be possible before then.

Do you think you would be able to send me two floral patterns before then? I would be most happy.

I am writing this letter in the first days following your return.[7] You did not tell me where you had been. Hopefully somewhere pleasant for a few hours and not too lonely. It is terrible how people have scattered in all directions. I have not heard from Teddie for some time either. But no doubt he is up to his neck in work over there.

I am sure I have told you that I have occasionally been seeing Werner Kraft, a former acquaintance of mine, also a former librarian in Hanover. I have before me now a fine essay[8] of his on two poems by Kraus, which appeared in the last issue of 'Der Brenner'.

I enclose two books[9] as a little diversion to ring in the summer. One of them – which I do not know – with a few pretty photos, and the other one rather well-behaved, readable and not exhausting.

Fond and fondest regards

Make sure you still write to me here
Yours Detlef

Original: manuscript.
On the dating: Gretel Karplus had received Benjamin's letter by 27 May, so he cannot have written it any later than 25 May.

1 Erich Lichtenstein (1888–1967), a literary and theatre critic, had founded a publishing house with Thankmar von Münchhausen in 1920; after the Second World War he worked as a critic for the *Neue Zeitung* and the *Tagesspiegel*. Nothing is known about the 'Jewish book society'.

2 Paulhan was editor-in-chief of the journal *Nouvelle Revue Française*.

3 The essayist, literary critic and translator Charles Du Bos (1882–1939). Benjamin visited him together with Werner Kraft on 10 June; see *Für Walter Benjamin: Dokumente, Essays und ein Entwurf*, ed. Ingrid and Konrad Scheuermann (Frankfurt am Main: Suhrkamp, 1992), p. 49.

4 This was the writer, critic and translator Pierre Abraham (real name: Pierre Abraham Bloch, 1892–1974), the brother of Jean-Richard Bloch (1884–1947) and the poet, writer and politician Marcel Abraham (1898–1955), who had acted as de Monzie's principal private secretary. Pierre Abraham was editor of volumes 16 and 17 of the *Encyclopédie Française*; he translated Brecht's *Furcht und Elend des Dritten Reichs* [Fear and Misery in the Third Reich], and Benjamin noted his book *Proust – Recherches sur la création intellectuelle* (Paris, 1930) in one of his book lists. He was music critic for the newspaper *Ce soir* from 1937 until August 1939.

5 The letter with this question has not survived.

6 Benjamin is presumably referring to the *Jüdische Rundschau* and the publication of his 'Kafka' there; it may have been mentioned in lost letters written by Benjamin or Gretel Karplus.

7 The letter in which she must have spoken of her absence from Berlin has not survived; it is not mentioned in her letter of 27 May.

8 The essay 'Zu zwei Gedichten von Karl Kraus' had been published in the April issue of the journal *Der Brenner* on the occasion of Kraus's sixtieth birthday.

9 Unknown.

59 GRETEL KARPLUS TO WALTER BENJAMIN BERLIN, 27.5.1934

27 May 1934.

My dear Detlef,

you will meanwhile have received the little pink note, the last that I wish to send you in Paris for practical reasons, but as soon as I have your new address I shall see to it that one is awaiting you there. – I have not heard any more news regarding your affairs, nor received your book greeting. I hope the recent negotiations were rather successful; I would like to hear about it at length from you. –

During and after Whitsun I had another horrible migraine attack from which I am only slowly recovering. Perhaps that was the punishment for my unwillingness to seek Dr Wissing's advice. After giving the matter a great deal of thought, I have decided to ask you to have him call me the next time he is in Berlin, if you – still – consider it advisable with reference to his condition. As I do not know if the short time will permit a second account, let me give you a quick report on my illness, even though I do not think one can effect a cure from a distance and do not wish to expect it of Herr Dr Wissing. What seems definite is that everything is fine organically, and that it is indeed a case of migraines resulting from my constitution. Now the problem lies in preventing the vascular spasms in the brain that trigger the migraines. I am now taking various migraine medications, though they must be introduced slowly and I cannot say anything about their effectiveness, such as Impletol injections, Luminal tablets, Decholin and a mixture of phenacitin and theobromine. With your aversion to medication, I can imagine the horror you must feel at so many names. The symptoms are typical: strong headaches, mostly at the right temple, nausea with vomiting, often to the point of being unable to retain any sort of nutrition, heavy depression and lethargy, accompanied by visual defects and sometimes also speech disorders.

Perhaps it is part and parcel of this condition that I am becoming increasingly disinterested in real life, which is naturally also helping me to get through this time and my great loneliness; it is only rather difficult to think of this condition as now being permanent. My early childhood wish to be no more than a figure in a novel – so almost Felicitas – is very much alive once more.

I was incredibly disappointed by the Kommerell. After reading it, your review seems much too good, not decisive enough in its rejection; I am very keen, on the other hand, on 'A High Wind in Jamaica',[1] which you recommended to me years ago.

I am somewhat fearful about your move to Denmark, and today I must touch on one of the most delicate subjects; I am reluctant to discuss it in writing, and am only doing so because it must be done. You of all people, who never uttered a word of complaint when I seemed so disloyal by not coming, who have always accepted my responsibilities and never hindered me, have every right to ask what gives me the right to overstep the boundary that has been set for us and intervene in your most personal affairs. Certainly you are right from your point of view, but I also have objective reasons for defending you, and I shall attempt to do so as best I can. We have hardly ever spoken about B., and I do not know him nearly as well as you do, but I have great reservations about him of which I shall mention only one, of course only in so far as I can identify it: his often palpable lack of clarity. Right now I am less concerned with discussing him in depth than with the feeling I sometimes have that you are somehow under his influence, which is a great danger to you. I remember very well a discussion evening in the Prinzenallee about the development of language and your agreement with his theories, when I felt this particularly strongly. I have fearfully avoided this subject, because I think that this relationship is very emotionally loaded for you and perhaps also stands for something entirely different, but here it would also be a step too far to say any more about it. And he of all people is the one friend who has supported you most in your current difficulties, and I can understand it so well that you need this contact to escape the isolation threatening us all, even though I might almost be tempted to view that as the lesser evil for your work. I know that I am risking a great deal, perhaps everything in our friendship, and it was only the long separation that could induce me to speak. Forgive me if you can if you feel I have gone too far. Today as ever fond regards and best wishes

your old

Felicitas.

Original: typescript.

1 This novel by Richard Hughes was published in 1929; the German translation appeared in 1931 under the title *Sturmwind auf Jamaika*.

60 WALTER BENJAMIN TO GRETEL KARPLUS PARIS, EARLY JUNE 1934

My dear Felizitas,

I had to gain a little distance in order to answer your last letter. The word has a dual meaning: distance from both your letter and my present work. You yourself, as is apparent in the former, have a clear awareness of how infinitely difficult it is to discuss in a letter the Danish question you brought up. You did so with great tact; not everything you say is untrue, but nor does everything you say prove that I should not go to B.

I shall address the most important question. What you wrote about his influence on me calls to mind a significant and recurring constellation in my life. A similar influence was exerted on me, according to my friends, by C. F. Heinle,[1] as also – in the opinion of my later wife, who at that time fought passionately against it – by Simon Guttmann.[2] A discussion relating to the latter has stayed in my memory to this day, despite taking place some twenty years ago. The most bitter of words were exchanged, and in the end it was claimed that I was under his suggestion. – Perhaps it surprises you that I am going so far back to explain these things. But I must do so for you to understand how – without denying your words – I can stand fast in the face of them.

In the economy of my existence, there are indeed a handful of decisive relationships that enable me to occupy a position that is the polar opposite of my original being. These relationships have always provoked more or less vigorous protest from those close to me, as now to B. – and voiced much less carefully – from Gerhard Scholem. In such cases I can do little more than ask my friends to trust that the fruitfulness of these ties, whose perils are evident enough, will become apparent with time. You of all people are by no means unaware that my life, like my thinking, is characterized by extremes. The breadth it thus asserts, the freedom to juxtapose objects and thoughts that seemed irreconcilable, takes shape only in the face of danger. A danger that is generally obvious also to my friends only in the guise of said 'dangerous' relationships.

Those are my thoughts on the matter; for I felt I owed you this answer, rather than one or two easier ones that could have taken its place. Let me at least hold on to the hope – and this brings me to the other motive that must be touched on here – that we shall be able to discuss these things together in the foreseeable future. Make sure you do not neglect to keep me informed in the matter of your papers.

Apart from that, I have postponed my journey – I shall depart from here on the 17th. Perhaps this will enable you to still send a floral pattern here before then, of which I am unfortunately very much in need. The first reason for this delay is the study on Kafka, and the distance I had to gain from it, which I mentioned at the start of the letter, is the second. I finished the preparatory work yesterday. I shall refrain from relating the extraordinary difficulties of the matter, except for the not insignificant ones residing in the circumstances. As I now simply had to tackle this long-planned investigation, it has turned out to be very extensive, and the manuscript, once finished, will have to be reduced to a third of its length in order to be printed by the Jüdische Rundschau – hardly an agreeable prospect. I managed to gather together all of Kafka's writings here, but it required an incredible effort.

A few days ago – or rather, more than a week ago – the small book parcel I had sent you came back. The manservant had written an incorrect address on it. You should still receive it, with the correct one, before my departure.

Wissing is in Berlin at the moment. Not in the best state, as I heard from a third party. But I shall at least enclose his telephone number here. And as your recovery has been interrupted once more after all, it would perhaps indeed be a good idea to call him: Steinplatz* – A few days ago I had the opportunity to take some mescaline.[3] This is the famous drug used by the Mexican Indians, made from the cactus anhalonium levinii.[4] The sacred hallucinogenic drink used in their rituals, Pulche, is based on it. Though my organism did not receive it quite as well as the hashish, it did offer me a long night with a whole series of highly important insights, but in particular a psychological explanation for catatonia that is of great interest. I produced an extensive log.

I have heard nothing from Wiesengrund. Why?

Be sure to write to me soon and definitely still here. Warm wishes for your recovery and many fond regards.

Yours Detlef

Original: manuscript.
On the dating: This letter is the response to the previous one written by Gretel Karplus on 27 May.

1 The poet Christoph Friedrich Heinle (1894–1914), who had been a friend of Philipp Keller and Ludwig Strauss since their school days in Aachen, studied first in Göttingen, then registered in Freiburg for the summer semester 1913 to study philology. He worked in the Freie Studentenschaft [Free Student Body] with Benjamin and was head of the 'department for art and literature'. Henle's suicide after the outbreak of the First World War was a factor in the composition of Benjamin's sonnets in the following years (see *GS* 7 [1], pp. 26–67).

* I cannot find Wissing's telephone number among my papers. But you can find it easily. He is living with Frau Sophie Cohn Kantstrasse 150[a]

2 Simon Wilhelm Guttmann (1891–1990) was a friend of Georg Heym, whose posthumous poems he co-edited, and co-founder of Der Neue Club in Berlin.

3 The experiment of 22 May 1934 documented by Fritz Fränkel; see *GS* 6, pp. 607–14; for Benjamin's own notes see ibid., pp. 614–16.

4 Mescaline – which was first produced in pure form in 1897 – is extracted from the top part of the cactus *Anhalonium levinii*, whereas Pulque, the intoxicating drink of the Aztecs, is produced by slitting open the stems of an agave species and fermenting the juice.

61 GRETEL KARPLUS TO WALTER BENJAMIN BERLIN, 12.6.1934

12 June 1934.

Dear Detlef,

many thanks for the books, which arrived exactly on my birthday,[1] so the porter's error in the address served a good purpose after all. – I am very glad you understood my letter as it was intended, and that nothing has changed between us as a result. And I shall learn from this, as we have no choice but to depend on writing, to express what must be spoken about as far as possible. This truly assumes a far-reaching and well-grounded friendship, but I think we can have this faith in each other by now. Your remark that Gerhard had written to you about the same subject confirmed my feeling. Denmark is certainly closer to Berlin than Paris is, and a weekend[2] there does not seem entirely impossible – with the low prices there I could very well imagine that you could risk a trip to Copenhagen, which would be easiest for me to reach. The only trouble is that my business partner is still gravely ill, so that I am even more restricted than usual in my dispositions. I am very worried about it; for his death could have considerable repercussions for me. For the summer holidays – if we still plan to stay in Germany – we are thinking of Baden-Baden in August; we would also be highly tempted to go to Madonna di Campiglio, one of the few places in the Dolomites where one does not have to take high-altitude mountain routes, though perhaps here too considerable difficulties with my passport. – Teddie is now in Oxford, waiting to receive your address, but will no doubt have written to you by now. He will stay in England until the beginning of July; his reports are quite interesting, especially those about the colleges, albeit tremendously foreign, though on the other hand I can well imagine him there. Being in Germany together in 1933 did have its advantages in some respects; I am much quieter than before and also feel genuinely entitled to be. –

Lichtenstein – I am almost tempted to say: to my joy – also failed, but to make sure no stone is left unturned I shall also make sure that Tau, who has returned from his Palestine trip for the FZ, sees the manuscript, although we are already familiar with his condition, which you sadly cannot fulfil; but if he found it very good, I am sure he could find some other possibility.

I have meanwhile heard from my future brother-in-law Ernst Schachtel that you might be writing something together with his best friend Erich F.,[3] the analyst, and I would be interested to hear more about that from you. Many thanks for Wissing's address, I am following a new trail at the moment and must wait for the results of that before I contact him.

Please forgive the bad behaviour of the typewriter on the previous page. – The floral pattern went out immediately and has hopefully long since reached you.

Please write to me soon at length about your life with B. and your work plans for the summer. Do you intend to return to Paris in the winter? And did Elisabeth ever mention my name?

I know so little about your past life, we would only now have started speaking about it, is Heinle the friend whose belongings I sent you and I do not know anything about Gutmann. But even with your current friends I sometimes only know their name, even if they live in Berlin. When I asked you to introduce me to him you refused, so it is your intention for me to know only certain sides of you, so then you must forgive me if I err now and again. And I certainly agree that keeping our relationship in this form does, alongside its great dangers, have very considerable advantages, above all the quality of being absolutely original and unique, and the impossibility of mingling it with any others and blurring its own special contours.

Good night, dear Detlef, it has grown late, I have spent a long time chatting with you and will now bid you a late farewell. Very warm regards and best wishes ever

Your

Felicitas

Original: typescript.

1 Gretel Karplus was born on 10 June 1902.

2 weekend: EO.

3 The psychoanalyst Erich Fromm (1900–1980) was an employee of the Institut für Sozialforschung. He had investigated Bachofen's theory of matriarchy, and Benjamin wanted to contact him for his essay on Bachofen.

62 GRETEL KARPLUS TO WALTER BENJAMIN BERLIN, 15.7.1934

15 July 1934, Detlef's birthday.

My very dear Detlef,

today is your birthday, and I was with you in my thoughts all day. I send you all my fond and best wishes, above all that the coming year might be easier than the last. This morning I spent a long time reading your letters, and was so close to you that I felt as if I could touch you. I had never before realized as clearly as I did today what the 'Du' in our letters expresses, a shy tenderness, a friendship that has grown and stood the test of time, and has become a sort of refuge in our lives. I am sure all this does not strike you as a sufficient reason for my long silence, for my unpunctual writing, when I normally like to think of myself as a particularly reliable person. I have had a great deal of turmoil and accompanying headaches lately, and it was so very important to me to write you a proper letter in which you would feel my closeness. For my business partner died from a stroke after 3 ½ months of illness and I have now been left alone to bear an enormous responsibility, and here too I have become isolated once and for all. I think I can deal with the situation mentally, if I manage to hold out physically. For that reason I went to see Wissing this morning, though he cannot help me at the moment as I am not having an attack, but he was very kind and intends to examine me when I have my next one. I can well imagine that he has a powerful effect on women, as they suspect depravity and sadism on his part, but I could never fall in love with him. And I do think I am in good hands with my current neurologist. Except that he still has some old, rather expensive and time-consuming methods to which I do not wish to be subjected, such as sanatorium and similar jests.

Teddie has been in Germany since last night, albeit not in Berlin. I hope we shall be able to travel at the start of August, I am having great difficulties with my entry permit for Italy, references, visa, foreign currency. In addition to that, I can only be absent from work for three weeks due to the change of circumstances, though I was thinking of spending – after a successful trip via Ultimo – a further week in Garmisch, where the Seligmanns[1] own a house, though not staying with them. Teddie has to go back again in mid-September to hand in the exposé for an epistemological study on Husserl that he plans to write for Oxford.

In the letter before last, you wrote about the pleasant children next door, and the other day I saw Alfred Sohn's little Brigitte,[2] who is now 12 years old and truly enchanted me, just as Daga did years ago. Do you still hear from her sometimes? – How is Stefan? – When you mention Hanns,[3] I assume you mean the composer; I never met any lady friend. He is quite intelligent, though slightly malicious, and was nicer 6 years ago than in '32. – Do you ever hear from Kurt and Lotte?[4] – Is Elisabeth still in America?

Do you still remember those strange houses in Berlin where the windows in the stairwells are decorated with large female figures, they look exactly as if they should appear in your stories, and today I spoke for a long time with one of them.

In the course of a conversation about our friend Ernst you once told me that a man only truly loves when he is faithful, but that this is different for a woman. At that time I did not really dare to ask any further, but I am so sorry that we did not talk more about love. Please do not misunderstand: it has nothing to do with gossipy curiosity, I am rather thinking of your beautiful words in Einbahnstrasse.[5]

Dear Detlef, do you really still think it impossible under the new circumstances to come to Berlin for a few days in the autumn. If I, Gustav,[6] Wissing and whatever other friend of yours would be willing joined forces and you perhaps stayed with Franz,[7] one could probably finance it, as a trip costs money, after all, and I have more to take care of than before. Please give my project some thought and give me a reply. If there is no change in the situation, my travel preparations would once again be tremendously complicated and uncertain.

In your last letter[8] you asked me about a man whose name I cannot read, something with 'Ko', do you remember? – You also wanted to write to me about your agreement with Fromm, who is incidentally the best friend of my future brother-in-law, whose existence I think I have mentioned to you before. He is a childhood friend of mine; his sister was a girl in my class, he was a lawyer here and is living in Switzerland at the moment, my sister has finally been admitted to the state examination, everything has been delayed for us by the unexpected change of papers.

Dear, I ask you once again to forgive me for my neglect, do not be cross with me and do not punish me for it with a long wait. I bid you a very warm good night, today and ever

your

Felicitas.

Original: typescript.

1 The family of Milton Seligmann (1866–1948) and his wife, Marie Bernhardine (1867–?), whose house in Frankfurt was open to guests and who accommodated many musicians passing through there on their travels.

2 This is the daughter (b. 1921) of Alfred Sohn-Rethel and Tilla Henninger (1893–1945).

3 Hanns Eisler.

4 Kurt Weil and Lotte Lenya.

5 This refers to the aphorisms bearing the title *Loggia*.

6 Gustav Glück.

7 Franz Hessel.

8 Not preserved.

63 GRETEL KARPLUS TO WALTER BENJAMIN BERLIN, 25.7.1934

b. 10 July 190(?) 25 July 1934.

Dear Detlef,

many thanks for the airmail letter;[1] am I merely imagining it, or have your letters from Denmark genuinely become a little more remote? No doubt I am simply jealous, and one is not always in the same mood, but this makes me sad and pensive. Please, tell me if something is bothering you. I am now going to the Dolomites on 1 August address: Golf Hotel Campo Carlo Magno Trento Ital. (it is situated above Madonna di Campiglio). Things are rather uncertain with my extra holiday time, but I think that Teddie will visit me in Berlin for a few days. Teddie has to be back in London on 15 Sept., so that I could really arrange a weekend[2] in late Sept. or early Oct., but it is almost out of the question for me to obtain a Danish visa, and it seems more than doubtful that my renaturalization will be complete by then. That is why I asked you if you could not visit me in Berlin, perhaps one could also meet in Warnemünde if you specifically want to avoid Berlin. –

It is very sweet of you to ask about my business matters; I shall attempt to give you a brief report and can only hope that it does not bore you too greatly. I just began here on 1 April 1933, was a trainee first, but was conferred with procuration after only two months and was made junior partner on 1 Jan. '34. Herr Tengler fell ill in March, i.e. right after I had been part of the business for about a year, and since then I have been managing the firm alone. The business contract states that his widow is the new partner, but I am sole managing director, so that under normal circumstances, i.e. if I can make a profit this year, hardly anything changes in practice. Naturally the responsibility is rather great and times are hardly easy, in terms of obtaining both loans and raw materials, but there are also great disadvantages to having a new partner, and I would prefer to take care of things by myself. I have hardly retained any of my technical know-how or chemistry, but my sound knowledge of leather is very useful when it comes to buying materials. I am supported by one of our senior employees: the head seamstress, the storekeeper, the 1st bookkeeper and the foreman. In addition we have a branch in Ziegenhals purely for stitching and cutting, in order to make the most of the much lower provincial wages. If my body survives it – psychologically speaking there are no problems, though it is sometimes difficult to have to make all the internal decisions alone without any consultations. If I do not think of something, it simply does not happen. If you were here I would like to take you on a tour of the company to give you an idea of my new world.

Else is in Marienbad, perhaps someone has forwarded the letter to you, have you heard from her in the meantime?

I would be very glad to hear from you again while I am still in Berlin. Fond regards ever

your

Felicitas.

Original: manuscript.

1 Not preserved.

2 *weekend*: EO.

64 WALTER BENJAMIN TO GRETEL KARPLUS
SKOVSBOSTRAND, *c*.26.7.1934

Dear Felizitas,

I am writing you only a few lines today, as my situation is becoming so incredibly critical. I do not yet wish to ask B., on whose hospitality I have depended thus far, for money except in the utmost emergency. On the other hand, I am lacking what I need for my daily expenses.

To be frank, I am drawing a degree of hope from the absence of any news from Else H or her nephew. I cannot imagine that they would terminate an undertaking of whose full significance for me they are aware without a word.

Meanwhile, however, time is passing, and with each further day I become more helpless. If I had anticipated these circumstances I would not have invested my meagre cash reserves in transporting my belongings from Paris. But now – to avoid storage expenses – I have done so.

See what you can arrange. Write to me directly.

Warm regards to you – as ever

yours Detlef

Original: manuscript.
On the dating: Benjamin had not yet received Gretel Karplus's letter of 25 July, in which she relates that Else Herzberger is in Marienbad; Gretel Karplus, in turn, does not seem to have received Benjamin's call for help before departing for the Dolomites, where she went on holiday with Adorno from 1 August. A reply from her followed only on 27 August – erroneously dated 27 July in her letter – after she returned from her holiday.

65 GRETEL KARPLUS TO WALTER BENJAMIN BERLIN, 27.8.1934

27 July 1934.

My dear Detlef,

our correspondence unfortunately suffered a small interruption through my trip, which I hope you will not interpret as betokening any ill will. There is simply never enough time; being together for only a few weeks and then separated once more for months is a state that will sadly continue for years in our case. But I surely have no right to lament to you about my future, for you have much greater and more immediate worries.

Teddie will speak to Else H., or in the worst case write to her, and I assume that something regular will happen once more from 1 October; we have not heard from Arnold in a long time either.

I would be very interested to know how you liked the little Threepenny book; cheeky as I am, the title makes me a little suspicious.

Above all else, however, you will be glad to hear that our expatriation has been revoked and we have been sent back our old passports. As I have quite a lot to do here first, I was thinking of the weekend[1] of 22/23 September. Now the trip to Copenhagen is still very long, unfortunately, so it would be splendid if you could relieve me of 4 hours by coming as far as Gedser. Only I am afraid I do not know if one can spend the night there and stay for a further day. With two night-time journeys it will be also be a rather strenuous and expensive business for me, as I do not want to be away for longer than Saturday. And I already know Copenhagen, so I would truly like simply to spend a few hours undisturbed with you, but it would be best if you made a suggestion once you have looked into the matter.

I am actually curious as to whether you will come up with any particular plan for this meeting again after 1½ years, but far more so about your appearance, your plans for the winter and above all the possibility of contact between us. It is far easier for me, I do not have so much to tell about myself, I simply have to bring up some thing, ask about another, but with you it is no doubt different and full of surprises, with new, unaccustomed things for me.

Despite my own tardiness, do not let me wait too long for your reply, so that I can duly look forward to our appointment. Please tell me if you should need any of the books I still have at my place, or if there is anything else I can take care of for you. Are any other preparations necessary?

Fond regards and many good wishes

ever your Felicitas.

Felicitas.[2]

I never encountered such refined gestures in France, let alone so tidy an appearance. It is actually a shame that you have lost touch with her; the influence you had upon her would only have helped her innermost nature to unfold with ever greater beauty. Sadly it is all too rarely that one finds women whose noble appearance is so perfect a depiction of their rich inner life.

Just as I am about to send this off, your last letter falls into my hands.

Original: typescript with a fragment of Benjamin's handwritten sketch for a reply on the reverse.

1 *weekend*: EO.

2 Gretel Karplus repeated the typed name by hand.

66 GRETEL KARPLUS TO WALTER BENJAMIN BERLIN, 3.9.1934

3 Sept. 34.

Dear Detlef,

unfortunately there are no return tickets to Copenhagen now in the autumn, and the connection is not very good – there are 2 trains:

from Bln.	Gedser	Copenhagen
8^{45}	14^{35}	18^{14}
19^{10}	1^{45}	6^{05}
19^{58}	14^{00}	10^{30} back
10^{05}	4^{08}	0^{08}

(out of the question, as I want to be at home the previous evening if I have to return to work early in the morning.) I would be very happy if the option with Gedser were feasible, then I can leave on Friday evening and would have until Sunday afternoon. After all, we simply want to have a good chat, and

I do not have any special requirements as far as lodging is concerned. Finally I can write 'auf Wiedersehen', warmest regards

your Felicitas.

Do you know any of Teddie's students other than Sternberger?

Original: postcard; stamp: Berlin, 3.9.34. Manuscript.

67 GRETEL KARPLUS TO WALTER BENJAMIN BERLIN, 11.9.1934

11 Sept. 1934.

Dear Detlef,

how I am already looking forward to the 22nd! I would ask you also to take a room for me in Gedser; it seems that the Bahnhofshotel is the only feasible option. I know it is only a short time, 1½ days, but we have certainly never been together for so long. I will definitely give you confirmation of my arrival shortly beforehand, please tell me how long you can still be reached in Skovsbostrand and how many days it takes for a letter from Berlin to arrive. We must not miss each other. Warmest regards

ever

your Felicitas

Original: postcard; stamp: Berlin, 11.9.34. Manuscript.

68 GRETEL KARPLUS TO WALTER BENJAMIN BERLIN, 21.9.1934

21 Sept. 1934.

My dear Detlef,

now I do have to write to you again at length before our meeting after all. I am particularly glad to do so, for I have the feeling that in recent weeks one or two things have forced themselves between us that can still be cleared away now, so as to avoid shortening the hours we have together. It was your telephone call that made this quite clear to me; now it is a difficult matter in any case with unprepared long-distance calls, one is so often disappointed, the other's voice does not sound familiar or tender enough, the questions seem like silent demands, and when it actually happened I was immeasurably amazed when it was Walter who announced himself, and not the Detlef of our letters.

But these concerns are less important at the moment than your pains, are you in good hands, are you being looked after, and is there anything I can do for you. – I would still much prefer Gedser, there are so many inner obstacles for me to overcome for the trip to Copenhagen, and in addition it can genuinely only be realized if I fly from here on Friday afternoon, as I have to go back early on Sunday, so that we can at least spend Saturday together undisturbed, but that also means a further expenditure of c. 40 RM that will be no use to either of us. Flying is simply still very expensive, roughly 1st cl., except for students 3rd cl., and I also think I would have to book my seat by Thursday at the latest. But dear, I would really be most reluctant to do so, and I ask you urgently once again to spare me that if possible.

At the moment I am very much in two minds as to whether I should perhaps take Wissing as my medical adviser after all, despite my earlier passion. After all, why should a doctor not be able to help simply because he also has other interests and one can have a conversation with him.

Please write to me soon, fond regards and best wishes as ever
your Felicitas.

Original: manuscript.

69 GRETEL KARPLUS TO WALTER BENJAMIN BERLIN, 3.10.1934

3 Oct. 34.

Dear Detlef, how are you, have you recovered properly? – 2 little patterns without any value are speeding to you separately. – Ernst Bloch may not be going to Paris again after all, but if so, here is his address: Madison Hotel, Blvd. St. Germain.* – W. knows the book, I have a guilty conscience because I lost the exact title on my trip. – We also forgot about the little letter for the J. Rundschau, which was, incidentally, attacked rather viciously in Angriff[1] yesterday. – The carnations are still alive and in full colour. Did you know that Brieger[2] will also be in San Remo? Unfortunately I forgot to ask if you are still able to talk to D.S.[3] properly these days. It will take me a while to get out of the habit of asking so many questions again! Fond and pleasant regards from your Felicitas.

Original: picture postcard: Kontinentet – Skandinavien – Via; stamp: not preserved. Manuscript.

* There is no harm in his knowing that I was in Gedser.

1 Translator's note: this means 'attack' (noun).

2 The writer Lothar Brieger (real name: Brieger-Wasservogel, 1879–1949), who spent the winter in San Remo and stayed at the guesthouse run by Benjamin's former wife, Dora Sophie.

3 Dora Sophie Benjamin.

70 GRETEL KARPLUS TO WALTER BENJAMIN BERLIN, 4.10.1934

4 Oct. 1934.

My very dear Detlef,

I was terribly happy to read your long-awaited letter,[1] and your affirmation of my own feelings was a joy I had truly yearned for. This almost encourages me to continue in writing our tradition of saying everything; you will then assume the role of an older brother, whom I would ask you to view not with familial affection, but rather as I do, namely as a tender father confessor. Then everything will be in order again. I have only one further request: do not conclude from my inquisitive behaviour that anything is amiss between Teddie and myself. This may sound like an excess of pathos, but here too the matter is truly worth every effort, and I never forget that, even if I sometimes have to find ways of passing the long periods of waiting.

I wonder if it would not make sense for Teddie to speak to your neighbour[2] in England, not least for your sake, so let me at least give you his address Oxford, 47 Banbury road, c./o Mrs Nye. I will send a detailed account of your last letter to England. You will hear from me as soon as I have some information about Sternberger.

Here is a quick list of the few *bound* books of yours[3] I still have:
Contes drolatiques
Your Balzac translation
Asselineau
Hauff's fairy tales
J. G. Schiebel
Fragmente des Nachlasses eines jungen Physikers./

I would be very pleased if you could tell me a few things about Gert Wissing, whom I sadly knew only in passing.

As for him, I find him very amusing, though I fear that he must find me much too bourgeois; for it hardly seems likely that he will produce the right imaginative horizon for me, one from which I can stand out in an advantageous and charming fashion.

Please make sure to write to me often before you leave, fond and warm regards.

your

Felicitas

Original: typescript.

1 Not preserved.

2 Brecht, who stayed in London from October until December in order to conduct publishing negotiations for *The Threepenny Opera*.

3 Balzac's *Contes drolatiques*. Benjamin's translation of *Ursula Mirouet* had appeared in the Rowohlt Verlag's Balzac edition, edited by Franz Hessel, in 1925. Asselineau's book is *Mélanges tirés d'une petite bibliothèque romantique* [Selections from a Small Romantic Library]: *Bibliographie anecdotique et pittoresque des éditions originales des œuvres de Victor Hugo, – Alexandre Dumas, – Théophile Gautier, – Petrus Borel, – Alfred de Vigny, – Prosper Mérimée etc.* (Paris, 1866). The book by Johann Georg Schiebel has not been identified. *Fragmente aus dem Nachlasse eines jungen Physikers* [Posthumous Fragments by a Young Physicist] was written by Johann Wilhelm Ritter (1776–1810).

71 GRETEL KARPLUS TO WALTER BENJAMIN BERLIN, 15.10.1934

15 Oct. 1934.

Dear Detlef,

a little pink bouquet should still reach you in time

All I managed to have done here was the duplicate of the Kafka, as it was already lying here half-finished. I cannot tell you anything about it, as the manuscript had to stay here in the safe until it was completed, and through the increased work this season the business took a little longer than intended. – I am not terribly keen on the study for the institute,[1] albeit for different reasons than Teddie. I think one can simply tell that it was meant for something else, the material would have merited more space. – Dolf is fairly stupid, unfortunately difficult to reach. – Have you sent off Fromm's essay[2] yet? It is still entirely uncertain when Max and Fritz[3] will be coming to Geneva; perhaps not at all. Their address: Hotel Oliver Cromwell, 12 West, 72nd street New York. – Unfortunately Teddie cannot come to Paris now, as term has begun, have you had any news from him? – After an extended late hibernation, Ernst B. wanted to come and take me there, but that would be a fine meeting,[4] my imagination is not sufficient to envisage all the complications. – Wi seems to be tightening my sails in the most varied ways, Teddie is in a distinguished monastery, and it seems that I have had enough of that now, the same time 9 years later. Strangely enough, it is temporarily increasing my appetite, and on the whole I am feeling better. You could tell me much more than I you. It is the first serious experiment, even including Ernst B., and I have had to get out of the habit of organizing things for more than three months at a time during this period.

As you can tell from my cheerful brashness, I am in quite good shape once again. Please write to me as soon as you are in Paris, bon voyage, fond regards.

Your

Felicitas

Original: manuscript.

1 Benjamin's essay 'Zum gegenwärtigen gesellschaftlichen Standort des französischen Schriftstellers' [On the Current Social Position of the French Author], which had appeared in the third 1934 issue of the *Zeitschrift für Sozialforschung*; see *GS* 2 [2], pp. 776–803.

2 See Erich Fromm, 'Die sozialpsychologische Bedeutung der Mutterrechtstheorie' [The Socio-Psychological Significance of the Theory of Matriarchy], in *Zeitschrift für Sozialforschung* 3 (1934), pp. 196–226 (issue 2).

3 Friedrich Pollock was assistant director of the Institut für Sozialforschung.

4 *meeting*: EO.

72 WALTER BENJAMIN TO GRETEL KARPLUS PARIS, 29.10.1934

Dear Felizitas,

I hope you find this card as pretty as I do. So you have now received my letter? Please do write very soon. I shall be leaving on Friday at the latest; if your letter no longer reaches me here, it will follow me to Marseilles, where I shall interrupt my trip in order to speak to Jean Ballard,[1] the editor of the Cahiers du Sud, where – as I probably told you – an essay of mine will be appearing. I had a meeting here with Paulhan – the director of the Nouvelle Revue Française: they have just turned down two essays on Bachofen[2] that were submitted, and are interested in taking mine. Where on earth will I find a secretary in San Remo? – My address there: Villa Emily. I spoke to Siegfried: he has finished his novel[3] and hopes to have it published here. I have written to Teddie,[4] but now that the letter is finished I have noticed that I do not have his address. It would be best if you could send it straight to me here. I have not moved, so Hotel Littré, 9 Rue Littré.

Fond regards as ever

Yours Detlef

Original: picture postcard: Paris – Porte St Denis; stamp: Paris, 29.10.34. Manuscript.

1 Benjamin had already met Jean Ballard (1893–1973) in 1926.

2 Unknown.

3 Kracauer's second novel, *Georg*, which remained unpublished during his lifetime.

4 No letter from Benjamin to Adorno is known from this time.

73 GRETEL KARPLUS TO WALTER BENJAMIN BERLIN, 31.10.1934

Berlin, 31 October 1934.

Herr
Dr Walter Benjamin
Paris VIe
Rue Littré, Hotel Littré.

My dear Detlef,

I am most excited that I am receiving so much mail from you at the moment. I feel I am clearly being given preferential treatment. I hope you have meanwhile received our joint cards.[1]

I am glad that various possibilities have transpired in France after all, and ask that you continue to keep me informed about them. I did not find E. F.'s Bachofen essay terribly thrilling. Your one is no doubt much finer.

The desired address is:

Th. Wiesengrund-Adorno Esqu., Oxford/England, Merton College

I have not heard very much from England lately, but I have the impression that the roses there have plenty of thorns too, and it really does not seem to be very rosy. But please keep this to yourself.

It may interest you to know that the F. Z. is not doing well at all. It will unfortunately be forced to cancel all the new appointments, and I am not sure whether Dolf Sternberger might not also be affected by this.

Ernst B. is in Vienna at the moment. He has now suggested a meeting[2] in Prague, but what I suggested myself only 5 weeks ago has sadly become impossible now.

I have only just started Célibataires.[3] I then read the Kafka essay straight away, and I was delighted by your idea of having the individual chapters as images. It is not without reason that 'das bucklicht Männlein' reappears here. But the text strikes me as so short. I still want to hear much more about it from you. All of its parts are so intermeshed, and it keeps such a hold on one after it is finished, that its brevity is almost saddening.

I am very eager to read your response to the second card. I will send the next messages to San Remo.

Fond and warm regards   ever your

Felicitas

Original: typescript.

1 Unknown.

2 *meeting*: EO.

3 Henry de Montherlant's novel *Les Célibataires* was published by Edition Bernard Grasset in 1934.

74 GRETEL KARPLUS TO WALTER BENJAMIN BERLIN, 15.11.1934

15 Nov. 1934.

Dear Detlef,

forgive me for keeping you waiting so long for a reply to your urgent letter,[1] but you will soon see what situation I am in. But first let me reply to your matters. I am afraid I cannot undertake anything at all on your behalf at the moment, the E. H. plan is also impossible, and at present it seems more than doubtful that I will be going to Frankfurt at Christmas. I return the letter from Max;[2] unfortunately you did not write anything about it. I assume from this that things are thus becoming still more difficult as regards your European plans, and detect that America is not so tempting for you. I do not know what you have to lose here, and would at least ask you to explain your reluctance to me, though I fear I shall – as in another famous case – hear an energetic 'no'.

Now to myself. I already came to you in a state of great distress in January 1933; today I find it much harder still, for I must write it, and I ask you to destroy these lines at once. Your letter arrived while

I was having the finest of migraine attacks, with all the trimmings, Wi had a look, likewise found me in good health organically, massaged me a little and alleviated the most pressing of the physical depressions. Perhaps you know that I had my 10th anniversary[3] recently, and everything is still as it was, in fact there is probably less chance than ever of any change. The Husserl study will take 2 years, and then I will find myself faced with a giant question mark like 11 years ago. Teddie has a great deal to do, is seeing new things and not finding any time to write, while I await any mail with trembling hands and sit alone in Berlin, wasting away from longing. My dear friend Detlef knew this, and the recommendation to Wi. strikes me as not entirely coincidental. He was not wrong. Naturally my family soon noticed, as we are together almost every day, and of course they took Teddie's side against me. In Oxford all this is unknown, and I have still had no news. Detlef, I am often so distraught that I can hardly do my work, I feel I can sense my ability to think declining. I love Teddie, and would be willing to betray my friends and do evil deeds for him. Forgive me, what I am writing is such a muddle that I do not know if you will find your way through it. I am tormenting E., whom I like a great deal, and who could use my love; in fact it is only with him that I am somewhat calm. I see no change, and I fear that Teddie might not be in accord with this Berlin revelation. Perhaps there will be no turning back then. The crazy thing is that everything is in the most wonderful state as soon as we are together, I am sure he has been fond of me these last few years, but something is amiss and it is not simply my imagination; he does not know what I am going through, and all I can see ahead of me is loss, which I cannot bear. You know him, you must know what he means to me. Every word I say is connected to him, and if I lose that bond I will no longer exist. I will probably ask him to come to Berlin in mid-December*, but the four weeks until we sort things out then will be torture for me. And yet I sometimes have the feeling that it would only take something very small to put everything in order again, even the trip with E,[4] so that he can finally feel healthy and free. As long as I knew for certain that I would be taken away, whether to England, America or the ends of the earth. Perhaps it is my fault, perhaps I have too little faith, but the reality is so infinitely hard to bear. Forgive me for burdening you with my laments now of all times, but perhaps you will find some tender words. Take my thanks and warm regards

your Felicitas.

* Christmas(?)

Original: manuscript.

1 Not preserved.

2 In his letter of 17 October 1934, Horkheimer had asked Benjamin whether he would be willing to come to America if an American research scholarship were found. In addition, Benjamin was probably somewhat shocked by the following statement: 'As our budget for the coming year has been greatly cut as a result of the increased workload through the branch office here and a number of other circumstances, we will probably not be able to commission any research projects for quite some time' (Horkheimer, *Briefwechsel 1913–1936*, p. 246).

3 Evidently Gretel Karplus and Adorno had become engaged in the autumn of 1924.

4 Unknown.

75 GRETEL KARPLUS TO WALTER BENJAMIN BERLIN, 21.11.1934

Day of repentance.

Dear Detlef,

at least one of us seems saved; I wish we too could begin our letters by saying:[1] 'finally I have found a way in which I can be helped'. The next four–eight weeks will culminate in the decision of which I cannot even imagine what (who?) will be left at the end?

Tomorrow I shall arrange no. twenty-five.

You asked me a few times about Walter Frank.[2] He is in Paris again. I have been told that you do not think much of him, and I must admit that E's friendship with him does not exactly please me.

It is a great shame that I cannot speak to you, there is so much to say and to clear up, and everywhere nothing but obstacles.

Let me hear from you soon

warmest regards
your
Felicitas

Original: typescript with handwritten addition.

1 An allusion to a lost letter from Benjamin.

2 Gert (Gertrud) Wissing's first husband.

76 WALTER BENJAMIN TO GRETEL KARPLUS
SAN REMO, *c*.25.11.1934

Dear Felizitas,

God knows I would give anything for us to be able to meet somewhere now. The last brief lines that came from you show me clearly that bad times are continuing for you. And, as careful as I tend to be in my assessment of your possibilities: it is certain that I could help you if we were together for a moment. Unfortunately it is almost equally certain that I can barely do so while absent.

I must therefore wait and be patient, as much as the current goings-on also concern me, having already told you my thoughts on the matter. Furthermore, I think you have reached a point where you should worry about travel difficulties least of all, and arrange Christmas in such a way that new surroundings can offer you new chances to take stock and take action.

These reflections are all the more sound, I think, for being culled from the noise of the bricklayers and plumbers who recently moved into the house. I sometimes ask myself whether it was preordained or determined by the stars that I should spend my days amid construction work. Perhaps you recall reading the description in my letters from Ibiza of my accommodation in a new building[1] that was, in fact, coming into being around me.

Naturally I have to do most of my work outside the house; now I have the possibility to do so, which I in turn owe to you. And it is precisely now, when I could show you my profound gratitude instead of simply telling you of it, that it must once again be in a letter. So as far as work is concerned, I have – perhaps my doggedness will amaze you – first of all resumed 'Berliner Kindheit'. There are still a small few parts that I have been planning for years. I think I have finally completed one of them; its title should tell you how central its position is for me. It is called 'Die Farben'.[2] As soon as I can find someone here to do some copying I shall send it to you. There are also others entitled 'Hallesches Tor'[3] and 'Weihnachtslied'.[4]

A Kafka selection[5] has been published in the little Schocken series. Perhaps this could resurrect that manuscript of mine slumbering in their editorial cupboard.

I have not heard from Berthold since leaving Denmark; I think he is still in London. Schoen sent me a lengthy but gloomy report from there. Ernst is supposedly in Vienna – but it was you who wrote me that! I asked the publisher for his book; it seems that will still take some time.

That is all for today. In the next letter perhaps a few words about André Breton, whose last collection of essays[6] on surrealism I now plan to examine in depth.

I send you my very warm and also comforting regards, and hope that you will write soon.

Yours Detlef

Original: manuscript.
On the dating: The 'last brief lines' from Gretel Karplus were from the German 'Day of Repentance', 21 November 1934, and her response to Benjamin's letter is dated 29 November.

1 See letter no. 21.

2 Benjamin had taken down a first, partial version of 'Die Farben' [The Colours] on the reverse of Leo Löwenthal's letter of 2 November 1934; see *GS* 4 [1], p. 263, and *GS* 7 [1], p. 424.

3 The piece called 'Hallesches Tor' [Gates of Halle] that dates from the time of *Berliner Chronik* and also exists in a verse version (see *GS* 7 [2], pp. 705f.) was later given the title 'Winterabend' [Winter Evening] (see *GS* 4 [1], p. 288, and *GS* 7 [1], p. 414).

4 'Weihnachtslied' [Christmas Carol] was either lost or never written.

5 See Franz Kafka, *Vor dem Gesetz*, compiled from Kafka's writings by Heinz Politzer (Berlin: Schocken Verlag, 1934) (Bücherei des Schocken Verlags, vol. 19).

6 See André Breton, *Point du jour* (Paris, 1934).

77 GRETEL KARPLUS TO WALTER BENJAMIN BERLIN, 29.11.1934

29 Nov. 34.

Dear Detlef,

a thousand thanks for your kind, understanding letter. I have meanwhile become calmer, and hope that I too will find a way of changing things. I have spoken with Oxford on the telephone, and assume that Teddie will come here around mid-December. There is just one thing I view differently; it is more likely that someone will be able to help me than that I could help in that most urgent of cases, even though I so wish I could.

In all haste just these few lines.

As a Christmas present I gladly await a new piece from Berliner Kindheit.

In old friendship warmest regards ever your

Felicitas

Original: manuscript.

78 GRETEL KARPLUS TO WALTER BENJAMIN
BERLIN, 10.12.1934

(1.)

10 Dec. 1934.

Dear Detlef,

have you received Ernst's book yet? You will get the shock of your life, but I do not want to give anything away. – I am terribly sad that I cannot reveal the greatest surprise, the new solution, but E. wants to have his turn too. – I would be very happy if you could send me a copy of Der destruktive Charakter. – How did your reply to Max[1] turn out? – Today Hermann Grab's book 'Stadtpark' arrived from Prague – I already knew it from the manuscript, almost too Proustian. Could Berliner Kindheit not perhaps be published in Vienna or Prague? – I wish you an enjoyable time with Stefan,[2] warmest regards ever

your

Felicitas.

Original: unstamped postcard with a silhouette of Gretel Karplus stuck onto the reverse. Manuscript.

1 Benjamin's letter from the end of October; see *GB* 4, pp. 520–2.

2 Stefan Benjamin, who was still going to school in Germany, was to spend Christmas with his father in San Remo.

79 EGON WISSING, GRETEL KARPLUS AND THEODOR WIESENGRUND-ADORNO TO WALTER BENJAMIN
BERLIN, 16.12.1934

(2.) (see letter)

In great haste warm Christmas greetings, I am going to Westend for a health cure and on 3 January for ½ year with a car expedition to Inner Africa (Egypt → Sudan → East *Africa* Tanganyika Nyasaland) I will come to Genoa on 5 or 6/7.1.

Write to me at: Kuranstalten Westend Nussbaumallee

Dear Detlef, I am feeling splendid, the other card is now quite obsolete, I will write at length. (20 start of the week.) Last night at

Kranzler's [?] the three of us became friends and cemented our friendship with snipe and crèpes suzettes.

Warmest regards from your Felicitas

Berlin, 16 December 1934 *error[1]

Dear Herr Benjamin, I have been able to read your Kafka essay thanks to Wissing*, and would like to tell you today simply that the motifs of that study made a quite extraordinary impression upon me – the greatest I have received from your work since the completion of the Kraus. I hope I shall find the time to comment at greater length[2] in the next few days, and I am touching on only a fraction of that when I emphasize the incredible definition of attention[3] as a historical figure of prayer at the end of the third chapter. I might add that our agreement at the philosophical centre has never been clearer to me than in this study! – I am having an enjoyable time here.

Yours ever Teddie W.

Original: unstamped postcard. – Manuscript.
On the dating: both cards seem to have been sent together in a single envelope on 16 December. Gretel Karplus writes on 16 December that 'the other card [no. 1?] is now quite obsolete'.

1 Written in Egon Wissing's hand.

2 Adorno did so in his letter of 17 December; see *Adorno–Benjamin Correspondence*, pp. 66–73.

3 'If Kafka did not pray – which we do not know – then he was endowed to the highest degree with what Malebranche terms "the natural prayer of the soul" – attention' (*GS* 2 [2], p. 432).

80 GRETEL KARPLUS TO WALTER BENJAMIN
FRANKFURT AM MAIN/BERLIN, 26.12.1934

Guesthouse
Fasaneneck am Kurfürstendamm

Express train Frankfurt–Berlin
Boxing Day.

Dear Detlef,

forgive me for remaining silent for so long, but I needed to have a little certainty before I could write to you again. Yes, I had a wonderful 3 months in Berlin, and even if I am quite calm now, I have by no means concluded everything safely. I am afraid I do not have the peace to give you a full report, so I shall fill only a few gaps: when E. was at the police station in December, it seemed entirely clear that something had to be done – but what? We pondered day and night how to find a way out, but every path seemed blocked; the only solution was voluntary self-denial. And I was sitting there helpless, forced to surrender a friend I had only just found. We waited for the end. – Naturally he did not want to wait until Christmas. We savoured the full intensity of the decline in all its agony and sweetness. I shall never forget the Sunday (2 December) on which we took the car to Brandenburg. – On Monday evening we met in the Bristol Hall and he reported that he had already received a telephone call in response to his letter (there was an advertisement in the BZ, someone looking for co-travellers for a trip to Africa etc., you know the rest.) Detlef, that was when I learned to believe in miracles again; I feel so small and modest and want to do everything in my power to bring the experiment to a good end. It is so easy to destroy a human life and so difficult to rebuild it. –

There will probably be changes for me too. Life in the Prinzenallee is becoming practically unbearable, and I am thinking of getting a small apartment of my own. I also think that Teddie will transfer his permanent residence to my place in Berlin while he is in Germany. –

How long do you plan to stay in San Remo? We are seriously considering an Easter trip to the Villa Verde. –

I did not receive the art nouveau essay by Sternberger[1] from you; you wrote to me back then that you had left it in Skovsbostrand. Should I get it for you here? –

The Kafka essay manuscript went off to Spitzer.[2] – I am writing these lines on 'The Master of Ballantrae',[3] but am still only at the start.

Forgive my horrible writing and the excess of pathos at the start; it is sincere. It would probably be best if you destroyed this letter too. I hope to hear from you very soon and wish you a good New Year's Eve, hoping for the best in 1935 and definitely to see you again.

In old, devoted friendship

your Felicitas

Original: manuscript.

1 The essay 'Jugendstil: Begriff und Physiognomik' [Art Nouveau: Concept and Physiognomy] had appeared in the September issue of the *Neue Rundschau*.

2 The Indologist Moritz Spitzer (1900–1982) was director of the Schocken Verlag in Berlin from 1932 to 1938; he emigrated to Palestine in 1939.

3 Gretel Karplus most probably read this novel by Robert Louis Stevenson on the recommendation of Benjamin, who had written the following to

Werner Kraft on 12 November: 'Before I close, let me draw your attention to a little-known book I recently read, and which I place above almost all the great novels in its importance for me, in fact directly after La Chartreuse de Parme. It is "The Master of Ballantrae" by Stevenson' (*GB* 4, letter no. 913).

81 GRETEL KARPLUS TO WALTER BENJAMIN BERLIN, 17.1.1935

17 January 1935.

My dear Detlef,

for days I have been meaning to thank you for your delightful New Year's letter,[1] and it is only today that I am finally getting around to it. But I shall spare you any long apologies and instead tell you a little about things here.

Teddie is back in England, and I am afraid I cannot yet tell you his thoughts on our spring plans. I am definitely expecting to see him in March, but I too am completely uncertain where. Perhaps it would be best for you to ask him about his intentions yourself. How soon do you have to know so that your other undertakings are not disturbed by pointless waiting? In fact I would generally like to know how and if things are proceeding for you down there. I have also spoken to E. about it, and we really wanted to make the joint suggestion that you might perhaps want to spend a little time in Paris looking after your sister Dora, who is apparently not at all well. Please do not misunderstand, this is naturally no more than a well-meaning suggestion born of my helplessness to undertake anything substantial, and all the more because you hinted to me in Denmark that your relationship with your sister has now become so much better.* – It is a crying shame that you will not have the chance to speak to E., as his ship was to leave for Antwerp tomorrow. I know only too well what this loss means for you. What is more, he would so have liked to tell you about the many fine ideas he has been having lately regarding Kafka. – Has anything transpired concerning your prospects in Palestine? –

I would, incidentally, be most grateful if you could write to me about your impression of Ernst Bloch's book. He did not receive Teddie's justified criticisms[2] at all well, as I had predicted, and I fear that in this case there is little more to be salvaged. It is a shame to lose him, but it goes without saying that I agree with Teddie both factually and personally, and I am fairly sure that you would be on our side if the worst came to the worst.

* and then the possibility of continuing the arcades study

For the next while, I am planning to lead a quiet life of serious work, of which there shall be no shortage owing to our balance, and I must also put more work into learning English and – as soon as the weather is better – look for an apartment. – Fare thee well, Detlef; an hour of friendly conversation with you would do me so much good. Thinking very warmly of you

ever your
Felicitas

Original: typescript.

1 Not preserved.

2 Adorno's letter to Ernst Bloch concerning *Erbschaft dieser Zeit* does not appear to have survived.

82 GRETEL KARPLUS TO WALTER BENJAMIN
BERLIN, 22.1.1935

22 January 1935.

My dear Detlef,

it is very sad that you have to lie in bed and are in such terrible pain, and I wish you a very, very speedy recovery. – I sent off the essay on Elective Affinities today by recorded delivery. – I never heard anything from Spitzer, nor was I given confirmation that he had received the manuscript. – It seems to me that the Easter meeting in San Remo is taking on ever more definition, if this prospect would at least make you a little happy and help you through the many other unbearable things. I remember your saying at some point that you would be going to Nice to meet a Frenchman who is of some importance to you[1] – did anything come of that? My health is in a bearable state at present, I still have frequent headaches, albeit not always with genuine migraine attacks. That one method of pulling my head up was quite helpful, but so far no one has found a truly effective means of doing away with my condition, and if anything the chances are worse now.

Wissing did not leave; he is in Paris at the moment. What now? It gave me a terrible shock; I suppose there are no miracles after all. It seems that no one knows about it yet here. If I could at least speak to you. If only everything did not become so small and lousy, so that one could at least hold on to the memory.

Today as ever fond regards and best wishes

from your
Felicitas.

Original: typescript.

1 This presumably refers to Marcel Brion (1895–1984), co-founder of the *Cahiers du Sud*, who corrected the translation of 'Haschisch in Marseille' and had met with Benjamin in late January 1934.

83 GRETEL KARPLUS TO WALTER BENJAMIN
BERLIN, 2.2.1935

2 February 1935.

Dear Detlef,

your questions[1] are quite difficult to answer, especially as they concern not only me. Essentially, I would not like to pre-empt E.'s explanation with my own. I am sure he has meanwhile written to you, in fact I even believe that you will see him again very soon – at least it was his firm intention. In short: for a variety of reasons, the East Africa trip he had planned has (unfortunately?) been called off. At the moment, E. is still in Paris, Hotel Littré, but he intends to travel on to Marseilles at the start of next week. Please ask him directly if you want to find out about his future plans. – Naturally my own stance in this matter is also a little complicated; my most private reaction consisted of a large amount of annoyance and a great deal of nervousness, which, as we all know, is no use to anyone. Now I can see a little more clearly and am calmer as a result, but there is still plenty of trouble, especially as I am in Berlin. I know very well that it is an incredibly difficult task for E. to change his entire way of life. Today there is still a faint hope that everything may turn out alright, though for now I find it difficult to wait so long, and still get annoyed about the daily events. You could do me a great favour: as you have known E. well for a very long time, you should be able to judge whether he changed a great deal through his marriage, so that many things could be viewed as symptomatic rather than as personal flaws. The success of our plan will largely depend on this, despite the incredible energy with which he is approaching the matter. But I would be very happy if it worked out after all . . .

As I am so handicapped and overburdened at the moment, I have passed the matter of the new glove design on to E., as I am sure he has seen the latest models in Paris. –

Please let me hear from you soon; even if I sometimes write to you in my initial excitement, you should never worry that it might make me forget the real nature of our friendship. Fond regards and best wishes

your

Felicitas

Original: typescript.

1 Benjamin's letter has not survived.

84 WALTER BENJAMIN TO GRETEL KARPLUS
SAN REMO, *c.*10.2.1935

My dear Felizitas,

as you hear so much from me about my material worries, it would be understandable – and perhaps desirable – for you to assume that I am 'otherwise' well. It would be an act of friendship for me to leave you in this assumption.

On the other hand, there are moments in which silence acts as a poison – and as it has been forced upon me, at least as far as my voice would reach, you too will now be confronted with it, and will not wish to withdraw from it.

I have been experiencing hours and days of the most profound misery, the like of which I do not think I have known in years. Not in the manner of the suffering one finds within periods of contentment, but rather full of a bitterness that flows away into nothingness and is fuelled by trifles.

It is entirely clear to me that the decisive reason for this is my situation here, my unimaginable isolation. Being cut off not only from people, but also from books, and ultimately – in the worst weather – even from nature. Going to bed before 9 every evening, making the same few journeys every day, on which one knows from the outset that one will not encounter anyone, going through the same stale reflections on the future every day: these are circumstances that, even with a very robust inner constitution – which I had always considered mine to be – must ultimately lead to a severe crisis.

The strange thing is that those conditions which should fortify me most – I mean my work – only heighten the crisis. I have now completed two substantial studies, the 'Bachofen' and the review of Bertold's novel,[1] and my inner burden is not becoming any lighter.

There is nothing to be done; my stay here will have to be terminated here one day in any case (my former mother-in-law is coming here), and I cannot even welcome that. There is only one thing that could help: for us to see each other. If only I could absolutely count on it!

I certainly do not count on Wissing, and it would almost surprise me if – after announcing his arrival from all points of the compass[2] – he actually arrived. (The last message notified me of the postponement of his departure for Paris.)

I received a pleasant letter from Bertolt, and there was even a message from Asja[3] – but that fills out my room only in a nebulous fashion.

May this letter, if nothing else, be a curiosity among my declarations, which are otherwise not entirely lacking in a more ascetic character.

très à toi

yours Detlef

PS I have just learned that P.[4] is going to Berlin. So he can round off the curious nature of this letter by handing it over himself.

Original: manuscript.
On the dating: the 'pleasant letter' from Brecht dates from 6 February, so Benjamin's letter must have been written around 10 February.

1 Benjamin wrote 'Brecht's Dreigroschenroman' (see *GS* 3, pp. 440–9) for Klaus Mann's journal *Die Sammlung* [The Collection]; it was not published there, however, as Mann considered the fee demanded by Benjamin too high.

2 Egon Wissing had written the following to Benjamin from Paris on 24 January: 'Mon très cher [paragraph] forgive me for not writing I have experienced the most adventurous and fantastic journeys and things (e.g. was in Zurich, in Basel, in Strasbourg, in Brussels, Antwerp then Switzerland again and now I am here for very real reasons, which I can, however, not explain to you in haste now. [. . .] I must (and this time I say "unfortunately" with all my heart) stay here until next Wednesday or Thursday (30th or 31st) Then probably (fairly definitely) Marseille & there I think there would be a chance of meeting, which would mean a great deal also to me.'

3 The letter dates from 4 January 1935.

4 This is presumably Lothar Brieger; see letter no. 69, note 2.

85 GRETEL KARPLUS TO WALTER BENJAMIN
BERLIN, 12.2.1935

12 February 1935.

My dear Detlef,

your disconsolate letter made me very sad, and I want to try to cheer you up a little; I wonder if I shall succeed? – Though I feel 'cheated' myself – my situation is desperately similar to that of the same month in 1933 –, but today I do not want to burden you with that too.

1.) I am fairly sure that you will now be receiving a visit very soon, and perhaps the roundabout is actually working better than you think.
2.) The business with your former wife will definitely be taken care of, albeit not yet, but surely in the near future, and it really is not so urgent.
3.) unfortunately I was unable to get the Benvenuto Cellini for you, as it is no longer published by Reklam and I sadly lack the time to go in search of it.
4.) Please let me know the cost of the Villa Verde for two nice joined single rooms with running water/bathroom and full board. If you think it would be better, I could naturally also write directly to Frau Dora Sofie. After all, this visit, from which she will be profiting, will only take place thanks to you.
5.) If there is still any point in doing so, I shall get the flowers for your friend P. next week.

I hope that now takes care of most of the business side of things. – Have you fully recovered your health? – Were you not able after all to arrange the trip to Nice with E's help? –

You could at least give me your private opinion of Ernst's book, even if I will then have to keep it to myself. Unfortunately he sent T. a bare-faced letter[1] – I cannot put it any other way – in which he also professed horror at the Rottweiler essay[2] you recently praised, so I fear that there is really nothing more to be done there, and I daresay that I, having declared my loyalty to T., will not be hearing a great deal more either. Naturally I know that you will be reluctant to break off a connection you had only just resumed, but on the other hand I know how important solidarity rightly is to Teddie, and that there is no one whose solidarity is more important to him than yours (I alone am naturally not enough). –

I wish with all my heart that the year 1935, which began rather unfavourably for all of us, will now finally show you its better sides. And I wish you above all a little joy and variety

warmest regards ever your Felicitas.

Original: typescript with handwritten closing sentence.

1 See Ernst Bloch, *Briefe 1903–1975*, vol. 2, ed. Karola Bloch et al., Frankfurt am Main, 1985, pp. 423–31.

2 Adorno's essay 'Die Form der Schallplatte' [The Form of the Gramophone Record], which he had published in the Vienna music journal *23* under the pseudonym of Hektor Rottweiler; see *GS* 19, pp. 530–4.

86 GRETEL KARPLUS TO WALTER BENJAMIN
BERLIN, 24.2.1935

24 February 1935.

I received your letter[1] by messenger on Friday, and hope very much that your situation has meanwhile improved: the weather is fine, your friend P. picked out five half-pairs of samples from my store that I hope you will like, and the distance between you and E. should now have diminished sufficiently for you to doubt no longer that the two of you will meet again. (The last message was from Marseilles, headed for Monte Carlo.)

My nervousness, which has a variety of causes, has reached a level that can hardly be surpassed; the impossibility of written communication of any prospect of change completely deadens, and I fear you would not have much joy with me. For today just this greeting

ever your

Felicitas.

Brieger's case
Suits
Lawsuit

Original: typescript with handwritten keywords by Benjamin.

1 Letter no. 84.

87 GRETEL KARPLUS TO WALTER BENJAMIN
BERLIN, 27.2.1935

27 February 1935.

My dear Detlef,

what good is it if we make the most wonderful plans, if things always turn out differently in the end. I am only glad that you are not alone at the moment; so my rather easy prediction that E. would still turn up[1] after all proved correct. – I hope my letter from Sunday still reached you; after your friend P's report of the family business, I almost suspected a sudden cancellation. After our discussions here, which I already told you about, I am not surprised by your decision to go to Paris. I would be very happy if you could speak to Max there. If only I knew whether you have any other connections in America, for I am too sceptical to consider any arrangement with the institute a lasting one. And what happened to the possibilities in Palestine? – And what would you think of Asja's home country?? Under the new circumstances I would very seriously recommend that we postpone our Easter plans for now, for we would not have any peace. If you are in Denmark in the summer there might be a chance to meet there, or perhaps at Whitsun for a few days. I am really not at all certain whether I can leave here directly at Easter, so I very much hope you will not be angry with me if it does not work out this time, and that you will not let your arrangements be disturbed by trying to accommodate me, when it would be for nothing in any case. Please do not misunderstand: I do not want to devalue our friendship, but at the moment I can be replaced by others. For now your unbearable loneliness has been interrupted. Today I am doubly happy that I at least saw you in September. – I am glad that you can confirm the good news about E's health; perhaps you could soon find the time to tell me a little more about your impression. And now for a request – and here I must naturally rely on your utmost discretion – please do not mention to Teddie that E. is coming to Berlin, or that I am corresponding with him at the moment. I am well aware that this is a somewhat delicate thing to expect, but after the failed trip to Africa, Teddie has become somewhat less favourably disposed towards him, and I have to juggle a little, as I know very well what is at stake on all sides. On the other hand, I want both to remain loyal to Teddie and absolutely avoid hurting E. I was able to depend on your tact and reliability in such matters once in the past: March 1933, so I am now turning to you once more to ask for your support. Please send me your Paris address soon. I would be happy if you had good news to report. Fond and warm regards from your

Felicitas.

Original: typescript with handwritten conclusion.

1 Benjamin and Wissing met in Monaco.

88 GRETEL KARPLUS TO WALTER BENJAMIN BERLIN, 7.3.1935

7 March 1935.

Dear Detlef,

many thanks for your report.[1] You can be sure that I too am greatly saddened by the failure of our lovely project; there is a great deal I would have liked to discuss with you, and now I always worry that one might never be able to make up for missed chances. But perhaps we can at least arrange for Teddie to return via Paris – I have already suggested it to him, so you could ask him about it if you like. Last night I spoke to one of my Viennese cousins,[2] the only one who arouses the faintest hint of familial sentiment in me, and we also got onto the subject of Ernst B., and I must confess that I now actually feel a great longing to see him. – I am only happy for you and E. that the two of you are together right now. Your help is all the more indispensable now that I am out of action, and WF.[3] in Paris is an absolute red rag to me anyway, and I am quite certain that I am right about him. He is spineless and inferior. Dear Detlef, it is entirely clear to me how things will end if the therapy goes wrong again, and even if I certainly do not mean to defend the good life – especially not now – it is a particular shame that this vitality and possibility would be lost through it. On the other hand, I am so very glad that you are no longer in such ghastly surroundings, and that I can at least contribute indirectly to making your situation a little more bearable. –

I find it so desperately hard to view this awful condition, which has grown worse with each passing day over the last two months, as final. If I succeeded in that, of course, there is little more that could happen to me, but it demands a level of self-denial that sometimes seems quite inconceivable to me, to say nothing of the utter futility. –

I gather that Else Herzberger is in Paris at the moment, XVIe, 38 quai d'Auteuil, perhaps it would be of some use to contact her? –

Write to me often and soon, I am so happy when I can feel that I am not yet entirely alone

your

Felicitas

Original: typescript.

1 Not preserved.

2 Unknown.

3 No further information could be found regarding Walter Frank, who later went to the USA.

89 GRETEL KARPLUS TO WALTER BENJAMIN
BERLIN, 17.3.1935

17 March 1935.

My dear Detlef,

thank you for your sweet letter,[1] in which you tried so touchingly to console me. And yet you cannot, of course, gain an accurate image from my intimations, and it is also somewhat difficult to relate coherently, while it would take no more than a quarter of an hour to explain it in conversation. It is not actually one grave situation that finally crushed me with its force, but rather an accumulation of so many things, for example all these long years of solitude, which has now degenerated into complete isolation, the less than rosy overall business situation, the abandonment of my plans for an apartment, and above all the lack of any prospect whatsoever of changing this situation; it all just continues hopelessly, and my only rays of hope are the letters. I know that one cannot, unfortunately, escape from one's own life, but it is only now that I have reached the point where I am prepared for anything, any loss, and without any joy at all. The one thing I should preserve is the possibility of a certain receptiveness, so that I do not end up missing a possible chance of joy at the decisive moment – if it should ever arrive. I have a very kind role-model, without whom I would hardly even have physically survived the last few months; you will not scold me for telling you in this way what a part you have played in my life during this time. –

My Easter plans are still uncertain, for Teddie's intentions are determined entirely by events whose outcome we ourselves cannot yet predict. I have now read The Last of the Vikings.[2] Did you also get that far north? I only managed to reach Lapland. Though I am not really so keen on books of that kind, I can absolutely understand your enthusiasm now. –

Sadly I have heard very little from Ernst in Vienna; unfortunately he is also cross with me, first because a meeting in October did not work out, and secondly because I was reserved in my comments on his book. It really is a shame that we cannot keep his friendship apart from his books. In Vienna he is spending a great deal of time with Piz von Motesiczky, but she never writes either. – That makes me think: might it not be practical for you to contact her brother Karl?[3] His address last autumn was: Copenhagen IX Andreas Bjørnsg. 21, he is in analysis there.* He is not the most pleasant of people – I consider him clearly pathological – but he might be able to help you, is interested and very helpful, and that is after all more important than amusement at the moment. If you cannot reach him at that address, I am sure the letters will be forwarded to him from Vienna: Vienna IV Brahmsplatz 7, Karl von Motesiczky. –

In my last letter to E. I suggested that he should talk to you about me; there are naturally many things that he would prefer to change, but you have known me for so much longer that I am sure you could make him understand my position in some matters where he perhaps

* [Marginal note in Benjamin's hand:] (Rich)

only views me as thoughtless and cynical. I have the feeling you understand me, even if I do not talk a great deal about myself, your friendship is so unegotistical. And where, ultimately, is the fine line between friendship and love? –

Detlef, always let me know how you are faring, and write to me often; that is the greatest comfort you can offer me. In old loyalty and friendship

your
Felicitas

Conscription	'it would take no more than a quarter of an hour to explain it in conversation'
Stefan	Journey here
Mountain climb	Role-model
Russia	Copenhagen
Brecht	Klaus [Mann]

Original: typescript with handwritten keywords by Benjamin.

1 Not preserved.

2 Benjamin had read this novel by the Norwegian writer Johan Bojer (1872–1959), published in 1921 (in German in 1923), in Skovsbostrand in September 1934.

3 Regarding the life of Karl von Motesiczky (1904–1943), a pupil of Wilhelm Reich, see Christiane Rothländer, ' "Und mit der Hausmusik ging er in den Tod . . .": Über das Leben des Wiener Psychoanalytikers Karl von Motesiczky' ['And with the death of family music he also died . . .'. On the Life of the Viennese Psychoanalyst Karl von Motesiczky], in *Werkblatt: Zeitschrift für Psychoanalyse und Gesellschaftskritik* 2/1998, no. 41, pp. 3–34.

90 GRETEL KARPLUS TO WALTER BENJAMIN BERLIN, 24.3.1935

24 March 1935.

Dear Detlef,

how sweet of you to greet me with a few lines[1] upon my return here. I had a good rest, despite the unfavourable weather, and found exactly what you so rightly wish me: new élan – I hope it will last for a while. But at the moment I do not have the slightest reason to be discontented, as Teddie is in blinding form, is making good progress with his work, is even more well balanced than usual, but has nonetheless understood – perhaps for the first time – what has been happening in my life. And then I have the prospect of seeing E. again, which I am greatly looking forward to; this interruption too will have to last for a very long while this time. – I skimmed through Krenek's article,[2] and would consider it wise if you wrote him a very friendly and lengthy letter, even if he has misunderstood you in every respect and moreover advances all sorts of banalities; but he is so full of good will and can perhaps help you, so why not indulge his vanity for once. – Else H. seems to be in Ascona at the moment, so perhaps it would be best for you to contact Teddie regarding her. How long will you be staying in Paris? Teddie's summer term will end around 20 June, would you not fancy luring him to Paris, for he does not know it at all yet and you are such an ideal travel guide. – I sent a nice letter to Vienna three or four weeks ago, but it has remained unanswered to this day; he is probably so deeply entrenched in matrimony that he no longer even dares to stray from the path enough to write to me – a shame, perhaps I would fancy meeting him in Prague now. Please forgive my cheekiness, but there is really nothing serious[3] there any more. –

I shall be very glad if, in spite of your workload, you find the time to write to me now and again. Detlef there is no one to whom I feel so close in letter, and there is nothing in the world as tender as the words you merely hint at. Farewell for today

your

Felicitas

Original: typescript on a sheet of Air France paper.

1 Not preserved.

2 Ernst Křenek's essay 'Künstlerische und wissenschaftliche Geschichtsbetrachtung' [Artistic and Scientific Examination of History], published on 24 March 1935 in the *Wiener politische Blätter*, contains quotations from Benjamin's book on baroque tragic drama.

3 Translator's note: this is a pun on Bloch's name, as *ernst* means 'serious'.

91 WALTER BENJAMIN TO GRETEL KARPLUS MONACO-CONDAMINE, *c.* END OF MARCH 1935 DRAFT

Dear Felizitas,

your little pattern arrived just now. Worth more than you can imagine. Firstly: the prospect of living normally again for two or three days. Secondly: proof of your – and *only* your – unmistakable and reliable presence, even in your absence.

It is stranger than I could have supposed how your not unproblematic, indeed precarious relationship with W has made ours – yours and mine – livelier than ever. I think a meeting would prove this. And it is a new motive for me to hope for our next one, which can only be a matter of time.

As regards W,[1] however, you may be seeing him sooner than you think, for his return to Berlin from here could be taking place very soon, without carrying out all the far-reaching plans you are familiar with, and in fact without even passing through Paris again. Certainly, this is only one possibility at the moment, but by no means an unlikely one. And as comforting as it might initially seem to you, it is ultimately a sinister one.

For the situation is as follows: he is being left in the lurch by everyone here, especially Frank, and also another Paris connection[2] which he would be entitled to count on to a certain extent. And as unbelievable as it sounds: for more than two weeks I have been supporting us both with my helpless means, which was admittedly possible only by lowering our standard of existence to a level I have never before experienced. Yes, it has been a memorable week for us (and who knows how many similar ones still lie ahead).

'Us' – that is not quite correct in the latter case – for if the situation does not change completely, W will be coming to Berlin. And then you will learn more exactly how it was. And more exactly – than I dare intimate to you what lies ahead of me.

And it is not as if I were leaving any stone unturned. But a paper as dubious as the one I am sending you[3] at the same time as printed matter (or enclose here) is, after all, only excusable or even comprehensible in a very indirect relation to the 'struggle for existence'.

I do not know how long this will continue. I would also rather like to know whether the Americans will definitely be coming to Geneva in May. For the meeting with them is for now the only event towards which I can grope through the darkness. So there would be a certain value in coming over here somehow in the course of the next month or one and a half months. We certainly cannot – as I learned three days ago – count on my sister,[4] who is quite ill and would not be able to accommodate me. So I do not see why I should undertake efforts to raise the expenses for a trip to Paris. I would arrive at the station and find myself no better off than here.

I plan to contact Else H. around Easter. But not before then, and not from here. For I had written from San Remo that I would stay there until Easter.

I know it is foolhardy to hope for any consequences of your conversation with Piz. But someone who is as rightly intimidated by the face of reality as I am can devote his strength only to the daring of his hopes. See what can be done.

The weather is fine. If one has ventured far enough into the morning or the afternoon on foot, one reaches a place where, for a moment, one is very glad to be still alive, in spite of everything. On the way back, however, one often lacks the courage to cross the threshold of the unpaid hotel, where one is greeted by the even more unpaid, in fact utterly unpayable, physiognomy of the patron.

And where will you now [breaks off]

Original: manuscript.
On the dating: Benjamin wrote the letter after receiving Gretel Karplus's letters of 17 and 24 March.

1 Egon Wissing.

2 This presumably refers to the neurologist Fritz Fränkel (1892–1944).

3 'Gespräch über dem Corso' [Conversation about the Parade], which appeared on 24 March in the *Frankfurter Zeitung* and which Gretel Karplus thanked Benjamin for sending on 2 April (see *GS* 4 [2], pp. 763–71).

4 Dora Benjamin had written to her brother on 13 March that he would not be able to reside in her apartment (which in fact comprised only one room) in the rue Villa Lindet, as she earned money looking after five children there in the mornings.

92 GRETEL KARPLUS TO WALTER BENJAMIN BERLIN, 2.4.1935

Happy Easter time and again!

2 April 1935.

My very dear Detlef,

as you enclosed your letters to me in a separate envelope, I am quite sure that you would not be at all in favour of sending joint letters to two people. I am certainly not one for exaggerated secrecy, but it is too easy to lose contact with joint messages. – I wonder how you survived my last letter? It was so full of terrible news and so lacking in consolation. I have already gone through all my acquaintances in my mind, but have not reached any new results. If I at least knew of an effective way to pressure the institute people. I will send you a pattern via a detour tomorrow. –

On Saturday we are going to Königstein for two weeks of peace and quiet. – Many thanks for the cutting from the FZ;[1] if only I came across the name more often. – My dear, when will your move to Denmark to the books be at all possible, I do think that your friend Berta[2] will at least help you out. And how will you live alone down there if E. is going to be called away sooner or later? –

Ultimately my relationship with E. is not really problematic, as I am always quite aware of the faults of my friends but remain loyal nonetheless. It was characterized by the intensity with which we both plunged into it, something I had always wished for, not waiting quietly first, but rather grabbing it at once with full élan and really achieving true pleasure. And I also went against public opinion – even ignoring your gentle warning – by placing unlimited faith in him, believing in the forces within him that were merely buried beneath all sorts of rubble. I myself have a great interest in the restoration of his reputation – out of vanity, out of affection, out of zeal, whatever you wish to call it – but it is neither out of charity nor out of friendship, but rather total dedication. Naturally this means a great deal, and my thoroughly considered decision that I would nonetheless *like* to remain on my previous path is in fact an almost inconceivable problem for E. You know all of us, so perhaps it is easier for you to understand me. You know how much I suffer, but you also know why I do it and can well imagine where I ultimately belong, despite great similarities and greater sympathies on the other side. I ask you very *urgently* to *destroy this letter immediately*, it is intended purely for you and it would be a disaster if anyone else laid hands on it. I think I can still deal with these things myself, but if I ever needed help I could think of no one better than you. –

Should you by chance no longer need the essay on Elective Affinities, I would like to have it here once more. E. could read it in the meantime, he hardly knows your most important things. If only I were rich enough to help you or at least had fine jewellery to send you for pawning. – Even if I do not know the exact connection, I do feel that I am responsible for your fate. – Detlef, I worry so terribly about you. –

I send you all my affection and friendship

ever your

Felicitas.

Original: typescript with handwritten Easter greeting.

1 The aforementioned piece 'Gespräch über dem Corso'.

2 Bertolt Brecht.

93 WALTER BENJAMIN TO GRETEL KARPLUS
PARIS, *c.*25.5.1935
FRAGMENT

[Beginning missing]
do not [think?] that one can light the torch of reason in the swamps of Prague with these will-o'-the-wisps. One also finds the same will-o'-the-wisps twitching around Kafka. At least, I consider a large part of his religion-philosophical reflections as nothing other than that.

So, even though I am entirely inexperienced in Jewish literature, I do think that authentic works would take you far away from your current reading. You should make use of the little Schocken series. I recall leafing through a charming volume of theirs by Tendlau[1] on 'Jewish Sayings'. I do not know if they have anything by Agnon that you do not know. But I can at least name 'Und das Krumme wird gerade', 'Die neue Synagoge', 'Die Geschichte vom Toraschreiber' – and, as I note these down, I recall that Schocken did indeed publish an anthology of such tales.[2] The second of those, which is beyond compare, was to be included in the first issue of my Angelus Novus many years ago.

Regarding the extremely far-reaching question of the renewal of the Hebrew language, my complete lack of knowledge naturally prevents me from saying anything on the matter. I suspect that the dangers involved in such an attempt are immeasurably hideous, and I do not know if they could be overcome. I only know that this question has been occupying important people on the other side for a very long time. Ernst has disappeared from Vienna, incidentally, and, as he has not surfaced here, he is generally presumed to be on the way to Palestine with Karola, who is planning to build something there.

Now I shall close for today with very warm greetings and little wishing-candles for your health.

Yours Detlef

Original: manuscript.
On the dating: Gretel Karplus's question about Jewish literature, which Benjamin answered here, has not survived. Presumably her letter of 28 May was written in response.

1 See *Sprichwörter und Redensarten deutsch-jüdischer Vorzeit: Aufgezeichnet aus dem Munde des Volkes und nach Wort und Sinn erläutert von Abraham Tendlau* [Ancient German-Jewish Proverbs and Sayings: Compiled from Oral Tradition and Explained According to Letter and Meaning by Abraham Tendlau], new abridged edn (Berlin: Schocken Verlag, 1934) (Bücherei des Schocken Verlags, vol. 10).

2 The Schocken Verlag had published *Und das Krumme wird gerade* [And the Crooked Becomes Straight] in 1934 (vol. 14); the two other tales named in the letter are contained in the collection *In der Gemeinschaft der Frommen*, which Benjamin had sent Gretel Karplus in January 1934 (see letter no. 41, note 4).

94 GRETEL KARPLUS TO WALTER BENJAMIN BERLIN, 28.5.1935

28 May 1935.

Dear Detlef,

your letter just arrived, and I am afraid I must confess that I found your news about E. extremely troubling. Not only was it from you – not him – that I learned he has finally been granted the visa;[1] there is airmail for such cases, after all. But you also do not seem so sure that Frank has not seduced him into turning to his previous consolation once again. Nothing could be worse for the friendship between myself and E., I not only asked him to be extremely careful, but also trusted him, and for him to disappoint me now would cause irreparable damage. Please do not be cross if I write to you at somewhat greater length about these things today, for I have the feeling that it concerns you too. But I ask you to tear up today's letter, i.e. this piece of paper, immediately. I am sure you have a fair idea of the situation from our conversations and my letters. Although E. often complains of my inexperience in practical matters and probably also life's pleasures, I am overall more mature than he is, in so far as one can still say that at our age. I think the most important thing is for E. to come to himself again, which would involve finding a steady employment that satisfied him; he finally has to achieve something again, and in his profession there is ample opportunity to do so. He must also support himself financially, and banish his abandon and licentiousness to the intellectual realm instead of retaining them in daily life as bad Bohemian manners. I am expressing myself very badly, but perhaps you can nonetheless deduce what I mean, intellectual particularity combined with an orderly life. Please do not consider it presumptuous, but following the results I have often had my doubts about the stability of his marriage, and wonder whether it would not have worked without M in the end. Oh Detlef, cross your fingers for me that these days in Berlin will turn out well. –

Thank you also for your information. – Bloch no longer considers it necessary to write to me, which makes me both sad and angry about the loss of another friend. All I know is that he wanted to meet his friends the Hirschlers[2] in Italy. – Have you met Krac[3] in the meantime, what is he working on? Have you read his novel? – Have you meanwhile told Teddie about your negotiations with Fritz?[4] I consider that absolutely necessary and advisable. Is he coming to Paris after the end of term? – I will see what I can do about the Kafka fragments tomorrow.

And now I shall come to the thing that is most important to me: the arcades study. I recall the conversation we had in Denmark last September, and I find it highly troubling that I have no idea which of your plans you will now be carrying out. It amazes me that Fritz is trying to find a possibility for the notes, are you thinking of writing something for the journal? I would actually consider that very dangerous, as you would have relatively little space and would never be able to write what your true friends have been awaiting for years, the great philosophical study that exists purely for its own sake and makes no compromises, and whose significance would help to compensate for a great deal of what has happened these last few years. Detlef, it is not simply a matter of rescuing you, but also this work. One should anxiously guard you from everything that could jeopardize it, and devote the greatest possible energy to supporting everything that might further it. I think you have rarely known me to be so enthusiastic about something, which shows you most clearly what high hopes I place in the arcades study. – I hope you will not resent my ecstasy. I await your news with longing and fear, please write to me about the exposé.[5] – I have so much time; if only I could keep you company a little in your hours of solitude and have you read to me from your notes. Fare thee well and kindly let me remain in good favour with you

your Felicitas

I must in some form

. . .

and I myself am not giving up the fight yet, as I . . .	Linda
Dora – that I am starving	Letter to Wiesengrund
There is really no evidence of the greatest possible energy	Exposé, once I have it back . . . Wissing

Original: typescript on a sheet of Air France paper with keywords added by Benjamin.

1 Egon Wissing had applied for a visa for the Soviet Union in order to work there as a doctor.

2 The doctor Maximilian Hirschler (1886–1963) had been a friend of Bloch since their school days; Hirschler's wife, Helene (1888–1977), was likewise a doctor.

3 This is Siegfried Kracauer.

4 Fritz Pollock had offered to meet Benjamin to discuss the financing of the arcades project, but was forced to end his stay in Europe prematurely. Benjamin wrote the exposé on Pollock's suggestion.

5 It is entitled 'Paris: Die Hauptstadt des XIX. Jahrhunderts' [Paris: the Capital of the 19th Century]; see *GS* 5 [2], pp. 1237–49. Benjamin sent it to Adorno on 31 May.

95 GRETEL KARPLUS TO WALTER BENJAMIN
BERLIN, 26.6.1935

26 June 1935.

Dear Detlef,

the character of our recent correspondence makes me so sad that I can no longer remain silent about it. I feel as if we can no longer find the way to each other, and, without realizing it, are often hurting ourselves a great deal instead. I cannot tell you how painful that is for me, for until now, ours was the one friendship I believed to be unshakeable. The blow is all the harder now due to great upheavals at work, a new monthly financial strain that makes it ridiculous to imagine a decent income, and the incredible responsibility; I feel very intimidated and am afraid of everyone. –

Can I still hope for you to send me the arcades exposé? Will I soon receive a response? Will it ultimately turn out that I was mistaken, or does your own feeling confirm my bleak suspicions?

Warmest regards as ever

your

Felicitas.

Original: manuscript.

96 WALTER BENJAMIN TO GRETEL KARPLUS
PARIS, *c*.1.7.1935

Dear Felizitas,

you are no doubt expecting a lengthy and open response to your letter, which is what I shall now give you.

After first reading it, I recalled the letter you wrote to me in Dragør shortly before our meeting; with a similar outburst of discontent, relating in particular to a telephone conversation which you did not stop to think that I might have had to conduct in the presence of third parties. That incident was without consequence: we saw each other directly afterwards.

Now it is different: but, once again, it is no more than a perhaps entirely explicable weakness, a surely well-founded exhaustion, that prevents you from opening your imagination to existential conditions that make my requests an absolute necessity. And a necessity not only for my sake, but also in a different – though no less decisive – sense for yours.

For what could have aroused your impatience other than the circumstance that I repeated a request in my last letter?[1] And do you not know that your fulfilment of such a request gives me much more than the compulsion to make it costs me? And have you forgotten – for I know that you have heard it from me and understood it in the past – that this compulsion is not purely a material one?

I shall say this much: your letter can only relate to that aspect. For in mine there has been no change, except for that which was expressed at the start of the previous month in the traces of total exhaustion and towards the end, when I was occupied with the writers' congress,[2] through a temporary silence. As a matter of fact, however, I had expected a very different letter when your last one arrived. For would it not have been natural to relate – as I had asked you from Monte-Carlo and Paris to do – how things were continuing with W?

I must admit that, at times during this gloomy and disconcerting development, I sometimes feared that my *one* violation of my old maxim in matters of friendship would one day cost me W's and yours. And it did not increase my confidence when I saw that – and how – W had already relapsed in his first days here. When one is separated for as long as you and I are, every person who travels between us inevitably becomes a *messenger*. And W cannot be the right one for me at present. The significance of his failure for me can only be understood if one imagines the way we lived together in the south and all the efforts I made for his sake. To add to all these doubts, I now do not know what level of communication you have found amongst yourselves.

What I do see, admittedly, is that E has vigorously aroused your interest in the 'Arcades'. In keeping with that last letter, however, this was no source of joy to me, for I cannot fulfil your request, at least not at the moment. The Geneva copies of the plan are still not finished. There are only two copies of it at present – T has one of them, which is presumably still in Oxford, and I am using the other for my work. There may also be other reservations in the matter; T will judge this himself. How infinitely more valuable it would be if we could simply speak about it!

If we have to wait until Denmark, however, it could take a long time. I do not think I shall be able to go there this year. For I wish to stay here – if it is at all possible – until I have completed the documentation for my book.

I hope I can give my next letter a more solid foundation, and will in particular give you a report of my discussion with Ernst,[3] which will most likely have taken place by then. The signs are not all too favourable; especially the fact that Karola and I are entirely incompatible.

I enclose, with a multitude of good wishes that you can use in an equal multitude of ways, the small blue sheets with the envelopes. In particular a rapid and true restoration of your health. And then I shall not forget to wish also for *our* recovery.

Yours Detlef

Original: manuscript.
On the dating: the addressee received the writing paper on 3 July.

1 Benjamin's previous letter dates from 25 May; it can no longer be ascertained whether a request was made in the missing part of that letter; nor has any further letter in which the request was subsequently 'repeated' survived.

2 The 'Kongress zur Verteidigung der Kultur' [Congress in Defence of Culture], which took place in Paris from 21 to 25 June. Benjamin wanted to report on this anti-fascist congress for the *Neue Deutsche Blätter*; he did not write about it, however.

3 See *GB 5*, letter no. 975.

97 GRETEL KARPLUS TO WALTER BENJAMIN BERLIN, 3.7.1935

3 July 1935.

Dear Detlef,

since my last letter I have spent two days in Frankfurt, where I found Teddie deeply dejected at the death of Agathe,[1] but where I also had the chance to look at your letter[2] and the exposé. After that letter, which was really directed at Teddie and me together, it seems to me that you do not appreciate it when your friends discuss your work in your absence, especially if they then report to you in the wake of that conversation. Therefore, to avoid any disharmony between us at all costs, I do not wish to pre-empt Teddie, not least because I know that I can only ever gain a proper impression from a finished text and am often fairly helpless when faced with a sketch. I find all sorts of details splendid, and at the moment I am most enthralled by paragraph V.,[3] but all this is only on the basis of my first brief impression; I am dying to read the book in its complete state as soon as possible. Is there anything new regarding its external chances of realization, what have you heard from America? – Has Fritz extended the conditions for May and June[4] to further months? You are so silent and are leaving me in the dark about your plans and possibilities; I would so like to hear from you very soon. Do not keep me waiting too long, as always ever

your

Felicitas

Might Krenek not be able to do something for 'Berliner Kindheit'? Many thanks for sending the writing paper, which is just arriving now.

Original: typescript with handwritten postscript.

1 Adorno's aunt had died on 26 June.

2 Benjamin's letter of 31 May to Adorno; see *Adorno–Benjamin Correspondence*, pp. 87–92.

3 This section bears the title 'Baudelaire und die Strassen von Paris' [Baudelaire and the Streets of Paris].

4 Benjamin received 1000 francs from the institute from April to July, then from August 500 francs.

98 GRETEL KARPLUS TO WALTER BENJAMIN BERLIN, 5.7.1935

5 July 1935.

Dear Detlef,

I am so glad our letters crossed this time. – My failure to send you the expected reports on the last four weeks is due only to the absence of anything to report. Those three autumn months, which were veritably packed with sensations, were followed by an extraordinarily calm period, with walks and the amusing evening game of competing for the largest pupils, in which I unfortunately had to admit defeat, as my eyes always remained brown, while E's often seemed to lose their last blue outline. The visa has now been in Paris for a long time and is expected here daily; until it comes, his days are filled by a medical study. I think the whole lies in the fact that E. is not – or at least is less – bored in Berlin than in P., so the month in Germany is more comparable to your stay in Monte-Carlo. I would be most grateful if you could give Ernst my little birthday greeting;[1] as I am unfortunately lacking his address, I must call on you. I am terribly proud of the blue writing paper; you are receiving the first greeting to be written on it. Let me hear good news from you very soon, warmest regards

ever

your

Felicitas

Original: typescript.

1 Not preserved.

99 GRETEL KARPLUS TO WALTER BENJAMIN
BERLIN, 12.7.1935

12 July 1935.

Dear Detlef,

I am afraid I cannot celebrate this birthday with you either, but only be with you in my thoughts. There are indeed a number of things I wish you: the successful completion of the arcades, a resulting alleviation of your material situation, better future prospects, bearable weather in that glorious country, and not least an imminent meeting with Felicitas, so all in all a year with more joys than the last ones. –

I plan to go to the Black Forest with Teddie at the end of the month; I have never been there before. – You will have received my chocolates by now, I hope they are to your taste so that I can send you some more soon. –

All my best wishes and even more fond regards

ever

your

Felicitas.

Original: typescript.

100 WALTER BENJAMIN TO GRETEL KARPLUS
PARIS, 29.7.1935

My dear Felizitas,

I admired this sheet away from someone in order to send you my holiday greetings on it. If fate handles me even half as artfully as the elephant handles his hat, these next weeks – and I hope so very much that they might – will compensate for many bleak ones in the spring.

The elephant, incidentally, is from the best of the recent French children's books, and is called Baba.[1]

I too am on holiday in my own way, and the pleasant thing is that it does not preclude work. But the best thing about it – and this is why I use the word – is that it gives me the feeling of living in a completed, closed space again for the first time after two years of furnished accommodation. From the good it is doing me, I can see that I probably need it even more than I realized while deprived of it.

I am barely concerning myself with anything except work. It has happened mostly involontairement that I am well informed about the penultimate or final stage of dissolution in Ernst's relationship with Linda[2] – unfortunately far more so than Ernst suspects and I would like. Linda – who has now left – was in such a state that I had to look after her a little. What I learned from her was sufficient to show me how entirely well founded the feeling of intense antipathy is which Karola aroused in me from the start. And it does not make my relationship with Ernst any easier that I have to avoid mentioning either his last book or his last wife. It is equally clear in either case, however, and I fear that, if Ernst stays here for much longer, no amount of skill on my part will be sufficient to prevent the crisis Karola must desire, for eliminating me from Ernst's life would seem to be the final step in securing her dominion over him.

Give Teddie, whom you must also greet heartily, my warm thanks for his last messages.[3] I am looking forward to Haselberg's 'Kafka'.[4]

If I went to the cinema, or even simply outside, if I were to come upon some reading matter for which you could find the time (in spite of your workload), then I daresay I could add a number of things. As it is, I must content myself with evoking the images for your mind's eye to make itself at home here in my room: I mean the posters you gave me during the last days in Berlin, which now adorn its walls, and between them two of the large tattoo panels you also know.

Time, which often flies once it has strayed onto the wrong path, recently showed leniency, and after an interruption of several years I have been able to resume my contact with Helen Hessel at a level that is more pleasant and appropriate than the one at which we separated, half by chance, long ago. If all goes well, then, I shall be able to treat myself to one or two fashion shows once again. She recently penned a little report[5] on the Paris fashion scene, incidentally, and it is absolutely first-rate in its demonstration of how socially conditioned that scene is.

Now I hope I shall hear from you very soon.

The warmest regards

29 July 1935 Yours Detlef
Paris XV
7 Villa Robert Lindet

PS Could you ask Teddie whether he will be (or has been) able to cast a glance at the text 'Triumphbogen' by Noack[6] (Studien der Bibliothek Warburg)? – I am awaiting his letter about the exposé with great anticipation!

Original: Manuscript on a sheet of writing paper decorated with an elephant that is driving a car and waving its hat; Benjamin's words of address to Gretel Karplus were written inside the car's tyres.

1 The author of the books featuring Babar the elephant was Jean de Brunhoff (1899–1937).

2 Bloch had divorced his second wife, the painter Linda Oppenheimer, in 1928; there is no further information regarding their relationship's 'stage of dissolution'.

3 The last surviving message is Adorno's card of 12 July, in which he thanked Benjamin for his letter of condolence, but made no mention of Haselberg's Kafka essay, so it can probably be assumed that a card or letter from Adorno was lost.

4 Peter von Haselberg (1908–1994), who had studied with Adorno from 1931 to 1933, wrote his 'Notizen zu Kafka' [Notes on Kafka] for the feature section of the *Frankfurter Zeitung*; although the text reached the proof stage, it was not published.

5 See Helen Grund, *Vom Wesen der Mode* [On the Nature of Fashion] (Munich, 1935). See also Benjamin's excerpts in *GS 5* [1], pp. 121–3.

6 See Ferdinand Noack, 'Triumph und Triumphbogen' [Triumph and Triumphal Arch], in *Vorträge der Bibliothek Warburg* (1925/6) (Leipzig and Berlin, 1928), pp. 149ff.

101 WALTER BENJAMIN TO GRETEL KARPLUS AND THEODOR WIESENGRUND-ADORNO PARIS, 16.8.1935

Dear Felizitas,

I think I am doing the right thing by entrusting these few lines to your hands.

If, contrary to my expectations, the two of you are no longer together when they arrive, I am sure you will see to it that they reach Wiesengrund.

They do not contain any discussion of your long and notable letter[1] of the 4th. This will be reserved for a later occasion – and certainly not one letter, but rather a series thereof in the course of our correspondence – a correspondence whose many rivers and tributaries will, in a future that is hopefully not too distant, flow into the bed of our shared presence.

No – this is not a discussion but rather a note of receipt, if you will. Its purpose is not, however, simply to inform you that the letter reached my hands. Nor merely the head along with them. What I rather wish to assure you in advance, before touching on any details, is how much joy I feel at this confirmation of our friendship and the renewal of so many friendly conversations that your letter provides.

What is so extraordinary and, for all the precision and insistence of your objections, so very special and stimulating about your letter is the fact that all its aspects relate to the matter in the most intimate connection with the conceptual life it has taken on for us; that every one of your reflections – or practically every one – points to the productive centre of the work, and hardly any of them miss it. In whatever guise they might continue to influence me, and however little I might know about the nature of this influence, two things seem clear to me: firstly, that it can only be a fruitful one, and, secondly, that it can only affirm and reinforce our friendship.

If I had my way, that would be my last word on the matter for today. For, at this point, anything beyond this would only lead into unclear and unlimited areas. As I wish to ensure that these lines in particular do not seem too sparse, however, I shall venture – not without an element of risk – a very few entirely provisional glosses.

You will have to take into account that they are of more a confessional than a directly factual character.

So let me begin by saying this: in the light of your highly emphatic comments in the letter regarding the 'first' sketch of the Arcades,[2] I can say that I have not given up any part, any word of that 'first' sketch. And the one you had is not, if I may say so, the 'second' sketch, but rather the *other* one. These two sketches have a polar relationship. They constitute the work's thesis and antithesis. To me, then, this second one is anything but a conclusion. Its necessity lies in the fact that the insights present in the first sketch did not allow for any immediate development – aside from an impermissibly 'poetic' one. Hence the long-abandoned subtitle of the first sketch, 'A Dialectical Féerie'.

Now I have the two ends of the spectrum – but not yet the strength to connect them. I can only gain that strength through extensive training, of which my work within the material constitutes one element (among others). Due to my unfortunate situation, these other elements have so far had to occupy second place in favour of the aforementioned one during this second period of my work. I know that. And I am taking this insight into account in [only preserved in copy from here onwards:] the dilatory manner of my procedures. I do not want to allow any mistake to affect my plans.

What are the other elements of this training? Those of construction. W's reservations about the chapter divisions[3] absolutely hit the mark. This disposition is lacking the constructive dimension. It remains to be seen whether it will be found in the direction you imply. This much is certain: the constructive dimension is for this book what the philosopher's stone is for alchemy. For now, the only other thing left to say about it is that it will have to summarize the opposition between the book and established, traditional forms of historical research in a new, concise and very simple fashion. How? is not clear.

After reading these lines, you will not need to ward off the suspicion that my resistance against other objections involves obstinacy or the like. I cannot think of any vice that is more remote from me in this matter. And I see clearly – but am saving for later examination – many points on which I agree with you. (Rarely to the same extent as in W.'s reflections on the subject of the 'Golden Age')[4] No – what I am thinking of at the moment is the passage on Saturn in your letter. That 'the cast-iron balcony would have to become one of Saturn's rings'[5] – I do not by any means intend to deny this. But I must nonetheless explain that the achievement of this transformation can on no account be the task of an individual examination – least of all that of Grandville's drawing – but rather the duty of *the book as a whole*. This of all books must not draw on forms such as those offered by 'Berliner Kindheit' at any point and to any extent whatsoever: confirming this insight to myself is an important function of the second sketch. In it, the prehistory of the 19th century, which is mirrored in the gaze of the child playing upon its threshold, assumes an entirely different guise from the signs it inscribes upon the map of history.

These entirely provisional remarks are restricted to a few general questions. They do not probe the concerns surrounding them, rather leaving all specific elements out of the equation. I will address many of these on later occasions. In conclusion, however, allow me – at the risk of doing this too in the form of a confessio – to point out what I feel is a decisive problem area. In bringing it up I am implying two things: namely how accurate W's definition of the dialectical image as a 'constellation'[6] is – and how inalienable I nonetheless consider certain elements of this constellation to which I have referred: the dream figures. The dialectical image does not replicate the dream – it was never my intention to make that claim. But it does seem to me that it contains the instances, the ingresses of waking consciousness, that it is in fact only through those very points that it can assemble its figure in the same way that many gleaming stars form a constellation. Here too, then, a connection still needs to be developed, a dialectic conquered: that between the image and awakening.

Original: manuscript and typewritten copy of one part by Gretel Karplus.

1 The 'Hornberg letter' of 2–4 and 5 August, which contains a detailed response to Benjamin's exposé; see *Adorno–Benjamin Correspondence*, pp. 104–16.

2 See *Adorno–Benjamin Correspondence*, p. 105; Adorno was thinking of individual elements from 'Pariser Passagen II' (*GS 5* [2], pp. 1044–59), which Benjamin had read to him in 1929.

3 'The division into chapters according to particular individuals does not strike me as altogether appropriate: it suggests a rather forced attempt at systematization that makes me a little uneasy. Did you not previously have sections according to various materials, like "plush", "dust" and so forth?' (*Adorno–Benjamin Correspondence*, p. 109).

4 'The Golden Age, p. 10, perhaps forms the proper transition to hell' (ibid., p. 110).

5 'The ring of Saturn should not become a cast-iron balcony, but the balcony should become the real ring of Saturn. And here I am happy not to offer you abstract objections of my own, but merely to confront you with your own achievement: the incomparable moon chapter in 'Kindheit', the philosophical content of which properly belongs here' (ibid., p. 111).

6 'The dialectical image must therefore not be transferred into consciousness as a dream, but rather the dream should be externalized through dialectical interpretation and the immanence of consciousness itself understood as a constellation of reality' (ibid., p. 106).

102 GRETEL KARPLUS TO WALTER BENJAMIN BERLIN, 28.8.1935

28 August 1935.

My dear Detlef,

you have had to wait so terribly long for a letter from me, but I think you sensed my absence from time to time nonetheless. Quite a number of things have happened in the meantime. It was very pleasant in the Black Forest, though in the low mountain range we certainly mourned for our beloved Dolomites, but I did have quite a good rest, and feel quite passable at the moment; I hardly dare say any more about my condition for fear of invoking a sudden change for the worse. – You asked me so kindly about my business; so far I cannot say anything at all; as I am mainly producing winter gloves, I am very much hoping that we will have a severe, early winter. Let us hope for the best. – As my father constantly has to mind his health, our apartment, with its two floors and the spiral staircase, has proved somewhat impractical, so we will be moving at the start of October to Westphälischestr. 27, by the Hochmeisterplatz. To avoid any resulting interruptions to our correspondence, you should then write to me care of Tengler at Dresdenerstr. 50. If you need any of your books and journals, I would gladly send them now, to avoid any unnecessary damage resulting from the move. – My sister just spent a few weeks visiting America, has incredibly interesting stories to relate and hopes she will soon be able to move there for good. – Teddie is in Frankfurt at the moment, will then be coming to Berlin for 2 weeks, and then return to Oxford around 10 October, though he will be in Frankfurt again and in London for a few days before he does.

I was so very happy to be able to discuss the response to your exposé with Teddie, and your reply is just as I would have wished – no, in its nuance of being directed at me it even surpassed my boldest expectations, and I am especially grateful for it. It is very reassuring to me that you yourself mention the first sketch and the other, thus preventing the assumption that you gave up after the first. Thus you share our opinion that the second is on no account final; one would never suspect the hand of WB in it. I already eagerly await your second letter to Teddie.

Have you meanwhile received the essay by Haselpeter? – Unfortunately I only spoke to him on the telephone in Frankfurt, and he told me of his plan for a new study on the Alps.[1] He is a great alpinist, you see, and knows quite a lot of the literature on the subject. He thinks that the Alps were only really discovered as a landscape in the 19th century, and then people recognized the models for the great cities and their buildings in them. – Regarding 'Berliner Kindheit', I would consider it most advantageous if you wrote to Krenek first, to see if he can find an opening for the manuscript. How are things in this respect with Ernst Bloch? He has always been superb at it with his own writings.

You made me extremely happy by sending Baba. And I am always up for a good detective novel. That reminds me: what do you think of the new Kafka edition with the different readings? – Do you think it would be possible to send me the book Machines en Asie[2] by Frédérix? – I know you cannot read English, but perhaps you have heard of T. S. Eliot, who has amazingly also written some very interesting surrealist poems in French?[3] –

How is your sister? I hope for your sake that she will not turn up very soon. Are you in contact with Fränkel, incidentally? Going on what I have heard about him, I could almost suppose it. – I would truly love to have a conversation with Helen Grund, and not only about the fashion products of the major companies, but also about the laws according to which fashions ultimately move socially downwards in the provinces and the middle classes. I am encountering this problem almost daily in my work, but I am not interested in it purely for professional reasons; this cycle has always interested me, and I would almost go so far as to say that the closer I am to it, the more difficult it seems to find the solution, and the more questionable I find the notion of taste. –

I hope this mammoth letter is not too boring to read, but I did want to compensate for the dearth of recent weeks. Fond regards

ever

your

Felicitas

Original: typescript.

1 Unknown.

2 See Pierre Frédérix, *Machines en Asie: Oural et Sibirie soviétiques* (Paris, 1934).

3 Gretel Adorno may be thinking of the four French poems 'Le Directeur', 'Mélange adultère de tout', 'Lune de miel' and 'Dans le restaurant' from Eliot's collection *Poems* (New York, 1920), which also included 'The Hippopotamus' and 'Mr Eliot's Sunday Morning Service'.

103 WALTER BENJAMIN TO GRETEL KARPLUS
PARIS, 1.9.1935

My dear Felizitas,

your letter was a source of great joy to me. Among the things it recounted, not one was truly unfavourable. And today, after all, we should already consider that a gain. What is more, I cannot imagine that a change of housing could be anything other than desirable for you. For you are hardly so attached to your current neighbourhood; and as far as the setting up of your new quarters is concerned, you will – I assume – be more or less able to fulfil your primary wishes and your independence. If a detective novel would make the first hours in the strange place a little more homely, then you can count on me to make this contribution to the ameublement of the hour. You can expect to receive 'Machines en Asie'.

I am afraid I cannot formulate any wish concerning my books on this occasion. My sister will return in the course of the month; the brief and pleasant time within my own four walls will then have reached its end, and I am faced with an uncertain situation, naturally without any support. With the great effort it requires simply to keep my few belongings together under these circumstances, I would not like to burden myself with any more. So I would be most grateful if you could continue to look after my things.

And now that we have arrived at the subject of my affairs, let me extend many thanks to you for your last rosy delivery and tell you once again, before I move on, what great confirmation of your existence emanates even from these little signs, which sometimes seem so much like great miracles.

Directing my stream of thoughts to loftier regions, I must nonetheless stay on the subject of myself for a moment. For you wrote about my 'second sketch' that 'one would never suspect the hand of WB in it', which I do think is going a little too far, and in doing so you are definitely crossing the threshold at which you can still be sure – certainly not of my friendship – but of my agreement. And I do not wish to be rash, but I hardly think you are speaking in TW's name here. WB – and this is not the case with all authors – but he sees his task and due right in it – has *two* hands. One day when I was fourteen years old, I got it into my head that I had to learn to write left-handed. And I can still see myself today sitting at my school desk in Haubinda for hours and hours, practising. Today my desk is in the Bibliothèque Nationale – I have resumed these writing studies there – temporarily! – at a higher level. Would you not like to *join* me and look at it in this *way*, dear Felizitas? That is all I shall say on the matter for now.

But though I cannot present you with any samples of the extraordinary finds these last few weeks have brought me, I at least wish to mention that I have found material in the works of Victor Hugo that is absolutely indispensable for the picture of Paris I am endeavouring to paint. In Germany we have no idea of this author, one of the most uneven and undiscerning geniuses that ever lived, but also one of the most powerful in language and images when dealing with the manifestations of elemental natural or historical forces. On the other hand, I have every reason to believe that the things I have discovered in Victor Hugo's works have remained unknown even in France, and it is only my old and great friend Charles Peguy who has said the most important things about Hugo in a brief passage.[1] And even that is hidden in an extensive essay about him that has little else to offer. – In any case, I think you know from one of my recent letters that I have long been approaching this object of examination. I have certainly written to you about Hugo's drawings.[2] At the moment I am dealing only with his prose works. I intend to contrast him with Baudelaire in one section of the book.

Perhaps TW will be with you when this letter arrives. Make sure you tell him that I would very much like to hear from him, and send him my warm regards.

Ernst cannot arrange anything regarding Berliner Kindheit with Krenek, if only for the reason that I no longer own a single copy of the book apart from my own. If you were able to gain possession of the one that was in Tau's hands, for example, it would be a great gain. Levy-Ginsberg took the last one, claiming he wanted to copy it out. Ernst is away, furthermore; he is staying in Sanary for a few weeks. He is working on his new book,[3] and doing so with the greatest vigour. Unfortunately my conversations with him have irrefutably confirmed the suspicion that his critical faculty can no longer be relied upon. Certainly self-criticism was never his forte; but he – to say nothing of his first wife – used to have a corrective for his behaviour. That is now entirely absent under his present circumstances.

To close, a glance at my correspondence to which I append the request to excuse the external state of the present sample – my only usable fountain pen is undergoing repairs. W. had an encounter with Asja,[4] and it is naturally very important to me to restore an indirect connection after so many years. Yes; as things stand, I think I would prefer an indirect one to a direct one through letters. He still has no accommodation; but he seems to be very well. Ernst Schoen is visiting a friend in Switzerland; I learned this from him after an almost year-long hiatus in our correspondence. I expect he will stop by here on his return to London.

I will tell you about my relationship with Fränkel[5] at some point. It has a long history dating back to my student days. And regarding Helen Hessel – my relationship with whom seems to be entirely re-establishing itself – also another time.

So: many best and even more fond wishes

1 September 1935 yours Detlef
Paris XV
7 Villa Robert Lindet

Original: manuscript.

1 Benjamin quotes twice from Charles Péguy's 'Victor-Marie, comte Hugo' in the Arcades (see *GS* 5 [2], p. 912f.), and once in the first version of his Baudelaire essay (see *GS* 1 [2], p. 587).

2 The letter has not survived.

3 Presumably this is *Theorie – Praxis der Materie* (later title: *Das Materialismusproblem, seine Geschichte und Substanz* [The Problem of Materialism, its History and Substance]); it is by no means out of the question, however, that he might be referring to the extensive lost manuscript 'Aufklärung und rotes Geheimnis' [Enlightenment and Red Secret], which Bloch mentioned to Adorno in 1937 (see Bloch, *Briefe 1903–1975*, vol. 2, p. 439, nn. 10 and 11).

4 Egon Wissing's letter of 28 August 1935, which evidently reached Benjamin very quickly, contains the following report: 'Mon très cher [paragraph] Yesterday I called Asja L. and arranged a meeting with her straight away. I am writing to you today in great haste, so only in brief (in the sanator. in a break between illuminat. two wards) – We spoke for a very long time and a great deal about you. She is – I can say this with certainty *very* favourably disposed towards you. She already made efforts *c.* ½ a year ago to get you a position here, got some quite influential people on your side. But the business – which was supposed to be a kind of surprise – fell through at the last moment (as a result of polit. constellations you will know about) Now we will both resume our efforts from different angles. A. K. will – I assume – even invite you over. You would have to get the visa yourself in Paris (not Intourist) I do not know what connections you have there, you could *surely* get it through Gide, who is incredibly popular here at the moment. [Paragraph] A. L. was very sorry that the deliberate criticism was not printed. The only thing she had to criticize about you was that you have not published any political essays, i.e. made *your* positions known cor. publico. I tried t. explain yr. stance to her. – [Paragraph] That is all f. today. From 1 Oct. I will probably be working only in Moscow proper. Maybe go away from 15.9.–1.10 answer as soon as possible. "Lu" was very enjoyable, please send me the next issues. Tonight I will call Felicitas in Bln. [Paragraph] How about paying a visit to W. Frank, he writes he is in very good health – is that true?! Where is Fr[itz] Fr[änkel] at the moment, I plan to write to him. [Paragraph] You know how living conditions are here, not easy or simple in any respect, esp. unbelievable housing shortage! I have still not found a room. [Paragraph] Best wishes and very warm regards yours E.'

5 Fränkel (1892–1944), who was already living at 10 rue Dombasle – the house Benjamin moved into in 1938 – at that time, was Benjamin's medical adviser for his drug experiments.

104 WALTER BENJAMIN TO GRETEL KARPLUS
PARIS, 10.9.1935

Dear Felizitas,

like this today. – The change of format will certainly not deprive you of anything I have to tell you, whereas your last message[1] was disappointing only in its brevity. I am indeed very reassured to hear that there is still one copy of 'Berliner Kindheit'. In addition, efforts are to be made on its behalf in Vienna at the moment.[2] Hence I would ask you to send it to me within the next few days so that I can make it presentable (without entertaining any great hopes, but not without making completely sure that the manuscript will be returned if it is rejected). Ernst's publisher[3] is out of the question for a hundred and one reasons. And without knowing whether the circumstances under which Ernst's book was published were significant, and in complete confidence, I can tell you – believe it or not – that it is a subsidized publisher; that is to say: they make – though there are apparently exceptions – the authors pay for the privilege.

I believe I already wrote that Ernst has gone to Sanary. The few hints he gave me about the new book give me little cause for optimism regarding its content. Incidentally, the opinions on the new book I have been hearing in conversations are mostly devastating. I am telling you this à pur titre d'information [purely for the sake of information].

In my work I have been blessed with considerable bibliographical luck in recent times. You should know in particular that I happened upon Koch's 'Zauber der Heilquellen'.[4] Furthermore, its content puts me in the same situation the little schoolmaster Wuz found himself in as a result of his poverty – if a title interested him, he had to write the book's content himself. All the author has to say about medicinal springs is that the presence of the potentates had a beneficial influence on the clinical condition of those who visited the springs. And he does a nice job of making that plausible through the example of Goethe, unfortunately without investigating the contemporary variants or the medical magic worked by the film stars in Carlsbad. I, however, who had hoped to hear something about the temples of Apollo and the spring-halls, as well as the relationship between them, am left empty-handed. I had better luck in a different case: there is a book with the highly peculiar title Heliogabal XIX ou biographie du XIX siècle en France,[5] which was published in Braunschweig in the forties and is extremely rare. Finally, after many months, I managed to obtain it from Göttingen through the Bibliothèque Nationale. And now I have established that my curiosity was not unfounded: it contains a series of allegorical images on French politics in which the most peculiar and hidden motifs from the mid-1800s appear. Now it should take another few months again until I am granted permission to have one of the plates photographed.

For this is a novelty: that I am taking notes on important and obscure images for my studies. The book – I have known this much for some time – can be adorned with the most important illustrative documents, and I would not like to cut it off from this possibility from the outset.

For the moment, however, I must turn to a different circle of images tant bien que mal [somehow or other]. Things are becoming serious with the Fuchs essay,[6] and this time I intend to tackle the matter in a fashion that is more suited to my aims: namely by starting with his studies on caricature, Daumier and Gavarni, which are at least related in their material to the other things I am investigating. Fuchs himself is not well, unfortunately, and his decline is palpable.

Why have I not heard from TW at all? – There is no shortage of less significant correspondents. Sternberger sent me an essay, 'The Saint and her Fool',[7] that proves he has become a diligent farmer, tilling the fields of art nouveau cleared by my winter kingship. Meanwhile I am dreaming of slightly more winding paths through that region. Did I ever speak to you about my idea of tracing Ibsen the apprentice pharmacist in the work of the later poet? I think I did. Well, now a psychoanalyst by the name of Tausk has had the same idea, and I have discovered an essay[8] on the subject in the 1934 Psychoanalytical Almanac. Now I only need the almanac! But there is no hurry.

As you can see, there is nothing but books, books, books today. That is partly an escape – I do not quite dare to think about the world outside; at the moment, the coming weeks are looking all too bleak again. As long as I am sitting here, everything can be done.

But for how long? If you are able, let one of your slips of paper appear to me in September.

Next week I shall send off the novels; they will include Machines en Asie. I will only be receiving them on Saturday – otherwise I would send them sooner. – Are you tending to your new domicile a little; and will you be able to secure – with regard to your fellow occupants – a highly self-contained existence for yourself?

Greet Teddie and accept my greetings too in the old way, that is to say: in a way that still includes the hope of seeing each other again.

Yours Detlef

Original: manuscript.
On the dating: date of the postmark.

1 Not preserved.

2 It is fairly unlikely that this refers to Franz Glück's attempt to find a publisher for the book; Benjamin's letter of 18 January 1936 to Glück (see *GB 5*, letter no. 1013) would appear to disprove this.

3 Oprecht & Helbeling, who had published *Erbschaft dieser Zeit.*

4 See Richard Koch, *Zauber der Heilquellen. Studie über Goethe als Badegast* [The Magic of Medicinal Springs: A Study on Goethe as a Spa Visitor] (Stuttgart, 1933).

5 See Count Hans of Veltheim, *Héliogabale: XIX ou biographie du dixneuvième siècle de la France dediée à la Grande Nation (en signe de sympathie par un Allemand)* [1843] [Heliogabalus XIX, or: Biography of the Nineteenth Century Dedicated to the Great Nation (as a Show of Sympathy by a German)].

6 Benjamin wrote the essay 'Eduard Fuchs, der Sammler und der Historiker' [Eduard Fuchs, the Collector and the Historian] for the *Zeitschrift für Sozialforschung* only in 1937; see *GS* 2 [2], pp. 465–505.

7 The essay was marked 'D. St.' and entitled 'Die vielen Tränen' [The Many Tears]. It was about the novel by Agnes Günthers (1863–1911), first published in 1913, and had appeared in the *Frankfurter Zeitung* on 27 August 1935 (issues 435–6, p. 10).

8 See Viktor Tausk, 'Ibsen der Apotheker' [Ibsen the Pharmacist], in *Almanach der Psychoanalyse* (1934), pp. 161–6.

105 GRETEL KARPLUS TO WALTER BENJAMIN BERLIN, 2.10.1935

2 Oct. 1935.

My dear Detlef,

warmest thanks for the book package, I have already started 'machines' with great interest. I will generally be finding significantly more time to read through the longer route to work, also because I take the city railway from Jannowitzbrücke to Halensee. – Teddie has just been here in Berlin for 2 weeks, we had a wonderful time. Teddie has recovered somewhat from the blow of Agathe's death, and is now in better shape than ever. If he does not write immediately, I am sure there is no other reason, and you can reach him in a week at London W1 Leinster Gardens, Albemarle Court Hotel and in 2 weeks at the usual Oxford address. I am sure he did not mind that you wrote the first letter about the Arcades to me, out of solidarity, and in any case, we are not so particular about individual property: Teddie has the original of your letter, for example, while I made myself a copy. – In spite of these dear visits I do often find it quite hard to stay here alone in Berlin, more and more people are moving away, the point of my sister's departure is also coming ever closer, and it is no trifle to be living alone with my parents in a spacious, yet one-storey 5-room apartment, especially as my father has become ill and does his best to make the atmosphere take on a shade of grey; this can certainly shatter a few nerves in everyday life. I hope that the longed-for change will take place in 36, or 37 at the latest. I have already prepared the 34 almanac for delivery, so I will send it off soon. – I heard you might be considering moving to E's current residence, how is that looking? Perhaps I could ask a few questions about these plans today, recalling your departure from Berlin, when I was also allowed to help you? Could you bear to live in the same city as Asja under these changed circumstances? Please do not take my questions as stemming from mere curiosity, but rather from genuine concern regarding matters that you may not want to think about at the moment. Do you have a good idea of the totally different living conditions in terms of living, eating, transport etc.? Would there be a sufficient chance of employment, as I can imagine that the aid which is still available now – albeit in short supply – will then no longer be possible. I was certainly in favour of the experiment in E.'s case, but you know the reasons for that: the danger of Berlin and Germany in general through the memory of things past and the family, also France, the incredible advantage through the new and unfamiliar, a great deal of work; let us hope that E. remains in good health, and that we can view the attempt as successful. But in your case things are much more complicated, even only vitally speaking, and I am very worried. Would you not like to write a little more about it? – For today let me send you the most friendly of greetings

your friend
Felicitas

Original: typescript.

106 WALTER BENJAMIN TO GRETEL KARPLUS
PARIS, 9.10.1935

My dear Felizitas,

I was indeed very glad to receive a longer message from you. Yes, it must be very difficult to see things becoming so empty all around you. But I would be very happy if a decisive change comes into view, as your letter suggests. And for you, in particular, I think that it will ultimately take on the most positive form. Your last reports, at least, do not prevent me from entertaining such hopes.

You are right to suppose that a change in my own situation – which is yet no more than a mere shadow in the distance – is a far more difficult affair. But it would be more irresponsible to avoid exposing myself to the danger of vital complications in favour of choosing the mere possibility of life out of excessive circumspection. I do not know if this possibility will still exist for me in Western Europe for much longer, however; all I know is that, if it remains in its present state, it will diminish by the square of its duration.

In short: what I need is support not for myself – an infinitely reducible quantity – but rather for my work, which makes modest, but definite minimum demands. If I had to abandon all hope of that, I would hardly find the courage to formulate it. At present, however, this is not quite the case. I have received a short and provisional, but nonetheless positive response to my exposé from Max.[1] And what is no less significant – perhaps not objectively, but for the moment at least subjectively – is the fact that I have made definite progress with the grid of construction that intersects, in a certain sense, with that of the documentation. I could tell you a great deal about it; and how little of that can be written! The things I could tell you, however – and I am sure of this – would also give you a new, in some respects more familiar perspective on the exposé you already know. I cannot address the specific content, but only tell you fundamentally that – during these last few weeks – I have identified the hidden structural character of today's art[2] – of the situation of today's art – which allows us to recognize that what is decisive for us, but only now taking effect, is to be found in the 'fate' of art in the nineteenth century. I have thus realized my epistemological theory, which has crystallized around the concept of 'the now of recognizability',[3] one that even you may be unfamiliar with and which I approach in a very esoteric fashion, using a decisive example. I have found that aspect of nineteenth-century art that can only be recognized 'now', which never was before and never will be again.

But, in the midst of all this, I must not forget to send you my warm thanks for sending the psychoanalytical almanac. If you happened to leaf through it, you will probably have entertained the thought that I make my bibliographical wishes rather lightly. For what use should the anecdote about 'Ibsen the Pharmacist' – as much as the title's motif might concern me – be for my work? You would be right. But less than you probably think. Sometimes I can simply be completely mistaken in book matters. And if I do, then the 'cunning of the idea', which checks that everything is in order, is there. In fact your package was much more important to me than the most decisive information about Ibsen as a pharmacist could have been. That brings me to the article by Freud on telepathy and psychoanalysis,[4] which I very much hope you read. It is wonderful, if only because it once again demonstrates the author's late style, which cannot be honoured enough – one of the finest examples of true general comprehensibility. But I am thinking of something quite specific. For, in the course of his reflections, Freud constructs – in passing, which is how he often takes up his greatest ideas – a connection between telepathy and language by phylogenetically making the former – as a means of communication – the precursor of the latter, referring by way of explanation to the insect state, which cannot exist without communication. In this I recognize ideas that form the heart of a small sketch from Ibiza, 'Über das mimetische Vermögen'. I cannot make any further intimations here, and consider it possible that I did not say anything to you about this important fragment when we last met – though I am not sure. I had sent it to Scholem, who has an old, traditional interest in my language-theoretical reflections, and who, to my astonishment, responded without the slightest comprehension. So the Freud passage in your almanac was a true present for me. My thanks!

Perhaps I can gain a little exposure soon with a language-theoretical essay – simply a collective review[5] – that is to appear in the institute's journal. I told you about it some time ago. There was no place for my own opinions there. But I did, at least, discuss a number of new theories of mimesis towards the end of this essay that support my own thoughts on the matter.

In between all this I am writing a tiny story entitled 'Rastelli erzählt . . .',[6] which I plan to send you in the next few days.

Now I await news from Teddie with impatience. If he does not have my address, he will surely acquire it from you. My new quarters have not changed since I first wrote to you from here. But Arnold L.[7] has promised me a few of the most essential pieces of furniture. As, apart from that, I am finding encouragement only in the realm of the intellect, I shall refrain from leaving it this time.

I place my arm around you, which has long been unaccustomed to this movement.

9 October 1935 Yours Detlef
Paris XIV
23 Rue Bénard

Original: manuscript.

1 On 18 September, Horkheimer had written: 'I can only give you a very brief summary of my judgement: your study promises to be quite excellent. This time, the method of grasping the period through small surface symptoms seems to be revealing its full potential. You go far beyond previous materialistic explanations of aesthetic phenomena. The excursus on art nouveau, but ultimately all other parts of the study too, make it clear that there is no such thing as an abstract theory of aesthetics, but rather that this theory always coincides with the history of a specific period. [Paragraph] The expectation of a discussion about the details of its execution is one of the things that make the European trip I plan to undertake in December seem a particularly important one' (*GS* 5 [2], p. 1143).

2 The first mention of the essay 'Das Kunstwerk im Zeitalter seiner technischen Reproduzierbarkeit' [The Work of Art in the Age of its Technical Reproducibility].

3 See the text of the same name concerning the 'Theses on the Concept of History' (*GS* 1 [3], pp. 1237f.) and the passages in 'Konvolut N' of *Das Passagen-Werk* (*GS* 5 [1]), pp. 578f., 591f., and 608, where the 'moment of awakening' also takes on a central role. Regarding the connection, see also the 'stage directions' for the Arcades exposé (*GS* 5 [2], pp. 1217f.). Translator's note: the original word *Erkennbarkeit* is based on the verb *erkennen*, which in a philosophical context denotes the gaining of insight and knowledge; hence epistemology is referred to as *Erkenntnistheorie*.

4 In the publication cited in the letter, Freud's essay bears the title 'Zum Problem der Telepathie'. Benjamin quotes from it in a paralipomenon 'Zu Sprache und Mimesis', which the editors of the *Gesammelte Schriften* assign to the essay 'Über das mimetische Vermögen' [On the Mimetic Capacity] (see *GS* 2 [3], p. 958).

5 See Benjamin, 'Probleme der Sprachsoziologie' [Problems of Language Sociology], in *Zeitschrift für Sozialforschung* 4 (1935), pp. 248–68 (issue 2); *GS* 3, pp. 452–80.

6 The story 'Rastelli erzählt . . .' [Rastelli Narrates]: appeared on 6 November 1935 in the *Neue Zürcher Zeitung*; see *GS* 4 [2], pp. 777–80.

7 This is Arnold Levy-Ginsberg.

107 GRETEL KARPLUS TO WALTER BENJAMIN
BERLIN, 21.10.1935

21 Oct. 1935.

~~Monsieur Marcel des Pompes funèbres~~
~~Rowohlt copy Ginsberg~~
~~Bloch's address~~
New York notification
Vienna 'Kindheit'
~~Oxford~~
~~Expectant position~~
~~Racking my brains over myself~~

Dear Detlef,

I like the story about Rastelli,[1] but do you really think that the motto is so well suited to me? I almost fear it is simply wishful thinking on your part. –

My days as a hostess, which had made a nice change from everyday life, will soon reach an end, and I cannot suppress the thought that this time we will be apart for a very long time. – I am dreading the winter. – Of the two detective novels, I liked 'chien jaune'[2] significantly better. – E. also mentioned a book with the subtitle pompes funèbres,[3] do you know what he means? – Did Arnold L. help you, he is still greatly indebted to us, for we were very nice to him here in Berlin, purely because we thought it might help you in some way. He also received copies of your books from Rowohlt to sell acquaintances at a profit for you, how is that looking? – Did you receive any response from Vienna regarding 'Kindheit'? – Do you happen to know whether Ernst B. has returned to Paris from Sanary? I owe him a letter, but have not yet found the time on account of the move and other distractions.

Have you heard any more news about the exposé from New York or Oxford? – I read what you wrote about the progress in the construction of your study *very* attentively and sent a copy to Teddie, as I am sure it was also meant for him and I wanted to spare you the effort of having to write everything twice. – I had already known the essay by Freud for some time from the new volume of lectures; unfortunately you did not tell me about your sketch from Ibiza last autumn. I already mentioned in the last letter that I have the feeling I will not be living in Halensee for long, though I was still lacking any rational justification for it. What makes it such a difficult decision for me is that I do not want to move even further away from T., so that we can at least see each other from time to time, even if all too briefly. Nevertheless, I do not know if I can maintain this expectant position for much longer. So I am, as it happens, racking my brains once again, and so far without any success or even clues. I do not like speaking about these beginnings from [x], but complete isolation is even worse, after all, so I preferred to speak to you about it. I shall keep my fingers crossed that November will look kindly on you, let me hear from you soon, despite endless separation

ever your
Felicitas

Original: manuscript.

1 Neither the surviving print of the story nor the typescript includes any motto; it thus remains unclear what Gretel Karplus is referring to.

2 A novel by Georges Simenon featuring the detective Maigret.

3 See Pierre Very, *Monsieur Marcel des pompes funèbres* (Paris, 1934).

108 WALTER BENJAMIN TO GRETEL KARPLUS PARIS, 30.11.1935 FRAGMENT

My dear Felizitas,

finally your letter arrived. And I read it most attentively, as you can imagine. Even though it now postpones our meeting,[1] it seems on the other hand to fix it. And that is a small consolation. I had indeed imagined that you would come much sooner, and had already spoken to my sister regarding that. I am sure you can now expect to be put up by her in the spring, if nothing happens to prevent it. And thus Paris should no longer present you with any great difficulties.

I received news about E from other quarters[2] at the same time as your letter. As he himself has still not written a word, I am finding it extremely difficult to make sense of the accounts. I am sorry to say that I fear something unfavourable, and ask you at least – if you can do so truthfully – to refute my worst suspicion: that he has succumbed to his old affliction. It offers me very little reassurance that a long letter from Asja did not even mention E. In my restless speculations on possible reasons it also occurred to me that the skin complaint might have returned. Unfortunately the one illness would not preclude the other.

At any rate, I intend to send E a letter in the same delivery.

[One or more pages are missing]

next week to visit Charles Du Bos, a friend of Hoffmansthal, by far the most important critic in France. The relationship with Monnier is developing favourably. Her excellent lending library[3] is of great use to me in my work. The travel connections between my area and the Bibliothèque Nationale are so poor that I take every opportunity to work at home.

In the next few days you will receive a detective novel and the latest issue of the Zeitschrift für Sozialforschung with my essay about language theory.

Write to me as soon as possible and sois bien embrassé

30 November 1935 yours Detlef

Original: manuscript.

1 The letter has not survived; the reasons for the postponement of Gretel Karplus's trip to Paris are unknown.

2 The source of this news could not be traced.

3 Since January 1930, Benjamin had been using the 'Bibliothèque de prêt' of Adrienne Monnier, to whom he had been recommended by Félix Bertaux: 'Madame, a writer and essayist from Berlin, M. Walter Benjamin, said to me yesterday: "Do you know the author of some poems that were published six years ago in the N. R. F. and intensely affected me? Of all the things I have read in French, this is what has made the strongest impression on me." I did not feel entitled to give him your name without your authorization; if, however, you do not absolutely insist on retaining your anonymity for M Benjamin (who has translated Proust), he would be delighted if you would send him word that he could see you. He lives at Boulevard Raspail, 232, Hôtel Aiglon. Madame, excuse the indiscretion of my approach, but I was so touched by the devotion of this strange reader that I at least wanted you to be part of it, at the same time as renewing my personal and lively homage to you' (*Adrienne Monnier & La Maison des amis des livres 1915–1951*, ed. Maurice Imbert and Raphaël Sorin [Paris, 1991], p. 43).

109 GRETEL KARPLUS TO WALTER BENJAMIN BERLIN, 3.12.1935

3 Dec. 1935.

Dear Detlef,

today I have a small piece of news for you: Teddie will probably be coming to Paris for a few days at the start of next week for a meeting with Max. You will no doubt speak to him then, and perhaps know more about my chances than I myself. – Could I today now ask you once again to maintain the discretion in which I know I can place such trust: Teddie knows where E. is and that he has a good position there, but not that he is not feeling very well. He knew about his presence in Berlin in October, but not in the summer, as Agathe's death pushed everything else into the background. Everything is peaceful and friendly, so you do not need to avoid the subject per se, but I am sure you have more important things to discuss than me. Meanwhile I found an opportunity to obtain the sequel to the novel for you. – Unfortunately Fräulein 'Else' cannot bring you any salami, nor in fact any food at all; she can best tell you the reasons herself, she is leaving on Saturday.

Your suspicions about E. are mistaken; firstly it is impossible there, and secondly he has overcome that illness – he would have to find the right opportunity to cultivate a new one. But his skin is indeed horrified at the cold, and I do not think that the wonderful time there will last forever. But what now? – Unfortunately none of us have so many possibilities.

I have a cold, and was plagued with the most unbearable neuralgic pains last week, but now I can at last move again.

So, dear Detlef, I wish you the best in every respect for next week – oh, if only I could be with you both. Please write to me about it in the greatest possible detail but also do not forget

your friend
Felicitas

~~Egon~~
~~Art theory~~
~~Asja~~
~~Wiesengrund~~
Carte de Presse
Flemish exhibition
Hauptmann
Hochschule
~~Condition~~
New art books

~~Discretion~~
~~Scholem~~

Original: typescript with keywords added by Benjamin.

110 WALTER BENJAMIN TO GRETEL KARPLUS
PARIS, AFTER 3.12.1935

My dear Felizitas,

thank you for your letter – in so far as one can be thankful for messages that offer so little information about your own matters. Have the neuralgic pains at least subsided for now?

And what about other, certainly equally important matters? I do not yet have any idea in what area you are seeking to secure a future, and thus probably know a little less than you yourself. Will I learn more from TW?

Incidentally, I have not heard anything about his trip here, and the letter you assured me he would write has not materialized. I continue to view this silence as mysterious. If we do indeed meet here, you can rest assured that the instructions of your last letter have found the most obedient and reliable recipient in me. –

I have meanwhile heard news about E[1] that, as incomplete or distorted as it may be, makes my worst fears seem like optimistic assumptions. And while I have a hazy idea of the catastrophic situation that has now transpired, I certainly have none about its causes. But it seems rather unlikely that it could have come about without any criminal recklessness on his part.

In this particular case I may be even more ignorant, and certainly no less helpless, than you. It is a great blow to me: firstly because of his person, and secondly due to the possible detriment to my connections there,[2] which – as you know – I made accessible to him.

At the same time as this, I am witnessing the formation of a dark cloud around something that had maintained a more or less friendly guise for decades. It is the figure of Scholem, to whom I had passed on by conversational means – through a third party[3] who is very close to him – information about my situation, which, if the forthcoming meetings do not effect a significant change, is very close to the point of hopelessness. These notions provoked a reaction from Scholem, whose pitiful awkwardness (to avoid speaking of falseness)[4] gives me the saddest idea not only of his private nature, but also of the moral climate of the country in which he has been educating himself for the last ten years. None of this had been made explicit in our correspondence, for since I have been faced with the possibility of defeat his approach to it has been as dilatory as it was once insistent. As you can imagine, however, my own desire to let him know what I think of the awkwardness, cloaked in self-importance and secrecy, with which he evades any active empathy with me is very slight. I do not consider it an exaggeration if I say that he is inclined to see in my situation the avenging hand of the Almighty, whom I have angered through my Danish friendship.

I continue to make great progress in my new study, which is nearing completion. The further it develops, the more convinced I am that I am forging a narrow path that is destined one day to become one of the most important main roads. As it stands now, the study will be divided into about twenty-five chapters.[5]

Please write whether you also have further volumes of the history of art[6] in your possession, and, if so, send them as soon as you can. The second came the other day; I have already finished it.

Je t'embrasse tendrement

yours Detlef

Original: manuscript.
On the dating: Benjamin is responding to Gretel Karplus's letter of 3 December.

1 The source of this news could not be ascertained.

2 It could not be ascertained whom, other than Asja Lacis, Benjamin might have had in mind. In his letters from Moscow, Wissing mentions only Asja Lacis.

3 This is Kitty Marx-Steinschneider.

4 Translator's note: there is a pun here, as the word used for 'awkwardness' is *Verlegenheit*, while that for 'falseness' is *Verlogenheit*.

5 The first version of 'Das Kunstwerk im Zeitalter seiner technischen Reproduzierbarkeit' has nineteen chapters.

6 It could not be ascertained which history of art is meant here.

111 GRETEL KARPLUS TO WALTER BENJAMIN BERLIN, 13.12.1935

13 Dec. 35.

Dear Detlef,

forgive these fleeting hurried lines from the city railway.

I have meanwhile been able to procure the 3rd volume of the history of art for you in a second-hand bookshop. – You are no doubt in the middle of your Paris conference, which is at least as important to all of us as the Geneva one,[1] but here is Teddie's address again just in case: Hotel Lutétia Boulevard Raspail. Please do not worry too much about his not writing; I have been fighting this evil for 10 years with very inconsistent success. – I wish you would take E's situation with the same grim humour you showed in your views on Scholem. He would certainly have been very pleased if the experiment had succeeded. No doubt he was already looking forward to inviting us over and helping us, full of pride about his good position and his achievements. If things have turned out differently, it has been very much *against his will*, for he tried everything he could. I am sure this does not affect his relationships with us, but I must tell you quite frankly that I would not be able to bear the climate there in any case, for even here I can hardly shake off my neuralgic pains, which have been wandering up and down my right side. – E is cured, at any rate, which must be acknowledged as absolutely positive, even if he is homeless. And can we, sitting in our own glasshouse, really reproach him for it? I am very curious about his next adventures; going on what I have heard, I would be in favour of South America e.g. Uruguay for a change.

At Christmas I am going to Frankfurt for 4 days, then Teddie will hopefully come to Berlin for a short visit. –

Let me ask you to view one of the Marburg books[2] as a Christmas present from me; I will have a replacement copy sent to you as soon as possible.

I await your next messages full of impatience, very very warm regards ever your

Felicitas.

Original: manuscript.

1 The former resulted in Benjamin receiving another 1000 francs and, from May 1936 onwards, also an increase in his research grant from the Institut für Sozialforschung to 1300 francs. The Geneva conference of the League of Nations addressed the Italian annexation of Abyssinia; England and France were against sanctions.

2 Unknown.

112 GRETEL KARPLUS TO WALTER BENJAMIN BERLIN, 9.1.1936

9 January 1936.

My dear Detlef,

this is now the first letter of the new year, which I hope got off to a good start for you. I would be especially happy if you could give me some details about your meeting with Max, in particular whether you were able to have the monthly sum increased following Teddie's emphatic advocacy. Perhaps you were even able to speak about the Eduard study and reach some agreement about that too, namely that it will not happen. – Teddie is gone, and I am spending so much time alone once again. He read a great deal of Hölderlin here and was completely fascinated by it, which inevitably led to a grudge against Berta. – The visit to London has been postponed until Whitsun on account of the fine weather, and I would stop by to visit you on the way back. – I must still thank you for a number of things: how delightful of you to send me a little cloth for New Year, I will hold it in high esteem. I read the detective novels, and I hope you will not be too cross with me if I confess that I ultimately find them too French, with too much eroticism; the purely matter-of-fact English ones are more to my taste in that respect. You still have not written anything about Haselpeter's essay, which Teddie told me you did not like. I certainly have enough points of criticism, but I nonetheless consider it highly remarkable, and would have been very pleased if you had given Peter some encouragement by sending him a response with your reservations. – Do you know one of your greatest admirers in Berlin, by the way, Hans Hennecke,[1] the former publisher's reader for Erich Reiss, have I not already written to you about him? –

E. is surprised he has not heard from you; he gave up his position on the 1st. As far as I know, his plans are currently directed at either Abyssinia or America, where my sister conducted enquiries on his behalf.

It really is a shame that you cannot speak English; I am so utterly captivated by the famous children's book 'Alice's adventures in wonderland' that I would almost advise you to read it in French, if there is a decent translation.

I look forward to your next letter, many fond and warm regards

your

Felicitas

Now I have more time to go in search of Marburg copies once again. –

Original: typescript.

1 The writer Hans Hennecke (1897–1977).

113 WALTER BENJAMIN TO GRETEL KARPLUS
PARIS, AFTER 9.1.1936

Dear Felizitas,

first of all, at the risk of getting various matters a little tangled up, I would like to address a number of things mentioned in your letter.

To begin as the alphabet begins: naturally I am familiar with Alice in Wonderland; it is in fact the only book of which I know a few pages in English. For it is those pages that I chose as the basis for my useless attempts to teach myself that language. Then, two years ago, I read it in German (or French) and took the opportunity to watch a film that was based on the book, and which I am sure I mentioned to you. It is an extraordinary affair, and is naturally also held in high esteem by the Surrealists.[1]

While we are on the subject, you will be interested to know that I shall be coming into contact with the Breton circle for the first time through the translator of my new text; an encounter that will naturally call for a great deal of circumspection. This Tuesday I will attend one of the group's meetings.[2] I learned with great interest that my translator is preparing a study of his own, 'From Sade to Fourier'.[3] The pace at which mine is proceeding gives me the pleasant certainty that – if I live to see the day – I will still be able to make use of one or two by other people before working on the text of my own.

To which I shall now return. This has been made easier for me because, though the text on Eduard has not been taken off my shoulders – which I had not expected it to be – the deadline has been postponed quite considerably. That, incidentally, has so far remained the only concrete result of my meeting with Max. The decisive meeting[4] is only supposed to take place following his return from Holland. Until then, a harsh wind will be blowing; and I would be very glad if I could forget my worries for a little while and immerse myself in the latest tome, which I thank you warmly for sending.

For this history of art, which is so ideally compatible with all my interests, harmonizes quite especially well with the studies of the last few days, which I have spent in the Cabinet des Estampes once again after an extended absence. There, guided by a Baudelaire passage, I discovered an etcher[5] whose Eaux-fortes sur Paris took my breath away when I saw them. He is a contemporary of Baudelaire – one cannot imagine what an edition of these copperplates adorned with texts by the latter would have been like. But this plan was foiled by the unpredictable nature of the etcher. His name is Meryon. The Parisian etchings are his magnum opus, and there are no more than 20 of them. But what remarkable pieces! You will have a chance to see them when you are here. Meryon died in a state of insanity soon after passing the age of forty.

But when is Whitsun? I fear this means that you have greatly delayed your visit. To say nothing of my plan to turn up in Denmark once again this year – a possibility that would admittedly have to be secured first, all the more so because I hardly wish to stay there as long as last time. But perhaps there will be time for that after Whitsun.

I am very glad the paperback was a source of plaisir to you. It is from a shop in which I used to buy more in better times. And you will take a look at that place too.

I would like to say more about Haselberg. But it is all more difficult if one does not know one another personally. Perhaps there will be an opportunity at a later point.

Best and warmest regards from

your Detlef

Original: manuscript.
On the dating: Benjamin is responding to Gretel Karplus's letter of 9 January.

1 Breton included 'Le Quadrille des homards' [The Lobster Quadrille] from the French translation in his *Anthologie de l'humour noir* [Anthology of Black Humour]. The film *Alice in Wonderland* was made in 1933 and directed by Norman McLeod; Charlotte Henry played the part of Alice. Adrienne Mounier had written about the film in the January 1935 issue of the *Nouvelle Revue Française*, pp. 172–4.

2 The group Contre-Attaque, founded by André Breton and Georges Bataille in the autumn of 1935, a union of the 'old' Surrealists around Breton and the members of Boris Souvarine's Cercle communiste-démocratique led by Bataille. In the winter of 1935–6 the group published a treatise, 'Appel à l'action' [Call to Action], directed against the right-wing alliance, especially Colonel La Rocque. Contre-Attaque disbanded in the spring of 1936. See also André Breton, 'Trois interventions à Contre-Attaque', in Breton, *Œuvres complètes II*, ed. Marguerite Bonnet with Philippe Bernier, Étienne-Alain Hubert and José Pierre (Paris: Bibliothèque de la Pléiade, 1992), pp. 585–611 and the accompanying notes. Nothing is known about Benjamin attending one of the group's meetings.

3 The writer, translator and painter Pierre Klossowski, born in Paris in 1905, spent his youth travelling through Germany, Italy and Switzerland, and in 1923 moved to Paris, where he associated with Rilke, Gide and Jouve and discovered the works of de Sade and psychoanalysis. He translated Otto Flake's book on de Sade (1933) and Friedrich Sieburg's *Robespierre* (1936) from German, as well as the latter's *Es werde Deutschland* [Let There Be Germany] (1933). His studies up to that point were: 'Élements d'une étude psychoanalytique sur le marquis de Sade' [Elements of a Psychoanalytical Study on the Marquis de Sade] (1933), 'Le Mal et la négation d'autrui dans la philosophie de D. A. F. de Sade' [Evil and the Negation of Others in the Philosophy of D. A. F. de Sade] (1934–5) and 'Temps et Agressivité: Contribution à l'étude du temps subjectif' [Time and Aggressiveness: A contribution to the study of subjective time] (1935–6). Klossowski, a member of Contre-Attaque, had announced a forthcoming essay in the group's only publication: 'The moral

discipline of a failed regime is based on economic depression, which rejects the free play of passions as the most terrible of all dangers. Fourier envisaged a economy of abundance resulting, on the contrary, from this free play of passions. At the point when abundance is within reach of mankind, rather than an escape from their moral misery, is it not time to break with the cripples and eunuchs who are imposing this misery today, and to make way for a mankind liberated from social constraints, open to all the pleasures that are its due – the way Fourier indicated a century ago?' (Georges Bataille, *Œuvres complètes I: Premiers écrits 1922–1940* [Paris, 1970], p. 391). Klossowski published an essay with the title 'Sade et Fourier' only decades later; see Pierre Klossowski, *Les Derniers travaux de Gulliver suivi de Sade et Fourier* [The Last Labours of Gulliver followed by Sade and Fourier] (Montpellier, 1974), pp. 31–77.

4 In a letter dated 22 January 1936, Horkheimer wrote to Adorno: 'I have already had a discussion with Benjamin. He completely denied that the content of his study has anything to do with Brecht. I convinced him of the correctness of my and also your objections to certain sections. He will look at them again thoroughly before the translation begins. The most depressing thing is my feeling that the shortcomings are partly due to his desolate material situation. I want to try everything I can to alleviate that. Benjamin is one of the few people whose power of thought forbids us to abandon them.' Adorno replied on 26 January: 'We had spoken of 1000 Francs – would it be indelicate of me to remind you of this figure? For as he cannot earn anything else at present, it would be impossible, even with the most resourceful money-saving, to survive in Paris with any less' (Adorno–Horkheimer, *Briefwechsel I*, pp. 108–11).

5 In 'Salon de 1859', Baudelaire draws the reader's attention to Charles Meryon (1821–1868): 'A few years ago, an impressive and unusual man – a naval officer, it is said – had begun a series of etchings depicting the most picturesque sights in Paris. Through the severity, the subtlety and the definition of his images, M. Méryon recalls the old etching masters. I have rarely seen the natural solemnity of an immense city represented in a more poetic fashion. The majestic accumulations of stones, the bell towers *pointing to the sky*, the industrial obelisks vomiting their concoctions of fumes into the sky, the prodigious scaffolding on monuments under repair, overlaying the solid body of the architecture with their own broken architecture of such paradoxical beauty, the turbulent sky, loaded with anger and bitterness, the depth of the perspectives accompanied by the thought of all the dramas contained there; none of the complex elements that form the mournful and splendid adornment of civilization have been forgotten. [. . .] His nascent glory and his labours were suddenly interrupted. And ever since then we have been waiting with anxiety for reassuring news of this remarkable officer, who had become an impressive artist in one day, and who had bidden farewell to the solemn adventures of the ocean to portray the black majesty of that most disquieting of capitals' (Charles Baudelaire, *Œuvres complètes II*, ed. Claude Pinchois [Paris: Bibliothèque de la Pléiade, 1976], pp. 666f.]).

114 GRETEL KARPLUS TO WALTER BENJAMIN
BERLIN, 25.1.1936

25 January 1936.

My dear Detlef,

before I begin these lines today, I must ask you to show me the utmost leniency. I have to appeal to the special status of our friendship to touch on matters that one cannot really sort out in writing. And even in conversation they would not be any less natural, that is all clear to me, and yet I want to undertake the experiment nonetheless. – As far as I have been informed, things are not looking bad for you with Max; he is absolutely intent on helping you, and in the right way: so that your productive energy is not diminished by external matters. It is not difficult to foresee that this would be inevitable in the long run, and I would consider it – quite apart from our friendship – a mortal sin if we did not do everything in our power to prevent it. Forgive me, I am really no advertising manager, but I think that you have a far more genuine friend in Teddie than you might assume. I see chances for both sides in your friendship that one does not find often. –

I think it would be simplest if you sent your new study[1] to Oxford. – I find the commemorative essay for Alban Berg[2] superb. Have you heard about the project of the jazz study?[3] –

Whitsun is on the last day of May, and our summer plans are still up in the air, as the Dolomites are probably out of the question at the moment. – I have had the last volume of the history of art sent directly to you. –

Please my dear, tear up these lines and think occasionally with old affection and warmth

of

your

Felicitas

Original: typescript.

1 This is 'Das Kunstwerk im Zeitalter seiner technischen Reproduzierbarkeit'.

2 See Adorno, 'Erinnerung an den Lebenden' [Commemoration of One Still Alive], in *23: Eine Wiener Musikzeitschrift*, 1 February 1936, no. 24/25, pp. 19–29; for a later, revised version, see *GS* 18, pp. 487–512.

3 In early January in Amsterdam, Adorno and Horkheimer had arranged for an empirical examination of jazz for which Adorno was to write the exposé. The plan was never carried out, but Adorno wrote his exposé, on which he had collaborated with the composer Mátyás Seiber (1905–1960), to form the essay 'Über Jazz' [On Jazz].

115 GRETEL KARPLUS TO WALTER BENJAMIN
BERLIN, 19.2.1936

19 Febr. 1936.

Dear Detlef,

so today I will do my best to give you an objective report, and if a few personal remarks should slip in towards the end, please forgive me. – Naturally I do not want to make your decisions for you, but I just have the feeling that you would not get a lengthy letter otherwise, and as I am at an advantage in this case through my location in Berlin, I wish to share my knowledge with you. Around the start or the middle of March E. plans to go to the USA, first to New York, everything else remains to be seen. Through his various orientations, and partly also through my sister, the prospects are at least not bad, particularly for his specialized area. His former boss is also over there, in Chicago, though I am not sure one should expect very much from him. What is more important is that E. received very high recommendations for N. Y. from his last place. For he knew how to secure an excellent departure, as he was the only one able to help a very important man from a major council, using precisely the substance that was later also mentioned in telegrams from Paris and America as the only possible cure. – It will certainly not be easy at the start, but a man of his abilities should manage really. What is more: despite the greater distance from his friends, he is in no danger of sacrificing his liberties for good over there, the climate is more favourable, even in residential areas, and one can buy everything. (We will have to wait and see whether the dream of Los Angeles can be fulfilled) As far as I can judge, he is completely cured; the last 6 months have not been wasted. Actually, in contrast to the others, the whole development has been very favourable for him, as he can now justify his new start with this plausible explanation, without even having to mention his private matters. – I could well imagine that he is now reaching genuine manhood, as he is no longer under the decisive influence of women, so I am sure he will be able to achieve something quite special. Time will tell whether this is just a pleasant dream of mine or a reality that will one day tempt me to visit. – At any rate, I can see a certain progress in your relationship, which encourages me to hope that I too will find a solution that is not too unfavourable. –

E. asked me to send you his warm regards, which I do equally intensely myself

ever your
Felicitas

Original: typescript.

116 GRETEL KARPLUS TO WALTER BENJAMIN BERLIN, 8.3.1936

8 March 1936.

Dear Detlef,

I am very sorry to hear that you are unwell, and I hope that you have recovered sufficiently to resume your work. I received a letter from Oxford[1] yesterday, and Teddie wrote that he has a very positive view of your essay; as it seems that you will be seeing him soon, he will be able to share his criticisms with you himself. I am dreadfully sorry I cannot see it yet myself, and must therefore content myself with fragments of a discussion. –

I genuinely do not know anything about a letter from roughly 10 days ago, nor the account of the lecture by Gide.[2] –

I do not think we have to agonize over E. any more. He has removed himself completely from that dull sphere of indolence, there is nothing left to remind one of 'la mort difficile',[3] and perhaps the USA is the most suitable area for a new field of activity in which one can and must earn money, where one may work, and which is no longer centred purely around women. Naturally the risk is great, but no greater than with all of us, and his attempt is at least being made in full awareness and not under duress. You knew E. in earlier times too: perhaps today he is more the way he was during his relationship with Gert, except that he is not so directly forward, but rather broken in a curative way. If you have any specific questions I will gladly answer them. Los Angeles is tempting because of the good climate, as there do not seem to be many prospects in San Francisco, but these are all just speculations; we should know more in a few weeks. –

We do not have any Easter plans yet, but I do very much hope to see Teddie soon, and as I can only take the public holidays off, he might come here. I only fear that he will feel Berlin has gone to seed once and for all, as the last of our acquaintances like Carlchen and Alfred Sohn[4] have meanwhile left. But he has so many sights to see in O., after all, that he can content himself with me here; I am very much looking forward to his accounts, in any case, and simply to seeing him, it is just always so short. –

But that is all I have to report about myself, at least my joys.

I constantly await your letters, do not make me wait too long for them and please give me some compensation for the lost letter, very, very warm regards

your Felicitas

Original: typescript.

1 The correspondence between Gretel Karplus and Adorno has not been recovered.

2 Benjamin's article 'André Gide und sein neuer Gegner' [André Gide and his New Opponent] appeared in the November issue of the journal *Das Wort* [The Word]; see *GS* 3, pp. 482–95.

3 An allusion to the story of the same name by René Crevel, published in 1926.

4 Carl Dreyfuss had emigrated to England in early 1936, and Alfred Sohn-Rethel to Lucerne at the start of February 1936.

117 GRETEL KARPLUS TO WALTER BENJAMIN BERLIN, 24.3.1936

Dear Detlef,

my situation has become clear for the time being, in such a way that you could far more easily surprise me with a little pink bouquet than vice versa. I will not starve, but it seems that my travel plans will not be feasible, a similar situation to spring 33. – E. left on the 19th, perhaps you have already had some news. – Nothing seems to have come of Teddie's Parisian excursion, a shame.

I am in such desperate need of a little encouragement, please write to me and tell me about yourself, let me imagine I am sitting in your room late in the evening and forgetting all my worries with you. – Only the weather has the comforting warmth of spring. A miracle has happened: I am going for many walks by myself. Please forgive my total self-centredness today warmest regards ever

your

Felicitas.

Original: postcard with printed Easter rabbit; stamp: Berlin-Charlottenburg, 24.3.36. – Manuscript.

118 GRETEL KARPLUS TO WALTER BENJAMIN BERLIN, *c*.24.4.1936

Dear Detlef,

the tone of your last letter[1] seems one of very slight annoyance, but I can assure you that you have no cause to feel neglected in favour of any of our common friends. I was just so utterly down[2] that even writing to my best friends was torture, and so I simply let everything pass me by. Now after Easter – I was in Frankfurt for 3 days, – Teddie as little in Berlin as in Paris, I am feeling a little better. – The dissolution of my business has been decided on, but what shall I do then? Do you think I would find some possibility in Paris? As you will have guessed, I am thinking of Paris above all because of you, and the less I know when we will see each other again, the more emphatically I want to pose this question. My Whitsun trip has been cancelled (postponed?), so I see little opportunity for us to meet at present. I am so sorry for you, as I know how much you were looking forward to our weekend,[3] but it is worse yet for me, for I have such a myriad of important things to tell you that cannot be properly discussed in writing. So, in case you happen to hear about something: complete academic training in chemistry, extensive business knowledge, 10 years of experience, speciality: glove leather – leather gloves. –

But now to you. I am very glad that the study[4] will be published in the foreseeable future; it is only a shame that I will not be reading it yet. Please do tell me a little more about Adrienne Monnier, for in her you seem finally to have found someone in Paris with whom you can have real contact, and whom you enjoy seeing. –

I have meanwhile had a long letter from Ernst; he was very cheerful, and had great plans. – I have just been to see Rowohlt, but unfortunately he was not there, although we had arranged a meeting by telephone, as he is ill. A friendly lady took care of the matter in his name; in Berlin they have no copies, so they plan to write to Leipzig and then tell *me* or send the books straight away. You will hear from me then. – I hope you have received word directly from New York,[5] so far E. is very optimistic; let us hope there will be no setbacks this time. It would be frightfully sweet of you if you could send me any books you no longer need; when one is alone as much as I am, a good read is of no mean importance. – I think that you will be more pleased with me today and expect to hear from you soon.

Very, very warm regards

your

Felicitas.

Original: manuscript.
On the dating: The letter was written shortly after Easter, which fell on 21 April.

1 Not preserved.

2 *down:* EO.

3 *weekend:* EO.

4 The abridged French translation of the 'Kunstwerk' essay appeared in the first 1936 issue of the *Zeitschrift für Sozialforschung* (see *GS* 1 [2], pp. 709–39).

5 The first of Ernst Wissing's letters from New York dates from 16 April 1936; in it, he writes: '*Here* I just about seem to have fallen on my feet. For we are getting the "licence" in the state of New York without a state examination, merely a language test, but it seems there is a law in preparation that will change that. I am here on a "visitor's" visa, but will probably manage a normal immigration via Canada. For we have no relatives here, but the connections of many different kinds I have here have already proved better than I had assumed. As you know, I am often together with Prof. Horkheimer (with whom I sometimes talk about you). [Paragraph] Here too, my career prospects are not bad' (unpublished).

119 GRETEL KARPLUS TO WALTER BENJAMIN
BERLIN, 19.6.1936

19 June 1936.

My dear Detlef,

thank you for your letter. – Once again there is a chance that you will see and speak to Teddie sooner than I shall, and unfortunately this meeting too will pass without my presence. –

Allow me to confess that I am just a little bit sad you forgot my birthday this year; at the moment I would have been especially grateful for a friendly thought. – But instead of bothering you with sentimentalities, let me ask just one thing of you. I know that Else H. has behaved in the most unspeakable way towards Teddie by accusing him of leaving you in the lurch. Only you know the true circumstances of our friendship (I mean Detlef – Teddie – Felicitas). I would be infinitely grateful if you could do your bit to do away with this horrible interference and thus confirm our mutual solidarity anew. –

With fond and warm regards in unchanging affection

from your

Felicitas.

Original: manuscript.

120 WALTER BENJAMIN TO GRETEL KARPLUS
PARIS, *c.* EARLY JULY 1936

Dear Felizitas,

why not the slightest news from you?

And this at a time when the absence of your letters coincides with an absence of various other things. I had already been greatly looking forward to Teddie's visit. Now I have been waiting in vain for the last two weeks for some word from him, and this meeting too seems to be changing from a specific expectation into an uncertain hope.

I think I shall leave Paris in the course of the month. To go where? I do not yet know. I do not wish to spend the holidays alone, at any rate, as that would create highly unfavourable conditions from which I am in considerable need of recovery. At the moment I am awaiting news from Stefan,[1] so that I can have him near me for a while if at all possible.

Before I leave here I hope to have the original version of the Lesskow[2] translated. An opportunity has arisen, and I wish to take advantage of it as quickly as I can. And so I must ask you to return your copy to me – if possible with the next delivery. You will not have to go for long without it – six weeks at the most. For the German text is to be published in Switzerland in September.

Take this first and foremost as an urgent request for some news and receive my greetings in the warmest, old fashion

from your
Detlef

PS And now, with wailing and gnashing of teeth, I shall turn to the text of my 'Eduard Fuchs'.

Original: manuscript.
On the dating: Gretel Karplus's last letter dates from 19 June, and her subsequent one, the response to Benjamin's, from 14 July.

1 The next letter from Stefan Benjamin dates from 13 July, but without an indication of the year.

2 This probably refers to Jean Cassou, editor-in-chief of *Europe*, which, according to Adrienne Monnier (*Rue de l'Odéon* [Frankfurt am Main, 1995], p. 149), was supposed to publish 'Le Narrateur'. In the summer of 1937 Benjamin translated the essay himself (see *GB* 5, letter no. 1172), and an unknown native speaker added handwritten corrections. In July 1938, Cassou read the French and German versions and asked Benjamin, who had not revealed that he himself had produced the translation, to ask the

translator to revise the French text. Cassou intended to have the revised version printed immediately, as he wrote to Benjamin on 15 July (see Nathalie Raoux, 'Six lettres de Jean Cassou et une lettre de la revue "Europe" à Walter Benjamin', in *Europe* 75 [1997], pp. 202–6; the passage quoted is on p. 205); it was never published, however. In October 1936 the essay appeared under the title 'Der Erzähler: Beobachtungen zum Werk Nikolai Lesskows' in the journal *Orient und Occident*; see *GS* 2 [2], pp. 438–65 (published in English as 'The Storyteller: Reflections on the Works of Nikolai Lesskow', in Walter Benjamin, *Illuminations*, trans. Harry Zohn [New York: Schocken, 1969], pp. 83–110).

121 GRETEL KARPLUS TO WALTER BENJAMIN
BERLIN, 14.7.1936

14 July 1936.

My very dear Detlef,

you should definitely receive these lines from me in time for your birthday, even if I am writing them rather illegibly on the city railway. All my fond and warm regards! I could send you a little something from here if it would bring you a little joy, but what? –

At the moment there is so much going on here that I broke down in utter exhaustion yesterday; today, after 12 hours of deathlike sleep, I was able to crawl out with great effort once more. Very important negotiations for 5–6 hours every other day, and they became such a burden that I asked Teddie to come to Berlin for the weekend, naturally a migraine attack, no proper sleep in weeks, but in spite of everything it was splendid to spend a few quiet hours with Teddie, who plans to come here for a longer stay in 10–14 days. – My sister is here from Boston too at the moment. She seems to be quite happy, and also brought good news about E. –

What bad behaviour to write so much about myself in a letter of congratulation.

Thank you very much for the 'Lesskow', I had passed it on to Frankfurt immediately, and Teddie will send it to you at once, and also has every intention of writing to you about it. You are quite right: your trains of thought are still very familiar to me, and it feels as if we have long since spoken at length about it, so there is really nothing left for me to say. I now also have your French reproduction essay here through Lotte, and am greatly looking forward to reading it. – Have your summer plans become clear? Where is Stefan living, and what is he doing? –

In the letter before last you wrote that, with the death of Karl Kraus, the last person who had some sort of influence on your work is now gone. I do not think we ever spoke about it, but did you not forget Rudolf Borchardt on your list? I not only have an incredibly high opinion of him, but also feel that there are very strong connections between his work and yours; he is one of the few people I would like to meet. Just recently I was looking at his Pindar translations[1] again and was completely enthralled, though I lack the prior knowledge to understand his prose afterword. Teddie also values him greatly; perhaps it would be possible to arrange something for him in Oxford.

Take very good care of yourself in good old friendship with warmest embraces

from your Felicitas.

Original: manuscript.

1 The book edition had been published in 1929–30.

122 GRETEL KARPLUS TO WALTER BENJAMIN BERLIN, 14.10.1936

14 Oct. 1936.

My very dear Detlef,

(I can hardly imagine that I should ever call you Walter in company, but who knows) here is just a little extra note. –

Your letter[1] made me very happy, as it showed me that the contact between you and Teddie has finally reached the completion I had long wished for. And even though I did not mention the subject directly, I do know that Teddie has always strongly desired to have you as his friend in the true sense of the word.

Now I know well enough that you naturally did not enjoy my previous letter. I would therefore be very grateful if you could tell me a little more about your conversations, as I assume they are the basis for your response, and as the matter really does concern me. I cannot possibly wait until we see each other again, that would be an excess of sadism. –

Could you please get me 50 small blue envelopes to go with this writing paper, I enclose the address.

With warm embraces from your

very glad Felicitas.

Original: manuscript.

1 Benjamin's letter of 27 September to Adorno; see *Adorno–Benjamin Correspondence*, pp. 148f.

123 GRETEL KARPLUS TO WALTER BENJAMIN
BERLIN, 9.11.1936

9 Nov. 1936.

My dear Detlef,

let me thank you with all my heart for sending your book.[1] I wonder if you know just how much it means to me right now? A comfort, a recovery – that is all too little, for it almost occupies the space of a living person for me. A friend who understands me, who knows what it means to feel completely out of place. And it is only natural that I should project all these melancholy and yet pleasing emotions onto you and think a great deal of our intense time together in 1932/33. When you turned from one I had marvelled at from afar into a friend, and I often had to ask myself how such a miracle could occur. –

I also like the book's external appearance, and it makes me happy whenever I recognize familiar passages, parts you have read to me. –

I am very glad that my relatives[2] did not bother you, though, on the other hand, our friendship made me take it almost for granted that I could ask you this small favour. –

It is a relief that you can begin this winter in the knowledge that you can at least cover the bare necessities. Very warm embraces

from your

Felicitas.

Original: manuscript.

1 *Deutsche Menschen* [Germans], which had just been published.

2 Unknown.

124 WALTER BENJAMIN TO GRETEL KARPLUS
SAN REMO, *c.*2.12.1936

Dear Felizitas, you will take as little exception to this medium of communication as to the fact that it was so lacking in recent weeks. I was not even able to thank you for your wonderful letter about my book. Let me do so very warmly today. – As it remained completely impossible to communicate with Stefan, both for myself and for his mother, and the situation could not continue in this fashion, we decided that I would travel to Vienna (via San Remo). Here this decision was overturned. After 2 weeks of the most difficult arrangements, my meeting with Stefan – first alone in Venice, then here – finally took place. Things are certainly not as bad as we had feared at the height of our uncertainty. But they are by no means simple, and I am very far from gaining full insight into them. And it is questionable whether I shall be able to do so before returning to Paris in a few days. So you will understand that I am currently in a state of great exhaustion and must therefore leave it at these few lines. Write to me here if you do so immediately (please letter, *not* postcard). I completed a study on painting and photography[1] here – that is all I could ask of myself. Let me hear from you right away. Very warm regards from your old Detlef San Remo Villa Verde

PS I am leaving for Paris at the end of the week

What is the horse[2] to do now. For simplicity's sake I am sending you the original Kisses G

Original: Picture postcard: San Remo. Città vecchia; stamp: covered. Manuscript with additional note on the picture side by Gretel Karplus, who forwarded the card to Adorno in Oxford.

On the dating: Benjamin left San Remo at the end of the first week of December, and Gretel Karplus sent the card on to Oxford on 4 December.

1 See *GS* 3, pp. 495–507.

2 Adorno's pet name for Gretel Karplus.

125 GRETEL KARPLUS TO WALTER BENJAMIN BERLIN, 21.12.1936

21 December 1936.

My very dear Detlef,

how glad I was to hear from you at least in the form of a postcard greeting, and I daresay I will soon get a report from Teddie. I am happy that you have been in such good contact, and am almost inclined to ask you whether I should be a little jealous of him for visiting you. – Perhaps you have already heard that I have sold the business; nonetheless, there will no doubt be not only a great deal of trouble, but just as much work until the end of March. What then? I do not know yet, but perhaps the next few days will bring clarity in this matter too. –

Even though I cannot say anything about your matters today, as I do not know anything yet, I can at least ask you for some advice. E. has now been gone for 9 months, and our exchange of letters has not really been continuing of late; it almost seems as if the friendship were slowly reaching its end. I do not want that, but what can be done without any prospect of meeting again soon? You know both of us, so perhaps you have some advice. Before he was in dire need of me, his recovery occurred for my sake, and I was drawn to his unusual, eccentric side. Nowadays he strikes me as too standardized, and the state of 'wanting to have' amuses me only for the moment (to explain my somewhat shortened train of thought: what I learned was the state of wanting to be, and the truly authentic state, whose advocates I need hardly name, is that of wanting to recognize); the question remains: where can one find the basis for a long-term relationship, the shared interests? I am sure you will know doubly what to answer: both through your long-standing friendship and the account of E's marriage to Gert, which you actually promised to give me 2 years ago. –

I need not tell you anything about Teddie and me today. I am sure he also told you how good it feels to us to be together; any word would be too much.

I wish you pleasant holidays, recover your strength a little and if, you have some time left over, finding a letter right after the festivities – I will be back in Berlin on the evening of the 27th – would bring a great deal of joy to

your Felicitas, in fond friendship

Original: manuscript.

126 GRETEL KARPLUS TO WALTER BENJAMIN BERLIN, 28.12.1936

28 Dec. 1936.

My very dear Detlef,

let me quickly send you these few lines from the old year – written in the train, to tell you that it was very enjoyable in Frankfurt, that I was especially happy about your letter,[1] and that Teddie is coming to Berlin for New Year. He did not tell me very much about your conversations, but he gave me a general idea. How I would have liked to hear the quotations from the Arcades and the big conversation with Alfred.[2] What is your impression of him now? In the past you had certain reservations about him. I still remember the meeting at Mampe's very well, Fräulein Freund[3] was also there, and yet you said that her book turned out well. – I must thank you quite especially for

'The Postman',[4] you hit the nail on the head once again. – Do you know anything else by Montherlant?

If you think there might be something to gain if I met occasionally with Franz H.,[5] then please give him my address, he can then find me easily in the telephone book. In the past I saw him only rarely at your place, but perhaps the change of circumstances will make it easier to be with him. – I hope Stefan's treatment proves successful; did Bernfeld[6] make a good impression on you? –

For 1937 I wish you good progress with your work and that we can finally see each other again.

Not entirely without hope

your Felicitas.

I can send you Ritter's 'Fragmente eines jungen Physikers' any time as a registered parcel if you need it, or give it to Teddie if I hear from him by 4.1., though I do not know when you will see each other again.

Original: manuscript.

1 This presumably refers to Benjamin's letter of 2 December to Adorno (see *Adorno–Benjamin Correspondence*, pp. 163–5), which Adorno gave Gretel Karplus to read in Frankfurt.

2 Adorno, Benjamin and Sohn-Rethel had met for a long theoretical discussion in Paris around 14 December centred around Sohn-Rethel's exposé *Soziologische Theorie der Erkenntnis* [Sociological Theory of Knowledge/ Epistemology] (Frankfurt am Main, 1985).

3 The Berlin-born Gisèle Freund (1908–2000) had come to Frankfurt in 1930 to conclude her studies in art sociology with a dissertation on the history of photography; she had to emigrate to France in 1933. She continued her studies at the Sorbonne and wrote the thesis 'La Photographie en France au dix-neuvième siècle: Essai de sociologie et d'esthétique', which was published by Adrienne Monnier. For Benjamin's review of the book see *GS* 3, pp. 542–4.

4 This probably refers to James Cain's novel *The Postman Always Rings Twice*; the French translation, published in 1936, which Benjamin had read late that autumn, bore the title *Le Facteur sonne toujours deux fois*.

5 This is Franz Hessel.

6 The Austrian psychoanalyst Siegfried Bernfeld (1892–1953), whom Benjamin knew from his days in the youth movement, was living in Menton at the time; Benjamin was considering consulting him regarding his son Stefan.

127 GRETEL KARPLUS TO WALTER BENJAMIN BERLIN, 12.1.1937

12 Jan. 1937.

Dear Detlef,

thank you for your lines from San Remo. – Now that you have brought up the subject, I would like to add one or two things by way of explanation so that you can understand why I am insisting at all. E. seems to be quite content in the U.S.A., he is working a great deal, having success and no doubt fits in well over there. He and my sister are often together, so I am fairly well informed through both. As I see it, the difficulty of having a friendship par distance with him lies mainly in the fact that he never really takes the time to write proper letters; but perhaps I should not complain so much, as my letters are no masterpieces either. – It is peculiar and almost exciting for me how important Gert has become in my life since her death. Not only my friendship with E, through which I have been granted the use of some of her possessions, but also now a quite close acquaintance with a woman who was a very good friend of hers,[1] so that I am once again encountering Gert's habits everywhere. Naturally I would be interested to hear what she was really like, apart from the failed 1st marriage, all the alcohol, illness and driving, and who better to give a pointer in that than you, who knew us both and can no doubt guess what I would like to know. Master of delicate details, please help me to solve this difficult problem. –

I hope your eyes are back to normal again. –

It may interest you to know that Dolf St. wrote a piece[2] for the F.Z. about a lecture by Heidegger, whereupon H. immediately cancelled his next speaking appointment, which is at least a success; the essay was very fine.

Every line of yours will be an equal source of joy to me in the new year too, and I will not object to any brevity.

Fond regards ever your

Felicitas

Original: manuscript.

1 Presumably Doris von Schönthan (1905–1968).

2 See Dolf Sternberger, 'Am Ursprung? Zu Martin Heideggers Frankfurter Vorlesung' [At the Origin? On Martin Heidegger's Frankfurt Lecture], in *Frankfurter Zeitung*, nos. 627–8, 8 December 1936, p. 11. Heidegger had given three lectures on the 'Origin of the Work of Art' at the Freies Deutsches Hochstift, the last of which was on 4 December 1936.

128 GRETEL KARPLUS TO WALTER BENJAMIN
BERLIN, *c*.18.1.1937

18th January

My dear Detlef,

I take it you are in Paris again, and as ever I am turning to you when there is something special on my mind that I cannot quite deal with by myself. – I am discovering a new – unfortunately bad – trait in myself: cowardice. I am referring to the planned legalization of the relationship between Teddie and myself. Certainly, there is nothing I have desired more these last years; in truth, I have adapted my entire being to this union, and I would no longer know what to do without it, and yet I have been having doubts as to whether I may have overestimated myself, whether I will be up to the task. I am no Else von Str.,[1] and at least had a chance to avoid being dulled by habit despite always being together. I know how much Teddie needs glamour, beauty and variety; where am I to get all that, now that I am long since not so young any more and have no income or property of my own? – Dear Detlef, do not read too much between the lines; I am very well, but just need your advice and your encouragement. – How happy I would be to know that I could sometimes also help you a little in matters that are not entirely insignificant. Tell me soon how *you* are, with fond and warm regards in close kinship

ever your loyal

Felicitas.

Original: manuscript.
On the dating: Benjamin noted either the date of the postal stamp or the day of receipt at the top of the page.

1 Else von Stritzky, Ernst Bloch's first wife.

129 WALTER BENJAMIN TO GRETEL KARPLUS
PARIS, 27.3.1937

My dear Felizitas,

I am now taking my Easter walk[1] to you – regardless of the circumstance that the sky over Paris has donned its frostiest watery countenance for my departure and you may have little better to offer me. I have planted myself next to the only stove on the terrace of the Select; now and again the sun protrudes from the clouds, thus providing the body with what the eye knows as twilight.

Perhaps these late lines are yet premature, for I can feel a bout of influenza brewing in my throat; should it force me into bed, I can expect a writing opportunity there, which I should not pre-empt now. Nonetheless – the yellow sheets are receiving their due attention once again. This time you have already heard much of what is normally reserved for them through Teddie. And this time we managed to gain many fine and important things from his stay in Paris. He will have told you about the feast of the exposition Guys[2] and certainly also about a special evening with Alfred,[3] and perhaps he also mentioned the literary find[4] I revealed to him. Friedrich[5] arrived on the day of his departure; I spoke to him only briefly. He assured me that Fuchs had been given a very warm welcome over there; I received a letter from Max[6] that same day confirming this. So the quarantine under which I had placed all correspondence was some use after all. It is possible that the study will appear at the same time as that by Rottweiler.[7] I still have the difficult visit to Fuchs ahead of me; I will bring it to him in the next few days.

As far as my next study is concerned, there has been a highly agreeable offer[8] that came from Teddie. Admittedly, it would be not unproblematic to accept it after Max's last letter. In the meantime I have been occupied with various new art-theoretical publications. After a long interval I have again for the first time taken up a volume purely for my own pleasure – English ghost stories from the previous century,[9] including some very fine ones.

Stefan is to come to San Remo at Easter. I will stay here. The news concerning him remains very unsatisfactory.

I have been receiving friendly messages from Ernst in Prague, albeit very sporadically. None from Egon for some time.

How do you like the Montherlant?[10] Allow me to interrogate you about it a little more closely for once.

I have set eyes – several years too late – on a letter by Rahel[11] for which I would very much have liked to write a commentary. She wrote it upon receiving the news of Gentz's[12] death. (They were long in love, as you know.) The letter has lent me an extra pair of eyes that are also giving me unexpected insights into the work of Proust.

I send you warm regards, which you should share with Teddie like a marzipan Easter egg.

27 March Yours Detlef
Paris XIV
23 rue Bénard

Original: manuscript.

1 The letter was written one day before Easter Sunday.

2 The exhibition of works by Constantin Guys (1805–1892) took place in the Musée des Arts Décoratifs. Guys occupies the central role in Baudelaire's 'Le Peintre de la vie moderne' [The Painter of Modern Life].

3 Alfred Sohn-Rethel; see also on this Adorno's letter of 23 March to Horkheimer from Paris (Adorno and Horkheimer, *Briefwechsel I*, pp. 322–39).

4 Benjamin had discovered the essay 'Die Rückschritte der Poesie' [The Regressions of Poetry] by Carl Gustav Jochmann (1750–1830), which he recommended for publication in the *Zeitschrift für Sozialforschung*; it was printed in 1940 with an introduction by Benjamin.

5 Pollock.

6 Horkheimer's letter of 16 March, see Horkheimer, *Briefwechsel 1937–1940*, pp. 81–8.

7 Adorno's Mannheim essay 'Neue wertfreie Soziologie' [New Value-Free Sociology] (*GS* 20 [1], pp. 13–45).

8 Adorno had suggested that Benjamin write an essay on the archaic and the dialectical image, which should simultaneously constitute a critique of Ludwig Klages and C. G. Jung. As things turned out, Benjamin then wrote the Baudelaire essay at the request of Horkheimer.

9 See *Histoires de fantômes anglais*, ed. Edmond Jaloux, trans. Georgette Camille (Paris, 1936).

10 Benjamin had sent Gretel Karplus *Les Jeunes Filles* [The Young Girls] (Paris, 1936) by Henry de Montherlant.

11 Probably Rahel Varnhagen's letter of 15 June 1832 to Leopold Ranke: 'I cannot, I must not let this day pass without writing to you. [Paragraph] How wrongly, how crookedly we say everything we wish to express; nothing can be understood if the other does not already know it. And so you cannot know that I *loved* my vanished friend only when, only because, he said or did something childish. It was *then* that I loved him; and so I repeated his words when he said: he was so happy to be the first man in Prague, because all the highest authorities had to send great ladies and gentlemen to *him*! etc. with a delighted smile while gazing into his eyes! Every well-bred and deceitful *beast* is clever enough to hide this: but who has the devoted soul, the dear heart of a child, to *say* it? *His* perfidies – he directed enough of them *against me* – are different to those of the others: he floated as if *flying* in a sledge of joy along a track that was his alone; and no one can compare themselves with him; and on this path he no longer saw left and right as one does on the earth: if he suffered pain or contradiction, he *was* no longer on this track; and then he demanded help and consolation – which he never gave. But no one *is allowed* to do such a thing while still remaining kind and lovable. I did not grant him impunity while he lived. But now, taking stock, all I have is pure, living love. May this be his epitaph! He always aroused my love: he was *always* disposed towards whatever he could grasp as true. He seized what was untrue with a

passion for truth. There are many people whom one can praise in parts: and they do not enter our hearts with love; and there are others, *a few*, whom one can scold a great deal, but they always open our hearts and move it to love. That is what Gentz did for me: and to me he will never be dead. [Paragraph] Furthermore, I now believe that we will know of each other after death: or rather, that we shall find each other. With these words I send you my greetings, and am certain that my letter will please you.' (*Rahel Varnhagen im Umgang mit ihren Freunden* [Rahel Varnhagen in Contact with her Friends] [Letters 1793–1833]), ed. Friedhelm Kemp [Munich, 1967], pp. 210f.)

12 Friedrich von Genz (b. 1764), a pupil of Kant, initially an advocate, then an embittered opponent, of the French Revolution, and ultimately Metternich's head man, died on 9 June 1832.

130 THEODOR WIESENGRUND-ADORNO AND GRETEL KARPLUS TO WALTER BENJAMIN WÜRZBURG, 31.3.1937

Würzburg, 31.3.1937

Dear Walter, this letter is to inform you of our safe arrival and send you greetings from a trip through the towns of Franconia that will still take us at least to Bamberg and Nürnberg. I am glad to hear of the success of your study:[1] may that success also remain loyal to you with its addressee.[2]

How I wish I could accompany you up the stairs of that suburban house a second time. May the view of this more urbane one offer you compensation from your warmly obliged

Teddie.

Dear Detlef

thank you for your Easter letter, to which I shall reply properly in Berlin. For today simply fond regards from your Felicitas

Original: picture postcard: Würzburg. Haus zum Falken. Manuscript.

1 Horkheimer had given a very positive response to the Fuchs essay.

2 Adorno and Benjamin had visited Eduard Fuchs in his apartment during his stay in Paris between 18 and *c.*22 March.

131 GRETEL KARPLUS TO WALTER BENJAMIN BERLIN, 22.4.1937

22 April 37.

Dear Detlef,

now that I am alone with peace and quiet in Berlin once more, let me thank you especially warmly again for your Easter letter. Teddie's reports have filled a gap that probably appears in every correspondence when one has not seen one another for so long (it has now been 2 ½ years for us).

Since 1 April I no longer have to stay at the office, only dealing with the liquidation of the business now and again, though unfortunately there is still no final agreement with the heirs of my partner in sight. – I want to make use of this breather, now that it has come at last after 10 years, first of all to rest thoroughly and overcome my previous fatigue and constant inclination to headaches. As I have to take things easy entirely for that, I will have little of interest to report for the next while. But I think this division of my strength is urgently necessary for my future plans.

At the moment, it looks as if we will probably marry in Germany at the end of August. I plan to visit Teddie in O. at the end of May to take a look at the terrain myself, and then we intend to return to Frankfurt together. Naturally it would be splendid if we managed to insert a detour of a few days to Paris on the way back, so that the meeting we have been planning for so long could finally take place. Perhaps you could contact Teddie, as we do not know how your summer plans are looking. I am already imagining the two of you showing me Paris, not least outdoing each other with discoveries at the world exhibition. As you know, I would forgo entire schools of pretty dancing girls for that. But we would also find time for conversations à deux, and thus the concluding discussion about chapter 2, which I dare say could then join many of our old favourite. –

Regarding Montherlant's 'jeunes filles': for today, I will only say that – alongside numerous details – I was slightly disappointed; we speak just as beautifully about love, and even the play on words of tombeau–tomber [tomb–to fall] and Falle–fallen [trap–to fall] has already been invented. French novels can often put one off altogether. But please do not take these as malicious comments, but simply – in the sense of the end of the previous paragraph – as a compliment. A bientôt, with warm embraces

from your

Felicitas.

Original: manuscript.

132 GRETEL KARPLUS TO WALTER BENJAMIN BERLIN, 30.4.1937

30 April 37.

Dear Detlef,

I see that my last letter already pre-empted some of your questions, so here are the remaining answers today: the 2nd Montherlant[1] has arrived, but has not yet been begun. – I am no longer in contact with the Tau Cassirer Verlag, the [x] costs 5–6 RM. – The Jean Paul edition by Reclam is out of print, and there is no other cheap one! – I hope I chose the right colours for the buttons. – Still a strong tendency towards headaches; once it finally stops raining I will include daily walks in my sanatorium programme. – The information about Jochmann[2] on the supplementary blue sheet. –

I have the feeling that you are establishing a good business connection with our transatlantic friends, and finally do not have to worry about every sous. No one is happier about that than I am.

Let me hear from you very soon, fond regards

ever your
Felicitas

~~Jochmann~~
~~Room furnishings~~
~~Dentist~~
~~Offenbach~~
~~Meeting~~
Theatre
Caillois
Levana /
~~French language~~
~~*Summer plans~~

Original: manuscript with handwritten keywords by Benjamin.

1 Probably the novel *Pitié pour les femmes* [Pity for Women], which was also published in 1936.

2 The 'supplementary blue sheet' has not survived among Benjamin's belongings.

133 GRETEL KARPLUS TO WALTER BENJAMIN
BERLIN, 15.6.1937

15 June 37.

My dear Detlef,

please, please do not be cross if there is too little in my letters, my life is really very monotonous and uninteresting, nothing to report, unless you also read my frequently gloomy thoughts between the lines. A telegram from New York just now, everything fine. I arrived here pretty exhausted, met by your friendly greeting, and to get a little rest at least I am going to Binz / Rügen, Villa Aegir until c. 5/8 July, if I do not unfortunately have to come to Berlin as a witness for an appointment. Then I will sit there all by myself and long for my good friends.

Books still in Westfälische Str.: Balzac Contes Drolatiques; Peau de Chagrin, Flaubert Madame Bovary; Asselineau Mélanges Bibliothèque Romantique.

Yes, I deserve your damning judgement:[1] reliable, but yielding little, and yet I even hope that you will nonetheless continue to count me among your friends. Very very warm regards your Felicitas

Original: manuscript.

1 Not preserved.

134 GRETEL KARPLUS TO WALTER BENJAMIN
BERLIN, 30.6.1937

30 June 1937.

Dear Detlef,

I suppose I should now really congratulate you (both), according to the telegram – the only news I have had at all for the whole time – we will be staying in England for a while. Recalling the 'squint of self-contemplation',[1] I am doing my best to prevent the Kafkaesque quality of my present situation from becoming apparent, rather imagining the purely subjective advantages of this judgement as far as possible. In all this, your friendship is one of the few objective, authentic ones.

It is pleasant here; this final taste of solitude has its advantages too. I am taking a lot of walks in the country, where the cornfields have not yet been cut; it is very much like July 31 (?), when we visited Asja and Daga in Ebertswalde.

And now that you know how things are here, one request: please do not go to Denmark. Perhaps you find it presumptuous of me and do not think I am entitled to say such a thing, but ultimately I do think you will understand what I mean without any further explanation.

I hope you will soon have good news for me about Stefan. I wish you a good recovery and a pleasant time, very warm regards

ever your

Felicitas.

Original: manuscript.

1 Benjamin uses this phrase [*der Silberblick der Selbstbesinnung*] in his book on German tragic drama to describe Hamlet's immersion in melancholy (*GS* 1 [1], p. 335).

135 WALTER BENJAMIN TO THEODOR WIESENGRUND-ADORNO AND GRETEL ADORNO
PARIS, 23.9.1937

Dear Teddie,

when I received your letter[1] of 13 September, for which I send you my warm thanks, I had been carrying in my pocket for several days a letter that I had written to you, yet without being able to decide on sending it.

On returning to Paris I was struck a blow[2] that was especially threatening under the present circumstances. Through an extremely disloyal, but entirely inexorable combination of events, I lost my room in the rue Bénard to a tenant who was deemed preferable; his offer could not be rivalled for the mere reason that he, being in possession of an expulsion order, had an interest in unregistered habitation.

This could not have been more dismaying than it is at a moment when, as a result of the exhibition, the Paris hotel prices, including even those of the lowliest dives, have increased by a half or more. A remotely humane accommodation would have been so far beyond the realm of my means that I had to decide to accept a compensation offer of a few hundred francs from the new tenant, so that I could pluck up the courage to find a decent room. This turned out as one could easily have foreseen: the 600 francs could not be obtained. My unfit attempts to do so and interviews in hotel offices, which were sometimes more like begging trips, took up all my time.

You will understand my hesitance to send you a letter written under such circumstances. Then finally a few days ago I received an offer from Else Herzberger to let me stay in her maidservant's room for the duration of her trip to America. rebus sic stantibus [Things being thus], there was nothing else for me to do but accept it. (The room is not within Else H.'s apartment, but rather by itself in the courtyard.) As soon as its current inhabitant has cleared it out, my address will be Boulogne (Seine) 1 rue du Château.

Yesterday I had an opportunity to speak to Max about all this. No one knows how strong my desire, how firm my resolve had been to refrain from taking any direct initiative in the economic realm better than you. But this most recent and unforeseeable incident left me with no choice.

It is my intention, as I told Max, to secure myself against such interventions – albeit on the most modest scale – as soon as possible and rent a closed studio or a one-room apartment. The furnishings will have to be found. Max received my account of the situation with complete understanding, and assured me that he will take the necessary steps as soon as he returns. He has now also told me of his own accord that – quite independently of the devaluation of the franc – he had already been intending to reach a new arrangement with me at the end of the year. Should it fall through before then, I have at least been circumspect enough to ensure that I shall get through even this extremely difficult September without having to ask Max for any direct help.

One of the immediate consequences of the situation is that the next few weeks will only partly be productive in terms of my work. I am starting my search for quarters, and it will not be an easy one. Let me extend my warm congratulations to you and Felizitas on the occasion of moving into your own. This brings me to your last letter. You will meanwhile have realized that my silence stemmed not from any offended sensibility, but rather from inevitable circumstances. So let that be the end of it!

I am extremely grateful to you for discussing my affairs at length with Max in London. Since then we have only had the one evening in Paris, and as it went particularly well and with a new homogeneity in our mood, we did not discuss all the technical aspects that would have merited it. So it is from your letter that I now know of the decision to set up a fund for the Arcades books, on which I can congratulate myself. As far as Adrienne Monnier is concerned, I will try everything to arrange contact between her and Max[3] in the next few days. At any rate, this matter has been settled as we had intended. The suggestion to receive the proofs for the journal from you in future is the most welcome one you could have made.

As I said, such questions were only touched on, if that, in my conversation with Max, which continued late into the night. It was of great significance for me, as Max told me for the first time about the notable economic and legal constellations from which he had to draw the resources on which the institute is based. The subject alone is fascinating; what is more, I have seldom seen Max in better humour. Before that we went to a small restaurant on the place des Abesses, which I have noted for the next visit from you and Felizitas. Unfortunately it seems we shall have to be patient for a little longer. But at least then I can hope to receive you in an apartment of my own when the moment comes.

As for the Berg,[4] I wrote immediately to my former wife with the request to make enquiries at the post office in San Remo. I have not heard anything yet, but I hope you have received the book in the meantime.

It would make me very happy – especially at the moment – if I could have some news from you very soon. You should send it to the rue Nicolo – it will follow me to Boulogne if necessary.

Warmest regards

yours Walter

Dear Felizitas,

the request that concludes my letter to Teddie should expressly apply to you too. Write soon, but above all at length.

Now you have seen how easily the rebus[5] was solved. So that similarly angry passages – which I hope will soon be a thing of the past – will not lead to a similar silence, please do your best to uphold our correspondence in a more lively fashion than lately in Berlin. I will not keep you waiting for a response.

For today fond regards

from Detlef

23 September 1937
Paris XVI
Villa Nicolo
3 rue Nicolo

Original: manuscript.

1 See *Adorno–Benjamin Correspondence*, pp. 207–11.

2 Ursel Bud had already written the following to Benjamin in San Remo on 27 August: 'I do not know if you are aware that my uncle [no further information], who has a semi-official position, has a special task to accomplish here with a number of high-ranking functionaries. The execution of this matter, which has been slightly delayed, requires that my uncle retain his current address. [Paragraph] Your letter [not preserved] stating that you will already be arriving here on 1 September has therefore put me in a difficult position; on the one hand, you know how happy I would be to have you here again, but on the other hand I cannot allow the clearing of your room on the part of my uncle

at the moment. For not only do I have an interest in the completion of his task here; associates of my uncle have also granted me the work permit I have been striving to obtain for years, as the accommodation of my uncle is causing me some problems. [Paragraph] You will probably not be able to understand all this entirely, but I cannot be any more explicit on paper, as you will understand if I repeat that it is a semi-official matter. [Paragraph] My uncle, who finds you quite especially likeable, has racked his brains with me to work out how we can spare you any inconvenience or discomfort. In the end, however, the only solution we could find was to ask that for a short while (it can only be a matter of two to three weeks) you either manage as you are doing at present, or in a different way of your choosing. Naturally my uncle will be happy to reimburse you for the expenses resulting from this interregnum.'

3 On Benjamin's recommendation, Horkheimer was planning to establish a close connection between Adrienne Monnier and the institute, not least to counteract the journal's lack of presence in Paris and the dearth of qualified French employees.

4 See *Alban Berg: Mit Bergs eigenen Schriften und Beiträgen vom Theodor Wiesengrund-Adorno und Ernst Křenek* [Alban Berg: With Berg's own Writings and Contributions from Theodor Wiesengrund-Adorno and Ernst Křenek] (Vienna, Leipzig and Zurich, 1937).

5 See *Adorno–Benjamin Correspondence*, p. 210.

136 GRETEL ADORNO TO WALTER BENJAMIN LONDON, 29.9.1937

Zweite Nachtmusik
(Aron's book)
New York decision — 29 Sept. 37.
Trip to England
Trip to Denmark
Chevaliers de la Table
Apartment (Dora)
Sternberger
Weil
(Brecht)
Topper

My dear Detlef,

you have indeed given me an incredibly difficult task: continuing a separate correspondence with you alongside Teddie. Here I am now, sitting between 2 scholars with my stammerings, constantly aware that, in dismay at all my faux pas, they are both trying to improve me. Is it not bold of me to dare nonetheless?

Do you think it impossible that you could come to London for a few weeks next year? I am sure one can live here for 100£. I thought of it because you yourself said that, for anyone with eyes, there is much to see here.

I followed your suggestion, and I do think you are right. The opera house with the market-hall and the splendid bathing-house not far from our future apartment alone are already worth the effort.

How are things progressing with your room? Can you not live with your sister for the time being? –

On Sunday I had my first taste of the English countryside, the famous Cots Wols.[1] Oh, what a peculiar country it is: the villages look like shabby towns, but there too one finds private houses, not farmyards; it is all old, but barely distinguishable from the new. And the gamekeepers hang animal carcasses (small birds of prey, rabbits, hedgehogs, moles) on the trees so that one can see how zealously they protect the pheasants from all harm for the landowner's hunting pleasure. I wonder whether the full-blown barbarism of America might not be preferable after all? Though I still feel well here and as Frau Dr. W.[2] There have been two rather nice films: 'Easy Money' and 'Topper'.[3] I have proved my good faith to you today, so do not look too sternly on my attempt. Fond regards

ever your

Felicitas

Original: manuscript with handwritten keywords by Benjamin.

1 This refers to the Cotswolds.

2 Gretel Karplus had left Germany in August and married Wiesengrund-Adorno in London on 8 September.

3 The first of these American films had been made in 1936, and the second, which featured Cary Grant, in 1937.

137 WALTER BENJAMIN TO GRETEL ADORNO AND THEODOR WIESENGRUND-ADORNO BOULOGNE SUR SEINE, 2.10.1937

Boulogne s. Seine
1, rue du Château, le 2/ 10/ 37

My dear Felizitas,

Though in future I may direct the letters sometimes to the one, sometimes to the other of you, they will for the most part be meant for you both. As I do not wish to deviate from accustomed forms of address, allow me to retain this alternation.

The irregular rhythm of my messages, the deviation even from their external norm, the change of address – all this should tell you that things are not in the best state for me. Max knows this, and I am reckoning with his intervention before the end of the month.

For now I am living, as I told you, in the chambre de bonne of E.H. As soon as Max sets me up I shall look for a one-room apartment.

The way things have been going in recent weeks, you will not be expecting any news on the Baudelaire or the Arcades. Through a happy coincidence, a newer study[1] is now on my daily agenda. Max introduced me to Oprecht,[2] and we arranged for an extended informational essay on the effectiveness of the institute for 'Mass und Wert'. We are not overlooking the editorial difficulties. But I think the influence of Oprecht will be sufficient to overcome them.

In the light of the current interruptions, I am doubly sorry that I cannot compensate with any older news. There is only a single copy of the final version of the reproduction study; that will have to wait until you come to Paris. – Teddie has raised my hopes for the second week of October. How I hope it is no vain hope this time!

I had a long evening with Max, as I related to you. This was followed by a brief afternoon, during which we paid Mme Monnier a visit. What Teddie prepared has thus been realized in the most welcome fashion. If October brings you here, then also to the rue de l'Odéon.

Now to your 'Husserl'.[3] (And here, dear Teddie, I hope you will allow a switch of address.) There have – Max volunteered this information without any questioning on my part – been objections to your study in New York. I have no idea whether they came from Löwenthal;[4] but Max did give me an idea of their content. The general attack on idealistic epistemology, which latter seems to have been entirely liquidated in the form of phenomenology, has evidently set things in motion through its far-reaching implications. At the same time, Max assured me that – as of course goes without saying – he plans to study the essay with the greatest curiosity and attentiveness. He is, no doubt as a result of your conversation in New York, entirely aware of its basic intention. Do not place too much value on these provisional impressions, however, especially as I daresay you will soon receive a first-hand account from New York.

I did not have a chance to borrow your 'Zweite Nachtmusik'[5] from Max. I hope I can expect a copy of it very soon. And my warm thanks again for 'Ensemble'.[6]

Dudow[7] was very happy to receive your letter. I would have liked to introduce him to Max. But there was not enough time. The idea of your essay collection on mass art made no less of an impression on him than on me. If only I knew how we could make progress in the matter, whether with or without him!

Sohn-Rethel has not been showing his face any more. Kracauer is also difficult to contact. And as I do not have a telephone, I am somewhat dependent on the initiative of others.

– As Teddie realizes, I agree with his criticism of Caillois,[8] especially his assessment of the political function of his study. I am not sure, however, that one should really characterize it as 'vulgar materialism'. Whatever diplomatic expenses a conversation with him 'inter pares' might incur, I might add, I would be in favour of retaining the plan to do so.

Tell me soon how you are settling in to your new apartment and what you make of London on closer inspection? and whether you will occasionally travel to Germany?

When you do so, will you please let me know what you have arranged for the French volumes you are still keeping for me? I would be happy if you had them with you in London. Otherwise, would it be possible to send them to me as a registered parcel?

To someone living in Paris, the political prospects seem extremely bleak. As soon as one crosses the road, one encounters the figurants from the American Legion[9] and feels entirely surrounded by fascism. I hope I can soon close myself off from these impressions in the material of my work.

Write to me without delay. And accept my warmest greetings

Original: typescript duplicate.

1 See 'Ein deutsches Institute freier Forschung' [A German Institute of Free Research], in *Mass und Wert* 1 (1937–8), pp. 818–22 (issue 5, May–June 1938); *GS* 3, pp. 518–26.

2 The Zurich publisher Emil Oprecht, who published the journal.

3 Adorno was intending to publish the final chapter of his Oxford Husserl dissertation in German in the *Zeitschrift für Sozialforschung* (see *Adorno–Benjamin Correspondence*, p. 176), The multiply revised essay version did not appear there, however; the 1938 version became 'Zur Philosophie Husserls'; see *GS* 20 [1], pp. 46–118.

4 Leo Löwenthal (1900–1993), born in Frankfurt and a friend of Adorno and Kracauer, had gained his PhD in 1923 with a dissertation on Franz von Baader and subsequently worked as a secondary-school teacher before becoming a member of the Institut für Sozialforschung. Löwenthal was editor-in-chief of the *Zeitschrift für Sozialforschung* from 1932 to 1941.

5 It was only published posthumously; see *GS* 18, pp. 45–53.

6 A set of musical aphorisms by Adorno; see *GS* 16, pp. 275–80, and *GS* 18, 40–4.

7 The director Slatan Dudow (1903–1963), who had made *Kuhle Wampe* with Brecht, was chosen as the film adviser for the institute's project 'Massenkunst im Monopolkapitalismus' [Mass Art in Monopoly Capitalism]. The project was abandoned.

8 See *Adorno–Benjamin Correspondence*, pp. 212–13; Adorno then wrote a critical review of Roger Caillois's 'La Mante religieuse: Recherches sur la nature et la signification du mythe' (Paris: La Maison des Amis des Livres, 1937) for the *Zeitschrift für Sozialforschung*; see *ZfS* 7 (1938), pp. 410f. (issue 3); *GS* 20 [1], pp. 229f.

9 An American veterans' association, founded in Paris in 1919, with right-wing leanings.

138 GRETEL ADORNO TO WALTER BENJAMIN LONDON, 1.12.1937

1 December 1937.

My dear Detlef,

so, we will most probably be going to the Villa Verde in San Remo during the second half of December and staying until January. The thought of having to spend Christmas and New Year in London is so dreadful that even packing and the long journey seem relaxing by comparison. Would it not be possible for us to meet down there? I cannot imagine that it would cost you more than in Paris, and we would then have plenty of time together, especially the two of us, as Teddie intends to continue his work in San Remo and finish the Wagner text.[1] –

As far as I am informed, the books are entirely beyond reach at the moment, together with mine in the big box. I am already greatly looking forward to seeing you again soon, warmest regards

ever

your Felicitas.

Original: manuscript

1 Adorno's *Versuch über Wagner* [Essay on Wagner], from which some chapters were published in the *Zeitschrift für Sozialforschung* under the title 'Fragmente über Wagner'; see *GS* 13, pp. 7–148. English translation: *In Search of Wagner*, trans. Rodney Livingstone (London: Verso, 1981).

139 GRETEL ADORNO TO WALTER BENJAMIN LONDON, 15.1.1938

15 Jan. 1938.

Dear Detlef,

after a few pleasant days in Brussels and a peaceful crossing between two storms, we are now back in our beloved London. According to some recent news, the departure from Europe with the Champlain has been postponed until 16 February. We do not yet know how we will divide our time; perhaps Teddie will still come to Paris after all, otherwise he will begin preparing the text of the Wagner at the start of next week. Good luck moving into your new apartment, fond regards

ever your Felicitas

Please do send us back the manuscript from Frick.[1]

Original: postcard; stamp: Paddington, 17 Jan. 1938. Manuscript.

1 No further information.

140 THEODOR WIESENGRUND-ADORNO AND GRETEL ADORNO TO WALTER BENJAMIN LONDON, 1.2.1938

1 February 1938.

Dear Walter:

Lazarsfeld,[1] the man who arranged the radio research commission for me, sent me a memorandum on the project and asked me to give him a response and compile a list of radio 'problems'. I will spare you his memorandum and my letter of reply. But this list has now grown into an exposé[2] not unlike the one I wrote on jazz, and as Sohn-Rethel had the friendly enthusiasm to copy out this exposé, I can send it to you and ask you to keep the duplicate. It goes without saying that I would be extremely interested in your opinion on the matter. If you wish to show Kracauer the exposé, I have no objections. I would only like to add that, for reasons you will understand, I have dealt with the one problem closest to my heart – namely, what happens to music that overflows,[3] that *no one* listens to – in a very watered-down form. In this context, the exposé essentially mentions only music that is pushed into the background, but not music that is not heard *at all*, and *that* is precisely the music most important to us. But I did not wish to hasten my admission to the lunatic asylum unnecessarily. In that sense alone, I am by no means certain about the effect of the exposé. But I do at least wish to share with you my view that music to which no one listens leads to disaster. I am still very much lacking a theoretical justification; but I do think that the relationship between music and our times is involved here.

Apart from that, I can also report that the first chapter of the Wagner is finished, and the second will be completed in the next few days. I have seldom found a study so enjoyable to write. I am, incidentally, seeking to keep the text as free from official philosophical jargon as I can.

As I have not received any telegram from New York regarding a possible trip to Paris, I assume that nothing will come of it. Which makes me await your response all the more impatiently.

Warm regards,

yours Teddie

Dear Detlef thank you for your card[4] and the Frick manuscript. Alfred Sohn has a theory[5] about radio and film as socialized sensory organs that complements Frick's ideas in a certain sense; apart from that he has the same ghostly brilliance as ever, but naturally we do not get to see any of the results of his work. Fond regards ever

your Felicitas

Original: typescript and manuscript.

1 The Vienna-born sociologist Paul Felix Lazarsfeld (1901–1976) had already moved to America in 1933; he directed the Princeton Radio Research project, in which Adorno had charge of the musical part.

2 It bears the title 'Fragen und Thesen' [Questions and Theses]; see Adorno and Horkheimer, *Briefwechsel II*, pp. 503–24.

3 For the passage in Adorno's exposé see Adorno and Horkheimer, *Briefwechsel II*, pp. 512–15.

4 The card does not appear to have survived.

5 See *Adorno–Sohn-Rethel Correspondence*, pp. 73–8.

141 THEODOR WIESENGRUND-ADORNO AND GRETEL ADORNO TO WALTER BENJAMIN NEW YORK, 7.3.1938

PRINCETON UNIVERSITY
PRINCETON NEW JERSEY

—

SCHOOL OF PUBLIC AND INTERNATIONAL AFFAIRS

OFFICE OF RADIO RESEARCH
203 ENO HALL 7 March 1938.

Dear Walter:

this is simply to give you a sign, in the inconceivable rush of the first weeks – which I have to devote entirely to the radio project – to say that we had a good journey and a safe arrival, and have settled in a very pleasant provisional apartment. The radio project is turning out to be a matter of extraordinary possibilities and enormous publicity. I am responsible for the entire musical side, and beyond that really the overall theoretical leadership, as Lazarsfeld, the official director, who brought me here, deals primarily with the organization of the work.

Today I would ask you to send me a very short report, 2 to 3 typewritten pages, with your name, about your experiments with 'listening models'[1] in Germany. I would like to take it into the archive and address it in the memorandum, and I think it is by no means out of the question that it will have some practical benefits for you.

Regarding my work at the institute, all I will say today is that I have had to put the Wagner on hold for a few weeks on account of the excess of work for the radio business; that Max's Montaigne essay[2] is entirely in agreement with our concerns, occupying itself not so much with a critique of Montaigne as with the functional shift of scepticism, and is quite excellent in my opinion, not least as an opportunity for political observations; that Gretel and I are labouring at Kracauer's manuscript,[3] though without seeing much potential in it. I am still uncertain as to whether any of it is publishable at all; it seems beyond doubt, on the other hand, that it would only be possible to salvage any of it by completely dismantling it and piecing together minute fragments. Kracauer has completely overlooked the major topic of advertising, which presents itself very clearly in the quoted material, for the sake of his socio-psychological platitudes. The theoretical construction is undisciplined and improvisatory, and the entire material is second-hand. – It seems that my Mannheim will be scrapped entirely, and will be disseminated among a few people merely in the form of typewriter manuscripts and proof copies; the

Husserl, on the other hand, should be appearing in some guise or other, admittedly with considerable cuts. A significant inhibiting factor is something I would also like to point out to you regarding the Baudelaire: that the journal will be reduced to its original length once again, which precludes the publication of texts that exceed a length of 2½ printed sheets.

As we both expected, we are not finding it difficult to adapt to the living conditions here. It is sérieusement much more European here than in London, and 7th Avenue, which is close to us, is as peacefully reminiscent of the boulevard Montparnasse as Greenwich Village, where we live, is of Mont St Geneviève. If you were over here, we would be as satisfied as one still can be in a world dominated half by Chamberlain's politics with Hitler and half by Stalin's justice. Letters will reach us most quickly and safely in our private residence: 45 Christopher Street, 11 G, New York City, N. Y. USA. So please do not be put off by the chameleon-like letterhead, and write to us very soon; also tell us when Scholem's arrival can be expected, and under what sign of the Cabbala one should most likely envisage his stay in Manhattan. Fond regards from us both your old

Teddie

Dear Detlef:

I not only like it better here than in London, but am also quite convinced that you would feel exactly the same. What amazes me most is the fact that things here are by no means all as new and advanced as one would really think; on the contrary: one can observe the contrast between the most modern and the most shabby things wherever one goes. There is no need to search for the surreal here, for one stumbles over it at every step. The skyscrapers are imposing in the early evening, but later, when the offices have closed and the lights are sparser, they remind one of insufficiently illuminated European mews. And just think, there are stars here and a horizontal moon and splendid sunsets like those in the height of summer. – E. was here for the weekend, he is genuinely in excellent shape; I am only curious how long he will be able to bear his relatively peaceful life. – You simply cannot imagine how much I wish you were here. But I fear you are so fond of your arcades that you cannot part with their splendid architecture, and once you have closed that door, it is possible that a new subject could interest you again. Please do not laugh at me too much and let me hear from you very soon.

Your old Felizitas, far from home.

Felicitas

Original: typescript with printed letterhead.

1 Benjamin's 'Hörmodelle'; see *GS* 4 [2], pp. 627–720, and the editor's note on pp. 1053f. The text 'Hörmodelle' (ibid., p. 628) may only have been written in early 1938 following the request made by Adorno in the letter.

2 See Max Horkheimer, 'Montaigne und die Funktion der Skepsis', in *ZfS* 7 (1938), pp. 1–52 (issue 1–2); in Horkheimer, *Gesammelte Schriften*, vol. 4: *Schriften 1936–1941*, ed. Alfred Schmidt (Frankfurt am Main: Fischer, 1988), pp. 236–94.

3 Kracauer had received a scholarship for his study 'Die totalitäre Propaganda Deutschlands und Italiens' [Totalitarian Propaganda in Germany and Italy], which he wrote in Paris. Adorno abridged the extensive text for a planned publication in the institute journal. Kracauer rejected this version, however, and it was not published.

142 WALTER BENJAMIN TO THEODOR WIESENGRUND-ADORNO AND GRETEL ADORNO PARIS, 27.3.1938

27 March 1938.
10, rue Dombasle
Paris (15e)

Dear Teddie!

I was very happy finally to receive news from you, and such good news. After all, neither you nor I have been spoilt with good news of late.

As you can imagine, I was glad to see that at least my son had escaped the miserable situation in Austria. One hardly dares think about what is going on in Vienna unless one is absolutely forced to.

I hope there is some truth in what I heard from Krenek: that he has essentially terminated his Austrian employment and gone to America.[1]

Scholem has also been there for some time, but has not written me a single line, so I do not know if he is in Newyork [*sic*], Chicago or wherever. If you have connections to Jewish circles in Newyork, you should probably be able to find him quite easily.

You can imagine that current events are prompting me to seek naturalization most vigorously. As ever with such matters, one is suddenly faced with difficulties one had not reckoned with; at the moment they consist in acquiring a vast number of papers. All this is also consuming a great deal of time.

As uncertain as the success of the undertaking may be, now is an especially appropriate time to pursue it – even if it were simply to contribute a further dossier to the files of the Ministry of Justice.

Perhaps Max told you that I have received the proofs of the institute essay[2] from 'Mass und Wert' – a result that was not easy to obtain from the dangerous saboteur that Lion[3] is.

It means a great deal that your new study is leading to the significant prospects you had envisaged with your exposé. In other matters, Felicitas's description of your area touched me in a homely fashion. It is an old desire of mine to be seduced away to certain cities, and it almost seems to me that you are on the right track for that.

I unexpectedly received some 10 or 20 volumes[4] from the remainder of my library that was left in Berlin. I am very much considering having the Danish books[5] around me too in the near future.

If, Felicitas, you should happen upon my French books while unpacking, please have them sent to me through the institute as quickly as possible.

I have been told that many people are fleeing from Prague. I do not know if it would be so prudent for Ernst to remain there. But perhaps he is going to Lodz!?

The listening models are among the manuscripts I had to relinquish when I left Germany. I have reconstructed the structure of those studies from memory as far as possible. I enclose the exposé.

Write to me soon at *great* length.

Greetings to the friends and warm regards to you both

Yours,

Walter

P.S. Let me name two book titles[6] here that might interest you in connection with your Wagner study:

Walter Lange: Richard Wagner's Sippe, Leipzig 1938, Verlag Beck

Eugen Schmidt's: Richard Wagner wie wir ihn heute sehen, Dresden 1938, von Baensch Stiftung.

Original: typescript.

1 Křenek arrived in America on 31 August.

2 'Ein deutsches Institut freier Forschung'.

3 Ferdinand Lion (1883–1965) was editor-in-chief of *Mass und Wert*.

4 Benjamin's sister Dora had notified him of the sending of three packages from Berlin in her letter of 8 March; she does not name the volumes.

5 These are the books Benjamin had left with Brecht in Skovsbostrand.

6 Benjamin made a mistake with the name of the second author; the complete titles are: Walter Lange, *Richard Wagners Sippe: Vom Urahn zum Enkel* [Richard Wagner's Family: From Ancestors to Grandchildren] (Leipzig, 1938), and Eugen Schmitz, *Richard Wagner, wie wir ihn heute sehen* [Richard Wagner as We See Him Today] (Dresden: Verlag Heimatwerk Sachsen, 1937) (Schriftenreihe Grosse Sachsen, Diener des Reiches [Great Saxons Text Series, Servants of the Empire], 2).

143 GRETEL ADORNO TO WALTER BENJAMIN NEW YORK, 1.4.1938

1 April 1938.

Dear Detlef,

why are we hearing absolutely nothing from you? Or at least, only very indirectly. For on Sunday we made the acquaintance of Scholem at Tillich's place. Aside from his strangely brash Berlin Jewish way of speaking, I was quite impressed; I particularly liked his intensity and passion. I hope we will see him more often once he is back from Cincinnati. –

Teddie is working like a real horse and dragging his Wagner along. Nine chapters have already been dictated, the fifth is being typed at the moment. What perhaps makes the work more difficult is the fact that an abridged version of only c. 40 printed pages is already supposed to be finished by the start of May, as the essay is urgently needed for the next issue. Naturally Teddie completed the complete version first nonetheless. As well as that, he has also written a big English memorandum[1] of 150–200 pages. I am simply trying to take some of the burden off Teddie, who works mostly at home, as best I can. For the moment, his labour is required more here than elsewhere, which is naturally extremely pleasing.

Have you meanwhile heard anything from Ernst Bloch? – Is there really no possibility of producing an extended German version of the reproduction study? I would be *very* happy to copy it out, so that I could at least make some contribution to its dissemination in German, even if it is only in the form of hand copies passed from reader to reader. The very fondest regards ever your old

Felicitas

Original: manuscript.

1 It bears the title 'Music in Radio'.

144 GRETEL ADORNO TO WALTER BENJAMIN
NEW YORK, 10.4.1938

10 April 1938.

Dear Detlef,

it is Sunday morning, Teddie is still sleeping; for we only returned home very late. First a small dinner party at Max's and then we all went to a nice little night-club [*sic*] for an appearance by Lenya. Yes, it is all here and in fact even more concentrated than in Berlin; there is such a strong feeling of being taken back to the years 25–32 that it sometimes feels quite eerie, and one asks oneself: what then? But I still do not know anything about America's domestic policy and its economic structure, perhaps everything is different here after all, let us hope that this hiding-place will remain for a while yet. –

Your letter about listening models arrived in good shape. I only heard that Max was singing the praises of your essay about the institute, which I am afraid I have still not seen. – did you receive the literary section of the FZ? – Have you by any chance set eyes on the new book by Dolf Sternberger?[1] – How is the Jochmann Literatur business looking, did Irmgard Kummer[2] prove of any use? My books did arrive in New York, but are still at the depot, so I am afraid I must ask you to be patient for another few months. – From what he has read so far, Max is quite impressed by Teddie's Wagner, the essay or excerpt (it is still not clear how the short version will be produced) will appear with a foreword by Max. I do not think one can bring about any changes in the structure of the institute through impetuousness, at the most through a good example and a persistent expression of one's opinion. –

Well, now that you were so careless again in San Remo as to encourage me to write, I do not know where to end and seek your advice in a matter where you probably cannot help me very much, as you are not familiar with the circumstances: the relationship between my sister and E has developed in such a manner that they will probably marry. (You see, in these letters on delicate matters it is always E at the centre.) She generally pays a great deal of attention to my advice, and I have told her about all my reservations. Naturally I cannot hinder her, but I do always feel a certain responsibility for her, and I simply fear that this marriage could go wrong. Though I should add that I am on excellent terms with E once again and have nothing against him. I also know that she will certainly have plenty of fun with him, as far as that is actually possible nowadays; but the question is, on the other hand, whether she will not be paying a very high price for it. I still remember very well the letter you wrote me back then. Certainly, there is no rivalling candidate in Lotte's case, but I do wonder if the sentence[3] 'in me you have someone you cannot rely on' is not also true of E. My mother, whose petty bourgeois character has given her a strong aversion to E after a single encounter, will naturally lay the great curse upon us all; but that is not significant; naturally she does not know anything either, just as everything has still been left open here. Lotte will now be coming to New York for three months and will then probably live here; but I hardly think that E will bear it in Boston in the long run, and would really expect him to move sooner or later.

What news do you have of Stefan?

Did the spa trip help your sister?

Let me hear from you very soon in all friendship

ever

your

Felicitas.

blonde Lenja
Literature section
~~Sternberger (Löwenthal)~~
Jochmann (Kummer)
Paris
My books
E's marriage
Stefan
Dora's spa trip
Scholem a Frankist?

Original: manuscript with keywords written by Benjamin on the left corner of the first page.

1 See Dolf Sternberger, *Panorama oder Ansichten vom 19. Jahrhundert* [Panorama or Views of the 19th Century] (Hamburg, 1938). Benjamin wrote a highly critical review of the book; it was not, however, published in his lifetime. See *GS* 3, pp. 572–9.

2 Unknown.

3 It is taken from Brecht's poem 'Vom armen B. B.' [The Tale of Poor B. B.].

145 WALTER BENJAMIN TO THEODOR WIESENGRUND-ADORNO AND GRETEL ADORNO PARIS, 16.4.1938

10, rue Dombasle
Paris, XVe
16.4.1938

Dear Teddie,

Your Gaston Easter card[1] arrived here yesterday.

Now I must tell you that I only learned of the relationship[2] to which you allude as if it were a known fact through that same allusion of yours. So there we are, you and I, waving at each other like little leaves on the family tree; and as we have already managed well enough before now in the language of the zephyr, we shall, with God's help, draw all the more from the storms that lie ahead.

I was especially pleased to see Egon now flanked by two helpers less fickle than those of K. but equally cunning, and of whom one can say that they are always more or less up to date with the goings-on at the 'Castle'. Feel free to pass this firm conviction on to him; may it compensate for the length of the congratulatory cable.

If I think about it, you are receiving this long letter only on account of the aforementioned new title; for I do not believe I have received a detailed response from you to my previous letter yet. Though admittedly I am not counting the Wagner, in which I have now reached the fourth chapter. I discovered a wealth of attractive, and in part very important motifs in it. I must, however, have access to the complete text and the chance to study it before you can expect any meaningful comments from me. The subject, as you know, places a few obstacles in my path, which are unfortunately magnified through the nature of the copy you sent me. It is pale, and makes for arduous reading; I hope you will send me a better one if you can spare it at all.

I was especially taken with the remarks on the 'guiding' quality[3] of Wagner's music. I also found your reflections on Wagner's language[4] in contrast to Schubert's word-setting in 'Forest and Cave' – a quotation from Faust that can certainly show its face here! – highly attractive. I need hardly add that your insights regarding allegory in the leitmotif[5] are particularly significant for me. – I am looking forward to the moment when I can wander about through the text and be able to find all my own thoughts within it.

Now it is time for a word to you, dear Felizitas, to send you my best wishes for Easter and all that accompanies it; and to thank you for your lines of 1 April, which made me very happy. Your willingness to copy out the reproduction study for me is of incalculable value. I accept your offer with the greatest joy. You will receive the manuscript as soon as I find the time to read it through again. It very much seems that your intervention has raised a lucky star over my opuscule. Yesterday I succeeded in recovering the manuscript of 'Berliner Kindheit' from Levy-Ginsberg,[6] and now there is even a prospect of obtaining the Rowohlt copies[7] you managed to make off with some time ago.

I have no difficulties in admitting that Elisabeth[8] is an extremely charming and remarkable creature. Unfortunately she floated away from here very soon; perhaps she will float back again some time.

The following news should be suitable for bridging the gap between this present note and our interrupted correspondence.

Dolf Sternberger has just put out his book 'Panorama – Ansichten des 19. Jahrhunderts' (published by Goverts – i.e. Claassens – in Hamburg). The title is in fact an admission of his attempt to plagiarize my work – and he is indeed the first to succeed in doing so – for the very idea on which the book is based; one finds the concept of my 'Arcades' filtered doubly here. Of the parts that managed to make their way through Sternberger's skull (filter 1), only those permitted by the National Chamber of Literature (filter 2) have become manifest. You can easily imagine what was left of it. The programmatic statement one can find in the 'Aphoristic Foreword' may also help you in doing so: 'Conditions and actions, compulsion and freedom, matter and spirit or innocence and guilt cannot be separated from one another when examining the past, whose immutable traces, as scattered and incomplete a form as they may assume, lie before us. For all of these are in fact always intertwined . . . We are dealing with the fortuity of history itself, which is merely caught and preserved in the fortuitous selection of quotations and in the fortuitous, unruly tangle of its characteristics, which nonetheless manifest themselves in the form of writing.'

Sternberger's indescribably impoverished conceptual apparatus has been pieced together from elements stolen from Bloch, from you and from myself. His references to the concept of allegory, which one finds every three pages, are a particularly shameful example. Two pitiful digressions on empathy[9] prove to me that he has also been dipping his fingers into the Elective Affinities essay. –

As he had to pander to the requirements of the National Chamber of Literature, he naturally did not dare to use any French, i.e. vital, sources. If you consider that it is the likes of Bölsche, Haeckel, Scheffel, Marlitt to whom he applies his imagined conceptual tools, you will have an accurate idea of what seems inconceivable when one has it before one's eyes in black and white.

It hardly seems surprising that the dear boy made his publishing debut with the Munich report on Hitler's speech[10] against degenerate art before setting to work on his present masterpiece.

I daresay you will order the book. Perhaps you can discuss with Max whether I should review – or, in plain German, denounce it.

I am entirely occupied with drawing up the scheme for the 'Baudelaire'; I have given Max a brief report on it. Having long piled up books upon books and excerpts upon excerpts, I am now seeking to lay the foundation for a completely transparent structure with a series of reflections. I hope it will have all the dialectical rigour of the Elective Affinities essay.

To conclude, a few months' worth of mixed post:

First of all a number of requests. To Felizitas, that she send me the French illustrated books as soon as she can, and preferably insured. And, to you, I repeat mine for your Kierkegaard. An equally important one would be for you to tell me a little about your encounters with Scholem, of which there have perhaps been more in the meantime. – I spoke to Jean Wahl[11] recently, right after his visit to Bergson. The latter is already imagining the Chinese marching into Paris – and this was while the Japanese were still winning. Wahl also reported that, according to Bergson, the railways are to blame for everything. (One might also ask what one will be able to get out of Jean Wahl when he is eighty years old.) – Grete de Francesco[12] passed through Paris. I only spoke to her on the telephone. She was terribly sad. Her parents, along with a sizeable fortune, are caught in the Austrian trap.

I hope I shall soon hear at great length from you and send my warmest greetings to you, Felizitas and the rest of our circle

Yours,
Walter

Original: typescript.

1 See *Adorno–Benjamin Correspondence*, p. 244.

2 The marriage of Liselotte Karplus (1909–?) and Egon Wissing took place on 30 May 1940.

3 See Adorno, *GS* 13, pp. 57 and 118.

4 See ibid., pp. 57f.

5 See ibid., pp. 43f.

6 As Benjamin's letter of 1 September to Gretel Karplus (letter no. 103) states, Arnold Levy had taken the last typescript duplicate of *Berliner Kindheit* with him in order to have a copy made.

7 See *GB* 4, letter no. 841, and the corresponding note.

8 This is Elisabeth Wiener, a friend of Gretel Adorno, after whom she had asked in her unpublished letter of 1 April.

9 They are to be found in Sternberger's book in the sections 'Die Religion der Tränen' [The Religion of Tears] and 'Edelblässe' [Noble Pallor].

10 See 'Tempel der Kunst: Adolf Hitler eröffnet das "Haus der Deutschen Kunst"' [Temple of Art: Adolf Hitler inaugurates the 'House of German Art'], in *Frankfurter Zeitung*, 19 July 1937 (vol. 81, no. 362), pp. 1f. (morning paper), and in the same issue, p. 3: 'Die festliche Stadt: Die Feiern zur Eröffnung des "Hauses der Deutschen Kunst"' [The Festive City: The Inaugural Celebrations for the 'House of German Art'].

11 The philosopher Jean Wahl (1888–1974), who had written on Kierkegaard, had taught at the Sorbonne since 1936.

12 This Austrian publicist worked for the *Frankfurter Zeitung*; her book *Die Macht des Charlatans* [The Power of the Charlatan] had been published in 1937.

146 WALTER BENJAMIN TO THEODOR WIESENGRUND-ADORNO AND GRETEL ADORNO PARIS, 19.6.1938

19.6.1938
10, rue Dombasle
Paris, XVe

Dear Teddie,

the time has come: I will now begin my letter regarding your 'Wagner', and will go straight to the heart of things, under the assumption that you are in less urgent need of learning the reasons for my letter's delay than what it has to say about the matter itself.

I have studied said matter to the extent that I can feel somewhat at home with it. I wish you had made these studies as easy for *me* as they will be for others; rebus sic stantibus, I sighed quietly to myself on several occasions: the copy is no source of joy to manuscript-lovers, and especially unsuited to detailed scrutiny.

The matter itself – to return to it now without further ado – is very rich in substance and possessed of the most amazing transparency. The unfavourable conditions under which I, being so unfamiliar with the material in question, have approached your essay serve as an excellent yardstick for it. I would not have thought it possible to gain a feeling for the most detailed technical examinations, let alone to have so clear a perspective on the other parts, on first reading. It goes without saying how much this testifies to the work's success.

As far as I can see, you have never written anything of comparable physiognomic incisiveness. Your portrait of Wagner is absolutely convincing from head to toe. You have shown masterfully how mindset and manner correspond in his case.

I cannot attempt, as I have sometimes done, to list individual elements that I consider especially successful in their content and formulation. (Though among the most compelling passages I will mention, at least in passing, the part in which you entwine the figure of Wotan and the beggar motif;[1] the 'German Socialism' in Wagner's stance;[2] the political illumination of the Ring motif; the portrayal of King Mark[3] as the forefather of the League of Nations, which I found every bit as vivid as the famous caricatures in the Evening News.)

As far as the central theme is concerned, I was especially captivated by how emphatically you reveal the specific 'formlessness'[4] that evidently pervades Wagner's works. The term 'guiding music'[5] – which I assume you coined yourself? – is a true find. I found your reference to the subtle shadings through which Wagnerian figures such as Wotan and Siegfried blend into each other equally instructive. In short, I have no doubt that the individual elements of your critique of Wagner stem from an overall conception that owes its compelling power to the authentic historical signature of your thinking.

And yet you have still not offered a conclusive answer to the question that established its ghostly existence between us during a conversation on a balcony in Ospedaletti.[6] Allow me to recall the memory of this question by posing it myself. In your first *experiences* with Wagner, did you always feel entirely at home in terms of your *insight* into his work? Let me use the analogy of a field and imagine someone who knows it well from the games of early childhood. One day, he unexpectedly finds himself there again at the very moment that it becomes the site of a pistol duel to which he has been challenged by a rival. It seems to me that some of the tensions that would accompany such a situation can also be found in your 'Wagner'. Should it not be precisely these that call into question the success of that 'recuperation' which formed the subject of our past conversation? You have shown both clearly and carefully what motifs could announce such a recuperation. I am thinking here of the most beautiful formulation in your study, that of the golden nothing and the silver wait-a-while.[7] It is certainly not the precision of your materialist deciphering of Wagner that loses any of its resonance through such passages; but they do not possess this resonance in full. Why? Would I be mistaken to answer: because they were not predestined to be a part of your conception? A work such as your 'Wagner' is hardly lacking ravines or caverns from which those motifs could echo back once more. Why do they not? Why do those fine passages in which one can sense their presence (the amazing one in which you quote 'The fair Holda stepped forth from the mountain')[8] stand out as much through their isolation as through their beauty?

If I have to settle on a succinct formulation, let me say this much: the underlying conception of the Wagner, which God knows is impressive enough, is a polemical one. I would not be surprised if it were the only one that is suitable for us, and which allows us to draw on the full resources as you do. It seems to me that your energetic technical analyses also – in fact especially – have their place in this conception. A polemical treatment of Wagner by no means precludes an illumination of the progressive elements in his work that you undertake, especially if those elements are as impossible to separate from the regressive ones as the sheep are from the goats.

But it seems to me – and here, dear Teddie, I daresay you will catch me with body and soul playing your favourite Indian game, the unearthing of the hatchet – that the historico-philosophical perspective of recuperation proves irreconcilable with the critical one of pro- and regressions. Or, more specifically, as reconcilable only in certain philosophical contexts we have sometimes discussed under the heading 'progress'. The unquestioning use of the categories of the progressive and the regressive, whose validity I would be the last to deny in the central parts of your text, makes these attempts to recuperate Wagner (which, on the other hand, I – especially after reading your text, with its devastating analyses – would be the last to insist upon *at present*) extremely problematic.

I am sure you will not wish to contradict me when I say that recuperation as a philosophical tendency demands a literary form that – to put it somewhat clumsily (as I cannot formulate it any better) – has a special affinity with that of music. Recuperation is a cyclical form, whereas polemic is a progressive one. I see the ten chapters of the Wagner more as a progression than a cycle. It is in this context that the socio-critical and technical examinations unfold confidently and independently; but it is also this context that impairs other longstanding and important motifs in your theory of music, for example opera as consolation or music as protest;[9] that pins down the motif of eternity in its functional connection with phantasmagoria[10] and must therefore disregard its affinity with that of happiness.

I think that all this, as I say, was present in one of our recent conversations[11] as a question. And I do not think that what I am speaking about here is any less in accordance with your concerns than it is with mine. Perhaps a recuperation of Wagner would have cleared a space for one of your oldest motifs – that of décadence and the Trakl quotation[12] you so love. The decisive aspect of recuperation – would you not agree? – is never a progressive one; it can resemble the regressive as much as the goal, which Karl Kraus terms the origin.[13]

The difficulties I have in the 'Baudelaire' are perhaps precisely the inverse of yours. There is so little space – even at first glance, and all the more in the matter itself – for polemic there, so little that is disreputable or outdated, that the form of recuperation could itself become a problem through its application to this subject. I hope that I will see this more clearly after a while.

Now to your letters and my silence. I have those of 10 April (that one was from Felizitas), 4 May and 8 June[14] before me. It would be more awkward for me if I were not able to assume that you had heard from me indirectly in the meantime, for since then I have sent a substantial letter to Max and a lengthy one to Scholem. During that time, I had intended finally to send you a copy of 'Berliner Kindheit', but suddenly found myself confronted with this same text once again and began a thorough revision. You can find several sections[15] of that in the last issue of 'Mass und Wert'.

To tell the truth, this catalogue of my hindrances is not complete. I was plagued by heavy chronic migraines for six weeks. Finally I decided to pay the doctors some visits; initially there was a suspicion of recidivist malaria, but there are no indications of that. The symptoms suddenly disappeared just as I arrived to have a thorough eye examination. And not a moment too soon, for I felt extremely weakened. It goes without saying that my work did not benefit from all this; I will do my utmost to make up for lost time in Denmark. I leave the day after tomorrow.

The various diplomatic representations required for my naturalization have been multiplying of late. I had told Max about it at length in my last letter of 28 May. I am almost certain that he did receive this letter before heading west. So I think he would still have been able before his departure to notify Pollock of my request for a certificate[16] that I require for my naturalization. In case I am mistaken in my assumption, I enclose a copy of the passage in question from my letter to Max, and would then ask you to pass it on to Pollock. He is aware of my basic intention. The bureaucratic procedures here are unspeakably drawn-out; the *sooner* I might receive the certificate the better.

In return for your sending the literature section[17] from the newspaper, I am sending you both, as printed matter, a prose piece by Claudel[18] that recently appeared in Figaro. A fine example of the magnificent vision and unprecedented skill of this terrible man.

In addition, let me give you – it will seem strange to you – a little tip for New York. At the moment there is a retrospective of American art[19] here. That is how I became acquainted with ten or twenty primitive pictures by unnamed artists from the period between 1800 and

1840. I have never seen pictures of this kind that made such an impression upon me. Those that are not owned by Mrs. John Rockefeller junior are mostly from the 'American Folk Art Gallery'. You absolutely must not miss having a look at them if they are there again. – Speaking of American matters: do you know Melville? A number of important works by him are being published here.

Two remarks concerning my recent literary activities. I daresay you will meanwhile have heard a thing or two from Scholem, especially about my study of Brod's Kafka biography. I have taken the opportunity to make a few notes on Kafka myself, from a different perspective to that of my essay. This prompted me to re-examine Teddie's letter on Kafka[20] of 17 December 1934 with great interest. Its soundness makes the Kafka essay by Haselberg,[21] which I also found among my papers, look all the weaker. – I read Ronsard for the first time, and found the motto for the 'Baudelaire'[22] there. I read 'Benighted' by Priestley[23] in translation. It has been made into one of the most remarkable films, 'The Old Dark House'. If you happen to find it in some retrospective or other, make sure you do not miss it.

Your description,[24] dear Teddie, of the visit paid to Behemoth by Leviathan, was read with the appropriate gaiety and will be preserved with the appropriate honour. It makes me feel all the shabbier for being unable to answer Felizitas's question as to whether Scholem is a Frankist. If I were to say no, which I would be authorized to do, it would be of little use to her. You must take into account that your first encounter with Scholem was a guest appearance on his part. That alone – to say nothing of other factors – already makes your chances of getting something out of him ten times greater than mine. I also hope that we will have a chance to meet in Paris again; but I am not sure of it.

Bloch is still in Prague; he is preparing for his move to America. He had a very nice essay on Brecht in 'Weltbühne', and an utterly appalling one about Bukharin's concluding remarks.[25] I must take this opportunity to tell you that the sort of news you gave me about Eisler and Bukharin is always extremely welcome.[26]

Else Herzberger's trip to America did not do *me* much good. Since then I have not got any further than a few telephone conversations with her, consisting mainly of intimations regarding the losses she has suffered. I am sorry about that, as you can imagine; but I do not see any real scope for action there.

Regarding your projects, I am of course extremely interested in your study on the new form of dialectic.[27] But I assume that 'Musik im Radio'[28] will take priority for now?

If I happen to encounter the Herr Greid[29] you mention, I will act accordingly. Fortunately your letter does not give me grounds to assume that this is particularly likely. Unless he is in Denmark?

So Sternberger is to be granted a reprieve?[30] – Now it is enough for today, so let me conclude with the very warmest greetings

Yours,

Walter

Original: typescript.

1 In chapter 9 of *Versuch über Wagner* (see *GS* 13, pp. 127f.)

2 See ibid., pp. 126f.

3 See Adorno, 'Fragmente über Wagner', in *Zeitschrift für Sozialforschung* 8 (1939–40), pp. 1–49 (issue 1–2); the passage referred to is on p. 40: 'Marke is the forefather of the League of Nations.' In *Versuch über Wagner* he then wrote: 'Marke is the forefather of Appeasement [EO]' (*GS* 13, p. 137).

4 See *GS* 13, pp. 38–40.

5 See ibid., p. 118. The term was not coined by Adorno.

6 During the Adornos' stay in San Remo at the turn of the year in 1937–8. Ospedaletti Ligure lies a few kilometres west of San Remo.

7 Chapter 10 of *Versuch über Wagner* originally contained the following sentence: 'The golden nothing and the silver wait-a-while belong together' (Theodor W. Adorno Archiv, Ts 2927).

8 See Richard Wagner, *Tannhäuser und der Sängerkrieg auf Wartburg*, Act 1, scene 3; Adorno quotes the passage in chapter 6 (see *GS* 13, p. 88).

9 'The true idea of opera, that of a consolation which makes the gates of the underworld open before it, has been lost' (ibid., p. 118). In the version Benjamin would have had, this passage read: 'In spite of all its expression, the musical experience here has an element of soullessness: the original power of opera, that of consolation, has been lost in Wagner' (Theodor W. Adorno Archiv, Ts 2897f.). See also the end of the tenth (and final) chapter: 'If someone is able to snatch away that metal from the dulling waves of Wagner's orchestra, its altered sound can help him to obtain that consolation which, for all its intoxication and phantasmagoria, it doggedly refuses to provide. By articulating the fear of a helpless human being, it could offer help to the helpless – however weak and artificial that help might be – and renew the promise made by music's age-old protest: to live without fear' (*GS* 13, p. 145).

10 See *GS* 13, p. 84.

11 At the turn of the year 1937–8 in San Remo.

12 In the summer of 1936, Adorno had been planning an essay on decadence for the *Zeitschrift für Sozialforschung*; regarding it, he noted: 'Motto for the decadence essay: "Wie scheint doch alles Werdende so krank" [How sick seem all nascent things]. Georg Trakl' (*Grünes Buch* [Green Book], p. 38). The line is taken from the first stanza of the third poem in Trakl's cycle *Heiterer Frühling* [Joyful Spring].

13 See Karl Kraus, *Worte in Versen I* (Leipzig, 1916), p. 69 ('Der sterbende Mensch' [The Dying Human], l. 40).

14 These have not survived.

15 These were 'Krumme Strasse' [Crooked Street], 'Pfaueninsel und Glienicke' [Peacock Island and Glienicke (a quarter in Berlin)], 'Der Strumpf' [The Sock], 'Unglücksfälle und Verbrechen' [Accidents and Crimes], 'Die Farben' [The Colours], 'Zwei Blechkapellen' [Two Brass Bands] and 'Winterabend' [Winter Evening].

16 For his naturalization application, Benjamin was required to prove that he had spent three years in France to carry out academic work for the institute.

17 One of the issues of the *Literaturblatt der Frankfurter Zeitung* was probably that of 17 April 1938, which included a review by Heinrich Zimmer of Dolf Sternberger's book *Panorama oder Ansichten vom 19. Jahrhundert*; Benjamin kept the cutting of the review.

18 Probably the essay 'Le poison wagnérien' by Paul Claudel (1869–1955), published in *Le Figaro* on 26 March 1938; see Claudel, *Œuvres en prose*, ed. Jacques Petit and Charles Galpérine (Paris, 1965), pp. 367–72 (Bibliothèque de la Pléiade 179).

19 Unknown.

20 Adorno's letter of 17 December 1934; see *Adorno–Benjamin Correspondence*, pp. 66–73.

21 In the summer of 1935, Peter von Haselberg had sent Benjamin his 'Notizen zu Kafka', which had been written for the features section of the *Frankfurter Zeitung* but was not published there.

22 The motto was taken from Pierre Ronsard's 'Hymne de la Mort'; see *GS* 5 [1], p. 301.

23 This novel by John Boynton Priestley (1894–1984) had been published in 1927; the American edition bore the title *The Old Dark House*; the film of the same name by James Whale, the German title of which is *Das Haus des Grauens* [The House of Horror], dates from 1932.

24 See *Adorno–Benjamin Correspondence*, pp. 249–50.

25 See Ernst Bloch, 'Ein Leninist der Schaubühne' [A Leninist of the Theatre], in *Die neue Weltbühne* 34 (1938), pp. 624–7 (issue 20, 19 May 38), and 'Bucharins Schlusswort', in ibid., pp. 558–63 (issue 18, 5 May 38).

26 See *Adorno–Benjamin Correspondence*, p. 252.

27 Adorno had written: 'As for the rest, my literary plans with Max are now beginning to assume a very concrete shape. It has already been virtually decided that we shall collaborate in writing a major essay on the new, open form of dialectic' (*Adorno–Benjamin Correspondence*, p. 255). The plan was never carried out.

28 The book Adorno was planning to write, which was to be entitled *Current of Music* and contain his radio studies, remained a fragment.

29 In January 1938, Adorno had written a report for the American Guild for German Cultural Freedom on the essay 'Optimismus' by the actor and director Hermann Greid (1892–1975), who had emigrated to Sweden. Greid, who also worked with Brecht in Sweden, did not receive a scholarship. In his letter, Adorno states: 'With my permission it was then made available to Herr Greid, who has written me an incredibly impertinent letter. All this would be of absolutely no consequence, of course, if the letter had not explicitly referred to Greid's relationship with Brecht, and then gone on to claim that Greid has never heard any of his acquaintances say anything whatsoever about me or my Marxist credentials. That is rather annoying, and I would be sincerely grateful to you if you could check that everything is in order, assuming that does not cause you any great inconvenience' (*Adorno–Benjamin Correspondence*, p. 255).

30 'As far as Sternberger is concerned, I have encouraged acquisition of the book, and I would certainly have nothing against such a denunciation. I would merely point out to you that, according to my latest and extremely reliable information, Sternberger's position at the newspaper [*Frankfurter Zeitung*] has become untenable anyway, and I am not sure whether one should pre-empt the world spirit here' (*Adorno–Benjamin Correspondence*, p. 251).

147 WALTER BENJAMIN TO GRETEL ADORNO SKOVSBOSTRAND, 20.7.1938

Dear Felizitas,

would you have thought that your birthday wishes[1] would arrive here precisely on the 15th, at 12 noon? Indeed they did, brought by the postman. Sadly, this joy at once intensified my awareness of my recent oversight.[2] This can only be forgiven, not excused. Now I will keep the date in mind all the better, and it is safe there.

I imagine that your memory will have been refreshed on the 15th for obvious reasons. This naturally makes me desire to know whether your sister's wedding has taken place or is yet to come. You had written to me at some length about it, and I had replied. I think it was in my last letter, to which I have not yet had a response from either of you.

You may have heard from Egon how things are with me here, as I wrote to him two weeks ago.[3] I am living in a reasonably quiet room in the immediate vicinity of Brecht's house. For my work I have a large, stable writing table – such as I have not had for years – and a view of the leisurely Sund, whose shores are passed by sailboats and also smaller steamers. And so I live in the *contemplation opiniâtre de l'œuvre de demain*,[4] in the words of Baudelaire, who is the subject of the *œuvre* in question.

For the last month I have been devoting between eight and nine hours daily to it, and intend to conclude the first draft of the manuscript before I return to Paris. As a result I had to abandon my plan to meet with Scholem, as much as it pained me: the interruption would have occurred at too important a stage of the work process. He has probably told you himself in the meantime.

This is followed by some news that I am reluctant to give you – to you first of all, and not so much into safe hands as understanding ones. In spite of all my efforts, I will not be able to observe the appointment of 15 September.

In a letter I sent to Pollock[5] from here, I mentioned to him that it might be necessary to exceed the deadline somewhat. Meanwhile I have had to decide on a restructuring of the work's scheme, which I had forcibly drawn up in Paris during a period of chronic migraines.

We agree, after all, that in studies such as the Baudelaire, the overall conception is of decisive importance; it is here that one must not force anything or look the other way. In addition, some of the fundamental categories used in the Arcades are developed for the first time here. These categories include, as I believe I already told you in San Remo, that of the new and the eternally same. Furthermore, the study – and perhaps this will best give you an idea – now connects motifs that had previously presented themselves to me only in more or less isolated areas of thought: allegory, art nouveau and aura. – And naturally, the denser the conceptual context becomes, the more urbane the language must be.

This is compounded by the difficulties that lie not in the subject matter so much as in the time, that is to say: in the period. How much I would give to see you, even just for a week! For in many cases it would take only half a word for you to understand me, and through that you would help me so much in gaining hold of its other half. There is nothing comparable here. On the other hand, I am very grateful that Brecht is showing such understanding for the necessity of my isolation. Without it, things would be rather less pleasant. But precisely that has enabled me to withdraw into my work to such a degree that I have not even read his new novel,[6] half of which is complete. Naturally it is not so much the time I am lacking, but rather the ability to enter anything that is remote from my work.

That same domineering character, which results in an incompatibility with any other activity, makes it difficult for me to impose temporal restrictions upon it. As much as I might take for granted that I will complete it before the end of the year – I would view 15 November as the latest date –, it would be foolish of me not to tell you already now that I will not be able to manage unless the deadline is postponed by at least five weeks.

Naturally I will have no choice but to tell Max the same. As my message would reach him much later than this one will reach you, however, and because, furthermore, I wrote to Pollock about the matter only recently, and because – and this is the decisive factor – I want to be sure not only of your understanding and your help with this editorial problem, but also Teddie's – that is why I am writing to you, and at such length.

But that is not all. Rather, let me immediately append a request that may conjure up my entire desk before your inner eye. I have found out that the famous R L Stevenson wrote about gaslight;[7] there is an essay by him on gaz-lamps. So far all my efforts to get hold of it have been in vain. I need not waste any words on the importance this essay could have for me. Might you try to procure it for me? – And finally: would it be possible for you to send me in the course of the next few weeks the French books of mine that you still have? It would spare me the customs difficulties that the French authorities love to create in the case of book deliveries. They would be shipped to Paris from here, along with the rest of my library.

I have heard that Ernst Bloch is in New-York.[8] Is this true? Tell me if so – and greet him from me. Going by the last issue of the journal, his student Joachim Schumacher is also there. His contributions to the reviews section seem to be of consistent quality; a book[9] he has published under the title 'Die Angst vor dem Chaos', on the other hand, does not reflect well on the training he has received.

I have encountered a little more writing that follows the party line here than in Paris; the other day I came across an issue of 'Internationale Literatur'[10] in which, with reference to my essay on the Elective Affinities, I am presented as a follower of Heidegger. The poverty of this literary scene is overwhelming. You will, I think, have the chance to hear what Bloch makes of it. As far as Brecht is concerned, he is doing his best to understand the reasons for Russia's cultural policy through speculations about the requirements of the nationality politics over there. But that naturally does not stop him from recognizing that the theoretical line is catastrophic for everything we have been working for in the last 20 years. As you know, his translator and friend was Tretyakov. It is highly unlikely that he is still alive.

The weather is gloomy, and does not exactly tempt me to go for any walks; all the better, for there are none to take. My desk also has a climatic advantage: it is situated underneath a slanted roof, where the warmth occasionally emitted by the sparse rays of sunlight lasts a little longer than elsewhere. One or two games of chess, which were supposed to bring a little variety into my life, are also taking on the colour of the grey Sund and of uniformity: for I win them only very rarely.

Take good care of yourself, my dear Felizitas; take into account that, due to my work, I require a particularly great amount of encouragement to write letters; provide me with this encouragement by reporting at length – your letters are *always* short – and send my warmest regards to Teddie and the others.

20 July 1938 Yours Detlef
Skovsbostrand per Svendborg
c/o Brecht
I recently saw – for the first time! – Katherine Hepburn. She is superb, and reminds me very much of you. Has no one ever told you?

Original: manuscript.

1 They have not survived.

2 Benjamin had forgotten Gretel Adorno's birthday on 10 June.

3 The letter has not survived.

4 This quotation [stubborn contemplation of tomorrow's work] is taken from the section 'Du Travail journalier et de l'inspiration' [On Daily Work and Inspiration] in Baudelaire's *Conseils aux jeunes littérateurs* [Advice to Young Men of Letters].

5 Only the sketch has survived.

6 The novel *Die Geschäfte des Herrn Julius Caesar* [The Transactions of Mr Julius Caesar], which Brecht had been writing since January 1938.

7 See Robert Louis Stevenson, 'A Plea for Gas Lamps', in *The Works of Robert Louis Stevenson*, Tusitala Edition, vol. 25: *Virginibus puerisque and Other Essays in Belles Lettres* (London, 1924), pp. 129–32.

8 Bloch had arrived there in mid-July.

9 Joachim Schumacher (1904–1984), who had known Bloch since 1933 and subsequently become his friend, had emigrated to the USA in 1937; the same year, Schumacher had reviewed the book *Die Verbürgerlichung der deutschen Kunst, Literatur und Musik im 18. Jahrhundert* [How German Art, Literature and Music Became Bourgeois in the Eighteenth Century] (Strasbourg, Zurich and Leipzig, 1936), by Leo Balet and E. Gerhard, for the third issue of the *Zeitschrift für Sozialforschung*, and for issue 1–2 (1938) Knight's *Drama and Society in the Age of Jonson* (London, 1937) and Newman's *Jonathan Swift* (Boston, 1937). His own book *Die Angst vor dem Chaos* [The Fear of Chaos] – written in France, where Schumacher had lived illegally with his wife – had been published in Paris in 1937.

10 The sixth 1938 issue of this journal (pp. 113–28) contained Alfred Kurella's review of *Le Romantisme allemand*, a special issue of the *Cahiers du Sud*; on p. 127 he writes the following concerning Benjamin's article 'L'Angoisse mythique chez Goethe' [Mythical Fear in Goethe]: 'Here he attempts to interpret Goethe's fundamental position in Romantic terms and declare a "power of archaic authorities", a metaphysical fear in Goethe's life, as the true source of his greatness – an attempt that does Heidegger great credit.'

148 THEODOR WIESENGRUND-ADORNO AND GRETEL ADORNO TO WALTER BENJAMIN BAR HARBOR, MAINE, 2.8.1938

From 15 August:
290 Riversidedrive, 13 D
New York, N. Y.

Bar Harbor, Maine
2 August 1938.

Dear Walter:

let me give you my warmest thanks for the letter of 19 June with your critique of the Wagner. First of all, I would like to apologize for the poor quality of your copy. But unfortunately only the original is more legible, and as I am constantly adding changes and improvements, I do not want to let go of it.

As far as your critique is concerned, I was exceedingly happy about your recognition. As for the negative aspects, I am forced to be somewhat laconic by the fact that I can only agree with you. Admittedly, the reason must be slightly different to that which you gave. I think it is simply because I have not had the sort of experiences that you – and Max too, incidentally, in exactly the same way – missed in the study. Wagner was not one of my childhood idols,[1] and even today I am unable to invoke his aura any more strongly than I have done in a few passages, such as the one about Robert Reinick.[2] But I would at least like to point out, as an extenuating circumstance, that I by no means related the motifs of Wagner's recuperation to his progressive traits unquestioningly, but rather accentuated the intertwinement of the progressive and the regressive. I think you will perhaps concede this if you look closely at the final chapter. It may also, in the sense you indicate, be a sign that the study has more of a cyclical form than you ascribe to it. The motifs of the final chapter correspond precisely to those of the first. [Note along the paragraph in Adorno's hand:] Please excuse this latest typewriter accident![3] I am *so* sorry![4]

The fate of the work is still undecided. At first, I imagined the difficulties of an abridged version to be so massive that I dispensed with them and instead began a substantial revision and abridgement of the

Husserl essay,[5] which is proving especially enjoyable, and I am inclined to think that you will also find it agreeable, though that does not mean it is of an agreeable nature. This new version will definitely be finished by 10 September, and I am hoping equally definitely that it will be published in the next issue. And I would be all the happier if the Baudelaire were also ready by then. That, incidentally, was also one of the reasons I set to work on the Husserl and put the Wagner on hold. I do not think it would have been very wise to have Baudelaire and Wagner in the same issue.

Our location here is especially pleasant by American standards: we are on an island whose character lies somewhere between the South of France, Rügen and Cronberg. Egon and Lotte were here for a week, and their car was as beneficial to our photographic experiences as their presence was in human terms. – Aside from that, I am re-reading Hegel's Logic, a truly incredible work; every part of it speaks to me today. You will find a reflection of that in the Husserl. I am also reading Hindemith's utterly abhorrent composition manual,[6] which I would like to rubbish either in the journal or in 23. While we are on the subject of abhorrence: Caillois has published an essay, l'Aridité,[7] in Mesures, in which he plays the strong-minded man on the one hand while at the same time enthusing about the regulation of ideas, yet without making it clear what authority is to determine that regulation. That makes it clear enough, of course. And yet the first page of the essay, which introduces a theory of the beauty of the Alpine landscape, testifies to quite extraordinary talent. One finds very few cases of such a tragic waste. The same issue also has Bataille railing[8] at the dear Lord again. I wonder if that will turn out well.

We would both be very happy to lay hands on a duplicate of Berliner Kindheit[9] very soon. We have still not seen the issue of Mass und Wert, and it would be very kind if you could send me one. I hope you have fully recovered from your migraine. I notified Pollock about the naturalization business at once; I hope it works out.

I will look at the American pictures you mentioned with Schapiro,[10] who has generally promised to initiate me into these matters a little. A very peculiar man. If I were you, I would contact him at all costs and not worry about Leyda.[11] It is probably only shyness that has prevented him from writing to you. The question he asked me will show you how intensively he has studied your work: what is the relationship between your critique of the auratic and the auratic character of your own writings? If anyone deserves an honorary copy of *Einbahnstrasse*, it is surely Schapiro. I might also mention in passing that he has a special interest in Grandville.

We are now in regular contact with Scholem, and his relations with the institute have entered a more friendly phase. During our last evening together he read out your extraordinary letter on Kafka[12] and told me about his favourite plan for you to write something about Kafka. I responded with great enthusiasm to this plan, and Löwenthal was also most delighted. I am sure a substantial Kafka essay could be published in the journal. The only problem is that Scholem is thinking of a *book*, as you probably are too, and book publications face the usual difficulties. Today I will merely pass this ball on to you in the hope that you take it: a scathing review of Brod's book in the journal would be highly welcome. Incidentally, to avoid misunderstandings: I would not have any objection to one of Herr Sternberger either, as he seems to be more firmly in the saddle than ever. Meanwhile he is paying tribute to Eisbein-Dacqué.[13] But the FZ has lately been spelling Baudelaire 'Beaudelaire', *ne ulla virtus pereat*.

Bloch has arrived in the meantime. Possibly on a ship with eight sails. But, at any rate, he is challenging the century arm in arm with Eisler. Unless he begins to find the latter's people's lectures[14] so unbearable that he ends up leaving the once-red flag after all. But even then his chances with the journal will not be especially good. Max was just as enraged by the Bukharin essay as you and I. With people like Bloch it is simply quite inevitable that they will get into hot water once they start being clever. But nonetheless: when Eisler tells me that Bloch is now so much better, so much clearer and no longer such a mystic, it is still the Indian[15] that is closer to my heart – even if I go along with Scholem's claim that the centre of Indian-Jewish mysticism is the German of Bubu de Montsalvatsch.[16]

I recommended to Scholem that he stay at the Littré, and so I can already see the two of you sitting in the Versailles,[17] and envy Scholem, you and the Versailles. Spare a drop of grenadine to drink in memory of me.

Write soon to

your old
Teddie

Dear Detlef,

it was so windy in the garden, that is why the letter is so very badly typed, please forgive me. – We will be staying here for about another ten days, and then I will return to New York – which is probably still as hot as a greenhouse – and set about furnishing our apartment: 3 rooms on the 13th floor with a view of the river. Even though we did not choose the furniture ourselves – we got hold of some old pieces from Frankfurt and Berlin – I do hope it will become a pleasant spot for us and a few friends, not for large gatherings. I am expecting to see you in the year of the world exhibition, even if you do not yet have all the documents from the institute's management. And just wait until I can lead you around a city, or perhaps even drive by then. (Though having a car is a big problem in New York: one can hardly ever find a parking space, everything is so congested on Sundays, the tax and insurance fees are fairly high, and actually I only really like very smart chauffeur-driven cars.) –

Lotte and E have not married yet; it seems they want to wait until the professional matters have been sorted out. E's time at the Mass Memorial Hospital will soon be over, and for a new position he will probably have to take the state examination first. I am sure he will tell you the details himself. I have heard nothing from them except for a brief greeting since the 20th, the day they left Bar Harbor, but I think we will be returning via Boston. Concerning my reservations about E: to be absolutely honest, I preferred him when he was on morphine. Despite all his merits, I could not bear being with him in the long run now; we will have to talk about it properly once you have met Lottchen and seen him in his present state. Very fond regards, with a kiss as in the good old days

ever your Felizitas

Original: typescript and manuscript.

1 Adorno only began studying Wagner's works under the tutelage, and on the urging, of Alban Berg, as a letter he wrote to Berg indicates: 'I am quite serious about my intentions regarding a reception of Wagner (nothing in the world but you could have enabled me to do so once more!)' (Theodor W. Adorno and Alban Berg, *Correspondence 1925–1935*, trans. Wieland Hoban [Cambridge: Polity, 2005], p. 29).

2 See *GS* 13, pp. 141f.

3 The carbon paper had slipped while Adorno was writing on the back of the paper, so that the mirror image of the text on the back imprinted itself between some of the lines on the front.

4 *I am so sorry!*: EO.

5 This refers to the essay 'Zur Philosophie Husserls'; see *GS* 20 [1], pp. 46–118.

6 See Paul Hindemith, *Unterweisung im Tonsatz: Theoretischer Teil* [The Craft of Musical Composition: Theoretical Part] (Mainz, 1937); Adorno's review of the book for the planned autumn 1939 issue of the *Zeitschrift für Sozialforschung* could not be published – like the entire journal – due to the outbreak of war. Adorno included it as the fourth part of 'Ad vocem Hindemith: Eine Dokumentation' in 1968 (see *GS* 17, pp. 229–35).

7 The essay was published in *Mesures: Cahiers trimestriels*, 15 April 1938, no. 2 (Paris: Librairie José Corti), pp. 7–12; for Benjamin's pseudonymous review within a discussion of several works, see *ZfS* 7 (1938), p. 451 (issue 3); *GS* 3, pp. 549f.

8 See Georges Bataille, 'L'Obélisque', in *Mesures* 4 (1938), pp. 35–50 (no. 2, 15 April). Benjamin speaks about Bataille's essay in his letter of 28 May 1938 to Horkheimer; see *GB* 6, pp. 93f.

9 Benjamin sent the manuscript of *Berliner Kindheit um neunzehnhundert* to the Adornos only in April 1940; see *GS* 4 [2], p. 968.

10 The art historian Meyer Schapiro (1904–1996) had been teaching at Columbia University since 1928.

11 Jay Leyda (b. 1910) had become assistant curator of the newly founded film department of the Museum of Art in 1936.

12 Benjamin's letter of 12 June 1938 to Scholem; see *Scholem Correspondence*, pp. 266–73.

13 See Dolf Sternberger, 'Verwandlung: Edgar Dacqué zum 60. Geburtstag' [Transformation: On the Occasion of Edgar Dacque's 60th birthday], in *Frankfurter Zeitung*, 8 July 1938 (vol. 82, no. 342–3), p. 10. Translator's note: *Eisbein* is a dish consisting of a leg of pork that is normally either cured and boiled, or simply roasted.

14 An allusion to Eisler's work as a composition teacher at the New School for Social Research in New York.

15 Translator's note: Adorno is referring not to natives of India (for whom the word would be *Inder*), but rather Native Americans (*Indianer*).

16 Presumably a reference to Martin Buber; the name is a combination of the title of Charles-Louis Philippe's novel *Bubu de Montparnasse* and the mountain in *Parsifal* named Montsalvat.

17 This refers to the Café de Versailles, which stood in the rue de Rennes opposite Montparnasse train station.

149 GRETEL ADORNO TO WALTER BENJAMIN BAR HARBOR, MAINE, 3.8.1938

De Gregoire
Bar Harbor, Maine

3 August 1938.

My dear Detlef:

your letter made me long for you so madly that I would most of all have liked simply to take the next ship to you, as if it were the most natural thing in the world. Yes, I would even go so far as to reproach myself – now that it is too late – for perhaps not treating you well enough in San Remo. There are certainly a few points in my defence: the guesthouse, my weakened state from moving between two continents, and probably most of all the feeling of being seen as a mere appendage now, which was naturally very difficult for my vanity to cope with. But still.

But now to the most important thing: the Baudelaire. As luck would have it, your letter arrived just as Leo Löwenthal came to stay with us here for a few days. We thought it best to show him your letter directly. (I know you will not view this as a breach of confidence.) Leo was quite beside himself and told us that he had to have the essay for the next issue at all costs, that he had no substitute, and would no longer be able to find one, as it was already too late. He said that this year they will only be publishing the double issue and the one at the end of the year, which should be first-rate with the 3 essays from you, Grossmann[1] and Teddie. The only other possibility he saw would be for you to submit the essay exactly one month later, i.e. 15 October to be read in New York. Dear Detlef, I know your arguments, and I agree with you entirely, and yet I would ask you to consider the following: at the moment, the institute is depending on you in order to maintain its renown, its unique standing. You should not pass up this opportunity under any circumstances. In your letter you mentioned a necessary deadline extension of roughly 5 weeks. That time would be more or less up by 15 October, so could you not manage it after all?

My dear, I hate to badger you, but for your sake: make the impossible possible. Do it also for my sake – for in accordance with American customs, I would have to say that I have bet on you.

And now I must compliment you especially on your letter, which is not only very fine and incredibly well considered, but also so subtly judged in its rationing of flattery; I am glad to have received it, I am proud of it, it makes me happy. At the same time, the letter also had the side effect that I am now held in much higher esteem at the institute. Perhaps I shall yet, after many years, be viewed there as a person in my own right after all, not simply as a 'lady of the institute'. –

Bloch is spending his summer holidays in New York State; we should be seeing him there in the autumn.

I also like Miss Hepburn a great deal, and am happy to hear that she reminds you of me; no one had ever observed that before. – A few days ago we saw the wonderful Hedy La Marr,[2] formerly Hedy Kiessler from Vienna, together with Boyer in 'Algier'. –

I will have the institute send you your books to Skovsbostrand in August. – We want to try finding the essay by Stevenson through Schapiro. –

I found what you wrote about Brecht extremely pleasing. If he has written anything that expresses this change of opinion, I would ask you to send it to me so that I can show it in black and white to everyone at the institute.

If you want to make me quite especially happy, please send me a copy of Brecht's pornographic poems[3] to inaugurate the first apartment of my own. –

How is your own apartment looking, has it turned out nicely?

Warm regards from Teddie and a kiss from your faithful

Felicitas

Original: manuscript.

1 Henryk Grossmann (1881–1950) had studied law and economics. He moved to Frankfurt in 1925 and was appointed professor in 1930. Like Adorno, Grossmann had gone from England to New York in 1938. No issue with this combination of texts was published.

2 Hedy Lamarr (1913–2000), whose real name was Hedwig Eva Kiesler, played the role of Gaby in said film of 1938. Charles Boyer (1899–1978) played Pepe le Moko, and the director was John Cromwell.

3 A number of these poems were first published in 1982; see Bertolt Brecht, *Gedichte über die Liebe* [Poems about Love], selected by Werner Hecht (Frankfurt am Main, 1982).

150 THEODOR WIESENGRUND-ADORNO AND GRETEL ADORNO TO WALTER BENJAMIN, ON A LETTER FROM MEYER SCHAPIRO TO ADORNO
BAR HARBOR, MAINE, *c.*12.8.1938

South Londonderry, Vt.
August 10, 1938

My dear Wiesengrund-Adorno,

I have just returned from a two-week visit to the city. Everyone was away, but the libraries were always crowded. I had hoped to find you in town – though I am glad you didn't have to suffer the terrible heat and humidity . . .

I took the liberty to recommend you to the Brooklyn Institute,[1] without finding out first whether you cared to lecture. By some odd confusion, the letter was first sent to the Rhode Island Museum, because the people at the NY Museum of Modern Art mistook your name for that of A. Dorner (over the telephone! you see what machine reception does to sound and especially to nuances in names). I also recommended Krenek for the lecture on modern music.[2] But since we couldn't reach him or find out when he would be in New York, and whether he spoke English well enough, we had to give up the idea. I liked his book very much, except for the social interpretation and the pathos.

Will Bloch remain in New York until October? I should be very sorry if I missed him. I will probably return to the city in the middle of September. Perhaps you might make an auto trip through New England during the next month and stop here for a day or two with Bloch. Sidney Hook[3] is not far away, and among our neighbours are Ernest Nagel[4] (who teaches philosophy at Columbia) and Selig Hecht[5] (the biophysicist who works on colorvision). I have read a part of the controversy in Das Wort on Expressionism[6] and although I agree with Bloch in much that he says, it seems to me the whole controversy masks other issues, of a political nature (evident in the attitude to Mann and in Lukacs' astonishing retraction of his old work on dialectics).

I do not know of an essay by Stevenson on Gas Light. If it is Robert Louis Stevenson that Benjamin has in mind, I can refer him to the sweet little poem in a Child's Garden of Verses called the Lamplighter. The collected works of RLS are easy enough to find; perhaps they contain an essay on Gas Light. You probably know the story about RLS, that as a student excited by ideas of adventure and mystery, he used to go about the streets at night with a lamp under his cloak . . . Benjamin probably knows that in the 70s there were critics who attributed Impressionism on the influence of gas-light! and that Baudelaire discussed the influence of gas-light on taste (see his Curiosités Esthétiques).

Do you by any chance know of Germans in New York who need the services of a competent English translator? I have a friend who for years has made first-rate translations from the German and French (he also translates Spanish) for Simon and Shuster and now works for the Oxford Univ. Press. He is an able literary man himself and could also revise English mss. for grammar and style. My friend is in great need at the moment. Is it possible that the Institute could employ him? He has experience with social and economic literature, history, biography and novels, also natural science; but not technical works of philosophy.

Best regards to both of you.

Cordially,

Meyer Schapiro

Dear Walter,

I am sending you this letter firstly for the information about this, but also because it tells you a few things about its sender – namely Meyer-Schapiro – that might encourage you to write to him. I am constantly thinking about finding new opportunities for you in America, and you would be doing me an enormous favour. And S. is truly at home in our climate. The address until mid-September

Prof. M. Schapiro
South Londonderry (Vt.)
U. S. A.

Tomorrow we are going to New York and moving into our apartment. I have now also written an essay directed against Sibelius[7] and 3 analyses of famous salon pieces.[8]

Fond regards from your old Teddie

Schapiro reads and speaks German very well.
Sohn-Rethel has meanwhile produced a new manuscript[9] in which I am represented as the prince of hell – flattering, but dissimilar.

Dear Detlef,

I hope I shall be able to send you the copy of 'The Seducer's Diary' with your books. Is Elisabeth Hauptmann not in New York too – what is her address? One more thing: does Brecht know 'Erewhon'[10] by Butler? There are some peculiar things said in it, for example that one should not finish any thought, and that one will be punished if one has no money. Today just this greeting. The very fondest regards ever your Felicitas.

Original: typescript and manuscript.
On the dating: The handwritten lines by Theodor and Gretel Adorno were added to a letter written by Meyer Schapiro on 10 August; as they returned to New York from Maine on Friday 13 August, and Meyer Schapiro's letter would have arrived on the 11th at the earliest, but probably on the 12th, one can take 12, or possibly 13, August – the day of their departure – as the date of the letter. Translator's note: the letter from Meyer Schapiro was written in English.

1 In January 1939, Adorno spoke on 'Aesthetic Aspects of Radio' at the Brooklyn Institute of Arts and Science in a series of lectures directed by Meyer Schapiro.

2 Meyer Schapiro, who had been given Křenek's book *Über neue Musik* by Adorno, tried in vain to have the former invited to lecture at the Brooklyn Institute (see *Adorno–Křenek Correspondence*, p. 130).

3 The New York-born philosopher Sidney Hook (1902–1989).

4 The American philosopher Ernest Nagel (1901–1985) had been teaching at Columbia University in New York since 1931.

5 The scientist Selig Hecht (1892–1947), born in Glogau, Silesia, taught biophysics at Columbia University.

6 See *Die Expressionismusdebatte: Materialien zu einer marxistischen Realismuskonzeption* [The Expressionism Debate: Material for a Marxist Conception of Realism], ed. Hans-Jürgen Schmitt (Frankfurt am Main, 1973).

7 Published as a review of the book *Sibelius: A Close-Up*, by B. de Törne (London, 1937), in *ZfS* 7 (1938), pp. 460–3 (issue 3); it was later included in

Adorno's collection *Impromptus* under the title 'Glosse über Sibelius' [Gloss on Sibelius] (see *GS* 17, pp. 247–52).

8 The analyses collected in typescript form under the title *Steckbriefe* [Wanted Posters] – 'Ave Maria von Gounod', 'Prélude cis-moll [C Sharp Minor] von Rachmaninoff' and 'Humoreske von Dvořák' – were later included in the first part of *Musikalische Warenanalysen* [Musical Commodity Analyses] (see *GS* 16, pp. 284–8).

9 The typescript that Sohn-Rethel sent with his letter of 8 July included the two first chapters of the unpublished manuscript entitled 'Kritische Liquidierung des philosophischen Idealismus: Eine Untersuchung zur Methode des Geschichtsmaterialismus' [Critical Liquidation of Philosophical Idealism: An Examination of the Method of Historical Materialism]; see *Adorno–Sohn-Rethel Correspondence*, pp. 87–93.

10 The novel *Erewhon, or Over the Range* (1872) by Samuel Butler (1835–1902).

151 GRETEL ADORNO TO WALTER BENJAMIN NEW YORK, 24.8.1938

24 August 1938.

Dear Detlef,

your books will be sent off in the next few days; I enclose a copy of the list.[1] Please send the Kierkegaard back soon. I am in a great rush and dead tired. We have been in the new apartment[2] for a week, and you can hardly imagine how much work it is. We have to find a space for furniture from two different cities, as well as vast numbers of books, sheet music and gramophone records in what is ultimately a rather small apartment. And then worst of all: Teddie's unsorted papers, 4 boxes of rubbish. I think we shall feel very much at home here; hopefully you will soon have a chance to visit us in our own stable. So far the only disadvantage seems to be the location, which is rather exposed [?] on all sides, but that is compensated for by so many advantages: letterbox in the house, naturally many new cupboards, very bright, well-equipped kitchen and bathroom, splendid view across the Hudson. My room is truly enchanting: from the big couch I can see the water, and in front of the window there is a lovely old writing desk and a table with two chairs, next to the couch a little chest of drawers, on the right-hand wall a glass cupboard and then also a carpet and typewriting table and chair, that's all.[3] While I was sorting things I also found many essays of yours from the FZ, the Voss and Literarische Welt – it is good to know that we have all that!

My dear, so much depends on the timely arrival of the Baudelaire here; I very much hope that you can make it possible.

Forgive the haste, but I am truly still half dead.

Fond regards ever your

Felicitas

All the best from Teddie, who is working on the radio project like a madman until Max returns.

Original: manuscript.

1 It does not appear to have survived.

2 The Adornos had moved into the apartment at 290 Riverside Drive on 15 August.

3 *that's all:* EO.

152 WALTER BENJAMIN TO THEODOR WIESENGRUND-ADORNO AND GRETEL ADORNO SKOVSBOSTRAND, 28.8.1938

my dears,

instead of a little fresh green, I am sending this black-speckled paper to your new apartment! there are orchids that have a similar effect.

The letters I have received from you of late have made me very happy. It would be a fine thing if Felizitas, who is so inclined to underestimate the significance hers have for me, were soon to try writing at greater length again. It would be one of the few things that I allow to interrupt my work!

Today I shall remain quite laconic – though your only conclusion from this should be that I have to make the most of every minute. The copy I enclose of the main passages from a letter to Pollock[1] that is going off with the same delivery will tell you why. I wrote it because a very detailed letter[2] about the state of the 'Baudelaire' that I had sent to Max on the 3rd of August was lost in the forwarding process.

I am highly tempted to tell you something about the Baudelaire – not so much about the forthcoming second part as rather its first and third parts. Those two parts supply the tools: the first presents allegory in Baudelaire as a problem, while the third deals with its social resolution. That – aside from the severe migraine period in Paris – was what made me get so behind with my work that I wanted at all costs to see clearly before me the comprehensive whole, in all its parts, prior to writing a single line of the final version. I reached that goal through a large collection of notes made in the first two months of my stay here.

The other side of the coin is that this pressure has now fallen on the completion of the second part; and perhaps I do not even feel its full weight; for I hardly dare imagine the full extent of this second part on its natural scale!

In addition to this, I have to move house; the noise produced by the children here makes the place in which I have been lodging unusable. I will exchange it for another, inhabited by a lunatic. Perhaps Felizitas remembers the great idiosyncrasy I have always had towards these sick people! – There is in fact no convenient accommodation anywhere here.

Many thanks for Schapiro's letter! I shall write to him once the Baudelaire is finished. Then I will be able to move freely among people once more; but not before then.

So it is all the more important that you extend my sincere thanks to him. The Stevenson essay in question is indeed in the collected works, and I have obtained it. I found his remark about the Impressionists very interesting, and the thought was new to me.

I liked Teddie's comment about Caillois. Compare it to a passage in my letter of 28 May this year to Max. Incidentally, Max was thinking of publishing that part of the letter and one or two others. My lost letter contains a declaration of full consent to it. I would be grateful if you could tell him that when he returns. (I would want only the passage on Bataille to remain unpublished, and could explain why.)

I will not forget to send 'Berliner Kindheit' and the Brecht poems. Because it is too late to do all that before I move, however, I enclose a picture[3] of myself standing in front of the door to Brecht's garden; his son took it. I trust you will find a place for it where it is no more exposed to the gaze of others than the products of the original have been thus far.

Make sure you do not forget to extend my greetings to Bloch, and to you I send warm and elegiac regards from the crumbling continent

28 August 1938
Skovsbostrand per Svendborg c/o Brecht

Yours Walter

PS After thorough consideration, I must append some remarks concerning the title of the second part as detailed in the letter excerpt enclosed. Last night I attempted to estimate the total length of the second part as precisely as possible. It transpired that it too substantially exceeds the number of pages that were to be allotted to me in the

next issue. I may therefore have to restrict myself to the two principal sections of the second part, namely the theory of flânerie and the theory of modernity. Accordingly, the title of the manuscript may differ from that mentioned in the letter to Pollock.

Perhaps it will interest Teddie to know – if he does not know already – that his Kierkegaard is mentioned in an important section of Löwith's 'Nietzsches Philosophie der ewigen Wiederkunft des Gleichen' Berlin 1935.[4]

Original: manuscript.

1 See *GB* 6, letter no. 1256.

2 See *GB* 6, letter no. 1254.

3 See fig. 3 on p. 243.

4 See Karl Löwith, *Nietzsches Philosophie der ewigen Wiederkunft des Gleichen* [Nietzsche's Philosophy of the Eternal Reccurrence] (Berlin, 1935), p. 166 (note 30).

153 GRETEL ADORNO TO WALTER BENJAMIN
NEW YORK, 12.9.1938

12 September 1938.

My dear Detlef:

a thousand thanks for your very sweet letter. From the first moment, I was certain that you would abide by the deadline and could not understand why the institute was so worried about the next issue of the journal. After your brief intimations I am more eager than ever to read the Baudelaire. I would almost go so far as to say that I am glad the institute is pressuring you; for this way we will at least see something of yours soon. Inquisitive as I am, I would like to know roughly when you expect to finish the entire Baudelaire. Please do not think me nosy, for I am thinking about the following: do you consider it at all possible or useful to judge how long you will still need for the Arcades study, or – and this perhaps interests me even more in this context – how long you will definitely have to stay in Paris for it. – Even though the political situation will probably iron itself out again now, things may still become a little too uncomfortable for you in Europe in the near future, and then the Arcades study should at least be in safe hands at all costs. So it has generally been assumed that you absolutely must live in Paris to finish your work. Teddie and I see things differently, however. Aside from the hope that you might be tempted by a few of the people here, we knew you for long enough in Berlin to be sure that New York would at least not be any more unpleasant for you. –

We were very happy to receive your picture; as a thank you I enclose one of Lotte and me[1] – though Lotte is actually much prettier and does not always have such a stupid expression on her face. This is just so that you have a rough idea of her. You will have heard that E's father[2] has died in the meantime. Aside from that, there is nothing new with him, it is all still uncertain. –

Bloch is coming to New York City only in early October; meanwhile he seems to be finding one or two things problematic due to his various articles in 'Weltbühne', especially the fact that we might have a different opinion, but I think it will not be too difficult to reach some agreement, in spite of Eisler and Karola. – What is the situation with Dora Sophie and Stefan, are they also affected by the new legislation in Italy?[3] – I have not heard from Elisabeth Wiener at all lately; she is cross with me because, in spite of everything, I had severe reservations about her emigration (as all her friends did). Have you heard from her? – I hope your books have arrived safely in the meantime; while I was sorting the shelf I also found Hauff's fairy tales and Madame

Bovary, which I would almost assume belong to you too. Can I continue to hold on to them for you? – I have just finished re-reading Kafka's 'America'. And – to be honest I was disappointed; in my memory it was much better, not so clichéd, and also freer. I have now given Teddie the last volume: letters and diary entries. – My days are now entirely filled out once again: in the morning household and cooking, or training my delightful half-Negro, half-Indian lady, in the afternoon Teddie's secretary, then also my quite extensive current correspondence. – I think your encouragement to write to you did me a great deal of good; there is hardly anything here that I like more.

The very fondest regards and embraces from your

Felicitas.

Original: manuscript.

1 See fig. 4 on p. 244.

2 No further information could be found about Alexander Wissing.

3 A decree stated that Jews who had immigrated to Italy after 1 January 1919 had to leave the country within six months.

154 WALTER BENJAMIN TO GRETEL ADORNO PARIS, 1.11.1938

my dear Felizitas,

as you can see, the familiar writing paper has reappeared – and with it, after an autumn full of news, a number of things have returned to normal. Should you desire a retrospective of my summer, I assume that it will soon reveal itself to you by reading the Baudelaire manuscript,[1] if that has not already been the case. It constitutes the quintessence of the past months. I am awaiting a report of its reception in Newyork in the next few days, and I hope very much that Teddie will contribute to it.

You must tell me soon what Newyork is like at second glance, not least as this second glance must also encompass a number of its brand-new inhabitants. In that regard I am especially keen to hear your account of Ernst Bloch and the relationship between him and you both. And I am no less eager to learn about your everyday routine and the manner in which you have arranged your lives, both as a couple and among our closer acquaintances.

I think it was apparent in my last letter from Svendborg that – for all the restrictions of my existence in Denmark – I was not enthusiastic about returning. I was expecting substantial changes; they are rarely for the better nowadays. So far I have not been able to see enough of my French acquaintances to assess how justified my fears were. I have only spoken to Adrienne Monnier, to whom these fears would never have applied. But then I encountered changes where I had not expected them. My sister is severely, in fact hopelessly ill. As well as the chronic complaint that has afflicted her for years, she now also has what appears to be an advanced hardening of the arteries. My sister's physical faculties have been reduced to the bare minimum, and she is often bedridden for entire days. Under these circumstances it is highly favourable that I am living so near to her. – My brother has been transferred to the prison camp in Wilsnak,[2] where he is occupied with roadwork. From what I have heard, life is still bearable there. The greatest nightmare for those in his situation, as I often hear from people in Germany, is not so much the dawning of each new day behind bars as the threat of being sent to a concentration camp after years of imprisonment. – As far as my wife is concerned, she passed through Paris quite suddenly shortly before my return, and is now in London. It seems she plans to make another attempt at opening a guesthouse there. I hope to see her here around Christmas and then receive favourable news about Stefan's chances in England.

To touch on the political developments again: the rapprochement between Germany and England that is at the centre of the current efforts will, I fear, inevitably drive apart the few French and Germans who are still close to one another. At the end of the week there is expected to be a 'statut des étrangers'. In the meantime I am undertaking my naturalization circumspectly, but without any illusions. If the chances of success were doubtful before, the usefulness of this measure has now also become problematic. In the light of the deterioration of the judicial system in Europe, the security of any kind of legalization is deceptive.

I have good reason to congratulate myself for every single piece of paper I placed in your hands in March 1933. So far, the only fruit – albeit an almost completely assured one – of my sustained attempts[3] to retrieve some of my books from Berlin, but primarily essays, has been the fact that both the writings left behind by the two Heinles, which I had collected in their entirety, and my irreplaceable archive on the history of the left-bourgeois youth movement, and finally also the works of my youth – including the 1914 Hölderlin essay[4] – have been destroyed.

To end on a merrier note, let me add the remark that the Lord, who can take so much away from the waking, gives it to his own in their sleep: Hessel,[5] who sat in Berlin like a mouse in the timberwork for five and a half years, recently arrived in Paris with great support and under powerful patronage. I think his story will be a notable one; I plan for him to relate it to me in the next few days.

Did you remember the pictures by American primitives that I recommended to you?

1 November 1938 Fond regards to you and Teddie
Paris XV Yours Detlef
10 rue Dombasle

Original: manuscript.

1 Benjamin's essay 'Das Paris des Second Empire bei Baudelaire' [The Paris of the Second Empire in Baudelaire]; see *GS* 1 [2], pp. 511–604.

2 'As part of his detention, [Georg Benjamin] was transferred to the "Aussenarbeitslager Abbendorf" [Abbendorf Outdoor Labour Camp] for the purpose of dyke-building. Abbendorf is situated in the floodplain of the River Elbe, fairly close to Bad Wilsnack (not Wilsnak). The camp, however, belonged to Brandenburg Prison' (letter of 2 May 1999 from Michael Benjamin to the editors).

3 Perhaps through Helen Hessel, who was staying in Berlin at the time in order to take Franz Hessel out of the country?

4 It has survived in a copy made by Scholem.

5 Franz Hessel had fled to France with a French visa that Jean Giraudoux, a senior civil servant in the Foreign Ministry at the time, had obtained for him; Hessel stayed with Alix de Rothschild, a distant relative of his, in the Avenue Foch.

155 GRETEL ADORNO TO WALTER BENJAMIN NEW YORK, 10.1.1939

10 January 1939.

My dear Detlef:

I hope your year got off to a good start. I would almost assume that Dora Sofie and Stefan stayed with you. How are they? Over here there was hardly any peace, even during the holidays. My activities are also starting to become much more intense through seminars at the institute, work with Teddie and Max, as well as teaching myself English shorthand, and I am very happy about that. – Today I sent off the Hauff to you by recorded delivery. – In a conversation with Max, there was mention of a children's book: M. Lionet, which Max thinks you recommended to him.[1] Who is the author? Is it difficult to find? Do you know 'Turn of the Screw' by Henry James? I am sure it has also been published in French, (tour d'écrou), and you absolutely must read it. Published in 1891, and it really anticipates much of psychoanalysis.

This time last year, our departure from Europe was not far off. Except for one piece of bad news from Germany – Teddie's parents will probably go to Cuba until they are let in here – that one year has more or less fulfilled our hopes for it. Hopefully you will soon have an opportunity to take a look at New York too.

The very fondest regards from Teddie, who will write to you himself soon

ever your old
Gretel.

Could you please send me a good recipe for mousse au chocolat? Teddie is so very fond of it.

Original: manuscript.

1 This is the novel *Monsieur Lyonnet* by Léopold Chauveau (1870–1940), published in 1930.

156 GRETEL ADORNO TO WALTER BENJAMIN NEW YORK, 2.3.1939

2 March 1939.

My dear Detlef:

now it has been a few days over a year since we came here. I have already grown so accustomed to it that there seems absolutely nothing new to me about being in New York. But there is still one person I miss here: you. Admittedly the immigration prospects are not looking too rosy at the moment, as the German quota has been exceeded, but in the long run you should definitely grow accustomed to the idea. This immediately confronts me with the great obstacle: learning English. Oh, if you could only set about doing so, the sooner the better. Here I am thinking above all of the fact that Meyer Schapiro will be going to France for 8 months in June. There is no question that you absolutely must see him. But it is equally certain that you would be able to discuss all the future prospects in America with him much better if you could do so in English. (For I know what an impression it made on him when a friend told him that Friedel Kracauer can already speak English so well.) You will get on superbly – he is very amusing, very learned and also very elegant! I am attending a lecture cycle of his at Columbia on Modern Painting,[1] it is a shame you cannot be there. Last time he said as an aside: Grandville, the Disney of his day, only more talented. With regard to Impressionism, the painter he regards most highly alongside Renoir and Cézanne is a young man named Bazile[2] (?) who fell in the Russian–French war. Do you know anything about him?

I have had very little news from Boston; sadly our interests increasingly diverge, and all they are interested in over there are neckties and the like. – Ernst Bloch is playing his nuisance[3] role only too masterfully, it is a crying shame. Alfred Sohn-R. is in Birmingham for the sake of hospitality[4] – with no end to his work in sight, of course. – Carlchen Dreyfuss, the poor fellow, is living among farmers in Argentina and feeling utterly rotten. – Have you heard from Scholem at all? We often talk about him. How are your siblings? And much more importantly, how are things with you? Let me hear from you very soon, fond regards also from Teddie

ever your Felicitas

Original: manuscript.

1 *Modern Painting:* EO.

2 Frédéric Bazille (1841–1870), from Montpellier.

3 *nuisance:* EO.

4 *hospitality:* EO.

157 WALTER BENJAMIN TO GRETEL ADORNO
PARIS, 20.3.1939

20 March 1939
10, Rue Dombasle
Paris XVe.

My dear Felizitas,

now I am forced to dictate the letter that has long been meant for you. I have been lying in bed (in my room, which has the elevator shaft going through it – sheer torture) for the last few days due to a bout of influenza, and the fever has still not abated. As always, everything has happened at once; and, in addition, I am unable to work, and can only spend the long hours reading. So I was all the happier to hear of the arrival of the books yesterday.

This letter, as I say, had long been intended for you. It kept being delayed through various pieces of work; most recently the long letter to Teddie whose receipt you confirmed yesterday. As you read in it, I met with Kolisch not long ago. There is a chance that I might see him again at the end of the month – in which case you would perhaps receive an account *de vive voix* from me soon after the arrival of these lines.

In some ways, you could certainly dispense with any couriers, and you have first-hand information regarding those things that determine my well-being. Shortly before your letter arrived, I received one from Max in which they play an important part. Max writes that the mobile part of the institute's assets has been used up, and that the majority of the properties owned cannot be converted into liquid funds at present. In the same letter, he tells me that the institute is seeking a scholarship for me in America – but asks me to do what I can from here.

Even without the ominous risk that he mentions, namely the termination of my research scholarship, it would still be self-evident that I must comply with his request. As soon as I am up again, I shall do what I can to set things in motion. I have been following things here for long enough, however, to know that, since the start of the emigration, no one who is working in a similar fashion and under similar conditions to my own has succeeded in making a living in France. I am not counting former professors such as Marck[1] and Gumbel[2] or the novelist Noth.[3] Their names form the complete list of those who, to my knowledge, could have lived off the earnings or the support available here.

There is therefore no question of my working here in the long run. I cannot afford to disregard the necessity you touched on, namely that of learning English, and I will begin this summer. – The question is whether *I will still reach America*. – I have just sought the help of Scholem, who, as you can imagine, has a certain influence on Schocken. What I would have to offer is a book on Kafka. Considering his Judaistic fixation and the mass of material forced on him by authors of Jewish orientation, however, the chances of bringing about a contribution from Schocken are slim.

And so I must place all the hope *that I so desperately need* in the efforts being undertaken on my behalf by the institute across the ocean. Three weeks ago, Max cabled me a request for a French exposé for the 'Arcades'.[4] It should have arrived by now, and will differ from the one you know in several respects. I tried, as far as I was able at such short notice, to make one of the basic conceptions of the 'Arcades' – the culture of commodity-producing society as phantasmagoria – its central focus.

To return to the questions concerning a more distant future: a number of people have advised me to put my name down on the list at the American consulate here. This supposedly guarantees a fixed place on the waiting list for potential immigrants. On the other hand, however, I have heard that in certain cases, e.g. if someone is being given an appointment, those exceeding the quota are disregarded. But one forfeits this chance if one is already on the list. – Now I do not know how I should proceed.

Have the last manuscripts I sent to Löwenthal found their way to you? I hope so, especially in the case of my review of the French encyclopaedia,[5] parts of which should interest you in the context of your current art studies. Let me take this opportunity to insist once more that you take a look at the wonderful American primitives in the American Folk Art Gallery. – I hope my review of Sternberger's 'Panorama' offers you a few appealing moments. I will send you the book very soon.

The author of 'Monsieur Lyonnet' you enquired about in January is Léopold Chauveau. Max owns the book. But if I find it here I shall send it to you.

I would very much like to know if Teddie's parents are finally in safety. – The health of my sister, whom you asked after, is unchanged. My brother sends an indirect report from time to time; they seem to indicate that life there has not defeated him yet.

Münzenberg has announced his exit from the Communist Party with an open letter.[6] At the same time as I read it, I received an official party pamphlet entitled 'The Path to Hitler's Overthrow'.[7] The idiocy of its authors exceeds my comprehension. This piece of propaganda is one of the most harmful documents the party can be confronted with. – The political situation seems to grow more threatening every day.

Will neither Max nor Pollock be coming here in the spring?

I am looking forward to meeting Schapiro.

Write to me soon. I am once again in great need of your presence.

Fond regards to Teddie and you.

Your Detlef

Original: typescript.

1 The philosopher Siegfried Marck (1889–1957), the social democrat councillor of his home town of Breslau, where he had held a professorship since 1930, emigrated to France in 1933. He worked at the Centre de Recherches Sociales, part of the École Normale Supérieure, until 1934, then taught at the University of Dijon until 1940. From 1936 to 1939 he held a scholarship granted by the Caisse Nationale de la Recherche Scientifique entailing between 17,000 and 18,000 francs per year (see Gilbert Badia, Jean-Baptiste Joly, Jean-Philippe Mathieu, Jacques Omnès, Jean-Michel Palmier and Hélène Roussel, *Les Bannis de Hitler: Acceuil et luttes des exilés allemands en France [1933–1939]* [Paris, 1984] [Études et Documentations Internationales], p. 155).

2 The mathematician and national economist Emil Julius Gumbel (1891–1966), social democrat and member of the Human Rights League, taught statistics in Heidelberg from 1923 to 1933, and gave lectures in 1929

at the Institut für Sozialforschung in 1929. From 1933 to 1940 Gumbel taught in Lyons. Gumbel, who remained politically active in exile, fled to the USA in 1940 and taught at the New School for Social Research.

3 Ernst Erich Noth (1900–1983); see his *Erinnerungen eines Deutschen* [Recollections of a German] (Hamburg and Düsseldorf, 1973).

4 See *GS* 5 [1], pp. 60–77.

5 Benjamin's review of volumes XVI and XVII of the Encyclopédie Française did not ultimately appear in the journal; see *GS* 3, pp. 579–85.

6 Willi Münzenberg, who had already parted company with the Communists in 1937 in reaction to the Moscow trials and Stalin's policies in the Spanish Civil War, had published his announcement with the reasons for his departure in his own journal, *Die Zukunft* [The Future], on 10 March 1939; see the excepts in Babette Gross, *Willi Münzenberg: Eine politische Biographie* (Leipzig, 1991), pp. 464–6.

7 No further information.

158 GRETEL ADORNO TO WALTER BENJAMIN NEW YORK, 26.3.1939

26 March 1939.

My dear Detlef:

I already told you some time ago how much I would like to produce a German typescript of your reproduction essay. You could hardly do me any greater favour at the moment than to send me the material as quickly as possible. For I am now unemployed, so to speak, and have all too much spare time on my hands. Teddie will be very busy with his English book[1] for the radio project for the next 6–7 months, and there in particular – despite my improving English shorthand – I am naturally of no use. The people at the institute have nothing for me to do either, and so I see a dauntingly long summer ahead of me. After 1 year of America I feel well rested and fresh, and ready – now that I am no longer sitting by my lonely self in Berlin – to begin something worthwhile. But what? Unfortunately I have no idea myself. Forgive me for bothering you with my needs, but I am more down than I have been for a long time. Let me hear from you very soon fond regards

ever your Felicitas

Original: manuscript.

1 This refers to the planned, but unrealized, *Current of Music*.

159 WALTER BENJAMIN TO GRETEL ADORNO
PARIS, EARLY APRIL 1939

my dear Felizitas,

I was troubled to read your little letter of 26 March. As happy as I am that you wish to take on my reproduction essay, it saddens me that this is to occur on the basis of boredom or even spleen. And Europe is a continent in whose tear-laden atmosphere the signal flares of comfort now ascend only rarely to announce good fortune.

The manuscript will be dispatched by the same post as a registered letter. It is in good order; I hope you will not have any difficulties finding your way through it. The text deviates from the one you know in several respects; first of all, it has been greatly extended. Admittedly I have also taken down a number of further reflections[1] on the matter since that revision. Assigning these reflections to their place in the overall context is one of the most important services your copy will do me. I would therefore ask you to leave a relatively wide margin in your copy so that it lends itself better to further revision.

Furthermore, one must now see it as an essential security measure to transfer all moveable goods – be they intellectual or material – to America as quickly as possible. For things are looking much more ominous than in September. The poorest devils – I will get to the rich people in a moment – are setting off to make sure they still reach the new continent. Fritz Sternberg,[2] as I heard yesterday, will be leaving within the next few days. – People here are saying – on the basis of information that will no doubt be out of date by the time it reaches you – that things will 'calm down' by 20 April. Then the operation against Poland is to begin, and no one knows whether it will be able to remain within the limits of mere blackmail.

In September, in the seclusion of Denmark, I was able to work well under similar circumstances. Unfortunately I cannot say the same now. In addition to this, a series of new decrees concerning foreigners are keeping everyone on tenterhooks. An increase in the obstacles to my naturalization should be the most harmless of the measures that apply to me. There is talk of a compulsory mobilization for foreigners[3] up to the age of fifty-two. – I now have a fundamentally new outline of the flaneur chapter that will, I would like to think, be of particular interest to Teddie. The flaneur now appears in the context of an examination of the specific characteristics assumed by leisure in the bourgeois period in the face of the dominant work ethic. – How much it would mean to me to speak about it with you, or even any reasonable creature at all; how much more quickly my work would proceed. My current isolation harmonizes all too well with the current trend, which goes against everything that is ours. It is not purely intellectual in nature.

This leads me back to the rich people I alluded to before. For in the next few days, the only truly affluent family I knew here, and who could have done a great deal to support me, is leaving for America. The man is a collector of Renaissance medallions – and there is no one with whom I find it easier to strike up contact than a collector. More importantly, I was able – falling back on my experiences with Speyer – to give his son, Ernst Morgenroth, who has been trying his luck as a novelist under the name of Lackner, a few hints. I am endeavouring to make the best out of losing this last crutch and to induce Morgenroth senior[4] to seek Max out. If one goes about it in the right way, I am sure one will be able to arouse his interest in my move to America, and perhaps eventually also in certain undertakings by the institute. I think the young Morgenroth will also follow suit. He is one of the more educated and benevolent members of his generation. He is willing to learn, and one should not be too rough with him.

Did I tell you that Brentano[5] was here for a few days? Grasset is publishing one of his books, and the journalists are taking the opportunity to woo the author. That was evidently not enough to ensure his peace of mind, for he showed an enormous resentment towards Russia and all other powers that gave the horse he had bet on such a bad start in world history. I could not bear the tone of his confessions for long. What unsettled me most about this visit was the fact that Brentano has a close connection to Silone.[6] I find it difficult to imagine how a political grudge such as Brentano's could be the daily bread of an author who is, after all, as significant as Silone. The notion that it is 'ten times worse' in Russia than in Germany is, Brentano would have us believe, the leitmotif of that Zurich avant-garde.

Thieme is currently in Paris. He is also a semi-fugitive, at the moment from Switzerland. He was active for quite some time in Germany in the Catholic opposition, and has been living out in the country near Basle for the last four years. It seems that the Swiss have stationed very significant amounts of troops on their border.

Schocken finally passed through Paris on his return journey to Palestine. I learned of it *post festum*. As I do not know Schocken personally, nor have any other connection to him other than through Scholem, I would not have been able to make use of his presence. Speaking of which, there are no prospects there. After Scholem's last letter, Schocken does not want to publish anything at all in German any more. A short encyclopaedia article about Jewish mysticism,[7] by Scholem himself, looks to mark the end of that production.

Which of my last manuscripts have you seen? Have you laid eyes on the new French sketch for the 'Arcades'? the review of the Sternberger? And the book itself, which I gave Kolisch to pass on to you?

I would wish you more leisure than copying the reproduction essay will afford you. But I am very grateful to you for it. I would like four copies.

Can I not hope that a longer letter from you is already making its way to me as I write this one? The tiny little notes form an endearing contrast to the great distances they cover. But now you should write a proper letter! I hope it will have good things to report about your present state.

My best wishes to you and Teddie

Yours Detlef

Original: manuscript.

1 Benjamin must have sent a typescript of the expanded second version of the reproduction essay (the second version without the additions; see *GS* 7 [1], pp. 350–84); the typescript of this version has not survived. The copy made on American typewriter paper, presumably by Gretel Adorno, and whose first half (including chapter VII) may be a carbon copy of a typescript, but is definitely an original typescript from chapter IX onwards, does not – contrary to the assumption by the editor of the *Gesammelte Schriften* (see *GS* 1 [3], p. 1056) – contain any corrections by Benjamin; it cannot be dated. There are no indications that it was produced in Benjamin's lifetime, nor is there any mention of the completion of the copy, let alone any sending thereof, in Benjamin's letters or those of Gretel Adorno. For the 'further reflections' written between 1938 and 1940, see *GS* 7 [2], pp. 673–80.

2 The politician and publicist Fritz Sternberg (1895–1960), author of a book on imperialism, had come to France via Czechoslovakia, Austria and Switzerland in 1938. He became an American citizen in 1950. In 1935 Sternberg published the book *Der Faschismus an der Macht* [Fascism in Power].

3 The decree dates from 12/16 April; the mobilization was to include all male foreigners between the ages of eighteen and forty-eight.

4 Ernest Gustave Morgenroth (1910–2000) had studied art history and philosophy in Frankfurt and Berlin. In 1933 he emigrated to Paris with his parents Lucie and Sigmund Morgenroth. Morgenroth wrote under the pseudonym Stephan Lackner; his novel *Jan Heimatlos* [Jan the Homeless] was published in Switzerland in 1939.

5 The writer Bernard von Brentano (1901–1964). Grasset published the French translation of his novel *Theodor Chindler*.

6 Ignazio Silone (1900–1978), author of the novels *Fontamara* (1930) and *Brot und Wein* [Bread and Wine] (1937), as well as the essay 'Die Schule der Diktatoren' [The School of Dictators] (1938) – of which a partial preprint was published in 'Mass und Wert' – lived in Swiss exile from 1930 to 1944. Silone, who, as a representative of the socialist youth movement, was co-founder of

the Italian Communist Party, was – together with Koestler – one of the main witnesses against communism after 1945, having abandoned it as early as 1930. (See Arthur Koestler, André Gide, Louis Fischer, Richard Wright and Stephen Spender, *The God That Failed* [London: Hamilton, 1950].)

7 There were in fact two articles, which were supposed to appear in the *Paris Yiddish Encyclopaedia* (*Scholem Correspondence*, p. 299), but were ultimately published only in 1946 in English translation: 'Jewish Mysticism and Kabbala' and 'Messianic Movements after the Expulsion from Spain' (in *Jewish People Past and Present*, pp. 308–27 and 335–47). Scholem had written that Schocken might arrange a private printing of the German manuscript.

160 GRETEL ADORNO TO WALTER BENJAMIN NEW YORK, 24.4.1939

24 April 1939.

My dear Detlef:

many thanks for the book by Sternberger. I will send it to you as soon as I have looked at it, or is it not so urgent? Rudi Kolisch was here before he left for Porterico (?), but was in such a terrible hurry that I hardly spoke to him. So unfortunately we have not had a proper oral account of you and how you are. – Sadly I am, of course, all too familiar with the institute's economy measures. At the moment I see a genuine chance for you if you meet with Schapiro, perhaps he can advise or even help you. Regarding immigration to America, there must also be people in Paris who know all about that, e.g. Kracauer. But I fear that you are no longer in contact with him (and rightly so). But how about enquiring at the consulate? –

Teddie's parents are to embark for Cuba the day after tomorrow, everything seems to have gone more quickly than we had hoped after all. –

I have just read The Autobiography of Alice B. Toklas[1] by Gertrude Stein.

I could imagine that you would enjoy glancing through the book; you would encounter many acquaintances in there, including Sylvia Beach and Mme Monnier. –

My prayers for something to do were answered a few days ago: Max's secretary has fallen ill, so he and I are working on his things together. Also, Teddie is preparing a study on 'determinism'.[2]

You know that your fate is more important to us than anything else, and that we are doing everything in our power. – I am already greatly looking forward to the new version and the 3rd part of the Baudelaire.

Do you have any plans for the summer yet? Are you intending to go to Denmark? –

I wish we could go for a walk together down by the Hudson and talk about everything at leisure. Unfortunately it does not look as if we will be coming to Europe in the near future. I do not think Max or Fritz have any plans either.

About 2 weeks ago we had a great surprise: Scholem sent the Sohar [*sic*] section[3] from Jerusalem. Have you had any other news from him? Did Scholem respond to the suggestion of a Kafka book?

Take good care of yourself, the very fondest regards ever

your Felicitas

Many greetings from Teddie

Original: manuscript.

1 This book, which describes the years in Paris from 1900 to 1932, had been published in 1933. Translator's note: title of book: EO.

2 Adorno never wrote it.

3 See Gershom Scholem, *Die Geheimnisse der Schöpfung* [The Secrets of Creation] (Berlin, 1935).

161 GRETEL ADORNO TO WALTER BENJAMIN NEW YORK, 1.5.1939

1 May 1939.

My dear Detlef:

I have read through your manuscript, and I must tell you that I like it substantially better in German than in translation. It was almost a shame that I could decipher everything so effortlessly, that there were no longer any handwritten notes. I also missed the addenda from which you read parts to us in San Remo. As I am working very intensively with Max at the moment, the copy will be slightly delayed, but I am sure that is not a problem.

Today Rudi Kolisch stopped off in New York for a day, and spent it almost entirely with us. We are very much looking forward to the reworked Baudelaire chapter – is it coming soon? I completely understand how attached you are to Paris, but I nonetheless think that you would not find it at all disagreeable here. Do not worry unnecessarily about your future; as Max says, on ne mourra pas de faim [one will not starve to death]. Teddie and I will do everything in our power for you (it is already troubling for us that we no longer have the financial resources simply to do it privately), and Max also knows what is at stake. And the circumstances *cannot* be allowed to disrupt your work.

(Kolisch has the most severe worries himself, as his fellow quartet members are showing an extraordinary lack of solidarity and jeopardizing the whole thing, but that must remain *entre nous*). –

Teddie's parents set sail for Cuba from Hamburg last Wednesday. –

The other day we heard, via a few other people, the rumour that both Eisler – who, incidentally, has meanwhile been expelled from here, and we do not know if he will be let in again later – and Brecht refused to sign a petition that was intended purely to glorify Stalin. Have you had any news from Denmark? Have a pleasant May in Paris and make sure to think often

of your little
Felizitas

Original: manuscript.

162 WALTER BENJAMIN TO GRETEL ADORNO PONTIGNY, 19.5.1939

my dear little one,

with a little luck, these lines will arrive right on your birthday. And if I am greeting you in this new fashion, my desire to do so stems as much from the pretty turn of phrase at the end of your last letter as from the wish to give you a sense of a place where the years to come will not make you older, any more than they would have made you bigger. For the rest of this opening, let me mention another inspiration that came from a close reading of Proust's correspondence.[1] Among his correspondents is a certain Madame Strauss; Teddie will remind you of some of her famous words.[2] She has a way of addressing Proust that I find enchanting. In particular her formulaic phrase 'my dear little Marcel', which has an inimitable tenderness.

The large library with 15000 books is the best thing about Pontigny – from where I am writing to you. It is at the free disposal of visitors, and you can imagine how I am profiting from that. As for the remaining features, they are infinitely less favourable. One could describe one of the more amusing aspects, concerning a gang of Scandinavian youths who raided it. One could also describe one of the more painful ones, namely the decline of the proprietor, Paul Desjardins, and the role of his wife in the matter. There are moments when the husband's situation in these cases irresistibly reminds me of my own in San Remo. Incidentally, I sent Max a letter containing a fairly detailed physiognomy of Pontigny.

Might it have been you who recommended to me, some years ago, the books of Henry James (the brother of William, the philosopher)? I recently stumbled on 'The Turn of the Screw',[3] which is remarkable. One day the three of us must get together to discuss the significant fact that the nineteenth century is the classic period of ghost stories. Then the figure of Henry James would take on a striking profile.

Another discovery I have made in this library is Joubert.[4] (He was the last of the great French moralists and experienced the Restoration.) His 'Pensées' truly astounded me. In Joubert's work I find exactly the style I would like to have in everything I write – not so much the model as rather the masterful definition of his writing.[5]

The 'Baudelaire' is progressing, slowly but now, I hope, surely.

I am delighted that 'The Work of Art in the Age . . .' has finally made its way to you. The numerous notes that are waiting to be inserted into the manuscript will find their place once I have your copy. That is one of the reasons it will be useful for me: I will not have to work on the *only* copy of the text.

There was nothing astonishing in the news you told me about Brecht. I have been very familiar with his thoughts on Stalin since last summer. Incidentally, Brecht has left Funen, where he no longer felt secure. He is going to settle in Sweden.

There are no fewer than three reasons for my writing to you in French. I mentioned the first at the start of the letter.

The second is that, in this French environment, it is quite natural for me. The third is that today, on your birthday, I wish to express my old attachment to both of you in a new guise.

(To conclude, I must tell you how much the words of reassurance in your last letter meant to me. They helped me to free myself from a terrifying feeling of entrapment.)

All the best

Abbaye de Pontigny Detlef

19 May 1939

PS Let me know when Schapiro plans to come to Paris. I will be returning on Monday.

Original: manuscript. Translator's note: written in French.

1 The six-volume *Correspondance générale*, published by Plon between 1930 and 1936.

2 Geneviève Straus (1849–1926), daughter of the composer Fromental Halévy, was married to Georges Bizet from 1869 until his death in 1875; their

son Jacques Bizet was a school friend of Proust. Her second husband, whom she married in 1886, was the lawyer Emile Straus.

3 See Henry James, *Le Tour d'écrou, suivi les Papiers de Jeffrey Aspern*, trans. M. Le Corbeiller, with a preface by Edmond Jaloux (Paris, 1929).

4 Joseph Joubert (1754–1824), who published only very little, wrote down his 'pensées' [thoughts] daily in notebooks that were published posthumously. Joubert had come to Paris in 1778 and struck up contact with Diderot, who seems to have provided the stimulus for his 'Essai sur la Bienveillance Universelle' [Essay on Universal Benevolence], of which a number of fragments have survived. The edition of *Pensées* used by Benjamin is that of 1883 (see *GS* 5 [2], p. 1302, no. 460); a two-volume edition of his *Carnets* [Notebooks] had been published in 1938, edited by André Beaunier.

5 See *GS* 5 [1], p. 604, and *GS* 2 [2], p. 579.

163 GRETEL ADORNO TO WALTER BENJAMIN NEW YORK, 31.5.1939

31 May 1939.

10 Juny
that's it[1]

My very dear Detlef:

your last letter was so wonderfully enchanting that I must answer immediately. Unfortunately Teddie failed completely: he could no longer remember the famous remarks made by Mme Strauss himself. – On Monday the young Morgenroth was here for a little discussion evening, as was Meyer Schapiro. Sch.'s travel plans have been slightly disrupted by his wife's illness, and he will now be leaving here only on 21./VI., but intends to spend a little time in England first. I am sure I will still see him before his departure, however, and will try to get him to tell me exactly when he plans to come to Paris. –

The big black-and-white picture by Picasso, 'Guernica', was on exhibition here until recently. Did you happen to see it in P. too? –

Teddie will be going to Cuba to visit his parents for 10 days, so I will be (as one says here) a grass-widow[2] for the first time. – I am well, and am enjoying my work with Max – especially now, on a political topic[3] – a great deal, though unfortunately the other institute business takes up a terrible amount of his time. – In the meantime I have read Sternberger's book. It reminds me very much of 'Our Father' by Allan Bott, a collection of pictures from 19th-century magazines. It is quite beyond me how a book like that – which is by no means a slim volume – can come about with so little text. I do not like such pure assortments of facts without any interpretation at all. –

Rudi Kolisch would also like to travel to Europe again as soon as possible, as his concert season is beginning there anyway. Unfortunately he still has terrible worries with the quartet at the moment. It almost sounds ironic, as he has been let down not only by one, but in fact by all his co-players. –

If you can think of some little gift that could bring you some joy on your birthday, please let me know post haste so that I can still get hold of it before then. (I hope we can go to Bar Harbor again as we did last year, but Teddie's summer plans are still completely undecided.)

Fond regards and best wishes

ever your Felizitas

Original: manuscript.

1 *that's it*: EO.

2 *grass-widow* [*sic*]: EO.

3 Horkheimer was working on his essay 'Die Juden und Europa'.

164 WALTER BENJAMIN TO GRETEL ADORNO
PARIS, 26.6.1939

Dear Felizitas,

today I shall return to my 'beloved German'. If, however, my letter from Pontigny left you with an occasional longing for French, it would make me happy if you could find a suitable moment to open a copy of les fleurs du mal and have a look at it through my eyes. As my thoughts are now focused on this text day and night, we would no doubt meet.

As far as the results of these thoughts are concerned, you will not find it easy to recognize the Baudelaire of last summer in it. The new version of the flaneur chapter – for that is all I am working on – will seek to integrate decisive motifs from the reproduction essay and The Storyteller, combined with some from the Arcades. Never before have I been so certain of the point at which all my reflections, even from the most differing perspectives, converge (and it now seems to me that they have always done so). I immediately reacted to the fact that you are determined to do your best with the most extreme of the ideas from my old reservoir. – Naturally with one qualification: for now it will always be dealing with the flaneur, not the total complex of the Baudelaire. This chapter will, in any case, far exceed the scale of last year's 'Flaneur'. As it will now be divided into three separate parts, however – the arcades, the crowd and the type – this should facilitate the editorial treatment of the text. I am still a long way from writing the final draft. But the period of slow progress is now behind me, and not a day passes without writing something down.

I recently received, to my joy, the proofs of my review of volume XVI of the Encyclopédie française. This reminded me once more of the universal silence that greeted my review of Sternberger's 'Panorama'. Not even you broke it when you mentioned the book itself in your last letter. (I am familiar with Alwin Bott's pretty photo collection.) I would have thought that my examination, quite aside from its critical orientation, offers something new in those reflections devoted to the structure of the 'genre'. Do you not have anything to write to me about it?

I have a small literary victory to report. It is ten years ago that I wrote an essay entitled 'What is Epic Theatre?'[1] at the request of the Frankfurter Zeitung. Then, after the proofs (which I still have in my possession) had already been printed, it was taken out of the issue by Gubler following an ultimatum from Diebold. Now it will be published, with a few minor changes, in 'Mass und Wert', who are initiating a debate on Brecht. You will find it in the next issue.

You enquired about my summer plans: they are dependent on when Schapiro can be expected to come. Or is he planning a longer stay in Paris? Then there would definitely be a chance to see him. – I will certainly not be leaving France this year, or even Paris, until the rough draft of the 'Flaneur' is completely finished.

I wonder if my birthday wish will still arrive in time? In truth, I would almost view the copy of the reproduction essay as precisely that. So that you do not think that you have a deadline for it, however, I would like to mention a little book.[2] I think it would make me happy if you gave me the last book by Robert Dreyfus, who has just died. He was an old friend of Proust; he entitled it 'De Monsieur Thiers à Proust' and it contains many stories about Madame Strauss, which I will gladly promise to relate to you.

I have not seen the picture by Picasso that you mention.

Give Teddie my warm greetings, with the best, tender regards to you

from your
Detlef

26 June 1939
Paris XV
10 rue Dombasle

Original: manuscript.

1 See *GS* 2 [2], pp. 519–31.

2 See Robert Dreyfus, *De Monsieur Thiers à Marcel Proust: Histoire et souvenirs* (Paris, 1939); for the chapter 'Madame Straus et Marcel Proust', see

pp. 13–36. Robert Dreyfus (1873–1939) and Proust had been friends since their time together at the Lycée Condorcet; he had published *Souvenirs de Marcel Proust* in 1926.

165 GRETEL ADORNO TO WALTER BENJAMIN NEW YORK, 7.7.1939

7 July 1939.

My very dear Detlef:

I am afraid I do not have the talent to write you a letter as beautiful as the one I received from you, but I hope nonetheless that you will receive my modest congratulations favourably. As it is rather difficult to obtain foreign books here, I must ask you to be patient a little longer. –

Lately we have been working so much again that I am still quite daft from lack of sleep. Max has just finished his essay about fascism. – Meyer Schapiro will provisionally be in London until August, address: American Express, London, in case you already want to get in touch with him. – We have to stay in New York for the time being, but I am sure we will be in Bar Harbor, Maine, again in August. –

Please excuse the brevity of this letter and accept all my kisses

ever

your Felizitas

Many warm congratulations from Teddie too

Original: manuscript.

166 THEODOR WIESENGRUND-ADORNO AND GRETEL ADORNO TO WALTER BENJAMIN NEW YORK, 15.7.1939

15 July 1939.

My dear Walter,

Max gave us the finest gift of all on the occasion of your birthday: the prospect that you will be coming here soon,[1] as well as the equally pleasing one that we will soon have the Baudelaire[2] in our possession. We can hardly tell you how happy we are: for the first time, we have adopted the local custom and performed a veritable Indian dance, and Max is just as glad as we are. Today just a few things in great haste regarding our plans: the French exposé for Tableaux Parisiens[3] reached me only yesterday, and I will write to you as soon as I have had a chance to study it properly.

Regarding the Baudelaire, first of all, its publication[4] in the first issue of this year (a double issue) would be a wish come true. For, in addition to the Baudelaire, this issue will feature an extremely important essay by Max – provisionally entitled Europe and the Jews, but it is in fact the first outline of a theory of fascism – on which I collaborated very intensively, as well as four chapters from the Wagner (I, VI, IX, X, connected by short text inserts). If the issue turns out as planned, it will indeed correspond to my vision of the journal, and I think I can say that Max feels the same.

Concerning the visit: we would suggest planning it for late September or early October. For the following reasons: firstly, academic activities will be in full swing again here by then. We hope you will present the central ideas of the Arcades study at an official institute event, and the more notables we can invite, the better. Perhaps we could also arrange a lecture at the Columbia philosophy department[5] on some aspect of aesthetic theory. I myself spoke there about the unavoidable Husserl[6] a few months ago, to great success. – Furthermore: Meyer Schapiro is very unlikely to turn up in Paris before 25 August. We all set the greatest store by your meeting with him, not only because his intellectual concerns are extremely close to our own, and because we not only make suggestions to him, but also receive them in return. The decisive point is rather that we see him as the most important intermediary either in arranging your definite move here or in procuring an American research scholarship for you in France. I think you should definitely have at least four weeks to spend with him. At the same time as this letter, I am also writing to him in London on your behalf. I daresay you are aware of his strong Trotskyist sympathies: it would be advisable to take that into account in the choice of people one introduces him to, as there could easily be fracas with people who are more loyal to the party line.

Max tells me that you might have to prove your ownership of a certain sum of money in order to obtain a visa, and asks me to tell you that the institute could substantiate this; but it goes without saying that this would be a mere formality. If I have understood Max correctly, you will bear the travel expenses, but will be the institute's guest as long as you are in New York.

We will probably spend August in Bar Harbor, as we did last year, and would be happy to hear from you before then. – I read the George–Hofmannsthal correspondence with the greatest interest, and am considering writing a substantial review[7] about it.

Forgive my haste; perhaps the prospect of our imminent reunion can offer some small compensation for it.

Fond regards from both of us

your old
Teddie

Dear Detlef:

I am quite beside myself for joy, and am already thinking constantly about the order in which we should show you the attractions of New York to make sure you enjoy yourself here in the land of the barbarians. Just think: in 2 ½ months we shall see each other again. I have never stood at the pier with such anticipation. The very fondest regards, a good summer and a very enjoyable time with Schapiro

ever your
Felizitas

Original: typescript.

1 On 24 June, Benjamin had informed Horkheimer in a letter that there were no objections from the American consulate to issuing a tourist visa for the United States. The purpose of the planned visit to New York was to discuss and examine the possibilities of Benjamin's moving to America.

2 Benjamin cabled Horkheimer to inform him that he would have the manuscript of 'Über einige Motive bei Baudelaire' [On Some Motifs in Baudelaire] by the end of July.

3 This refers to 'Notes sur les Tableaux parisiens de Baudelaire', which Benjamin had given as a lecture in Pontigny in May 1939 (see *GS* 1 [2], pp. 605–53).

4 The essay 'Über einige Motive bei Baudelaire' appeared in the *Zeitschrift für Sozialforschung* vol. 8 (1939), pp. 50–89 (issue 1–2); see *GS* 1 [2], pp. 119–34.

5 *philosophy department*: EO.

6 Adorno had given the lecture 'Husserl and the Problem of Idealism' in May 1939; for the text, see *GS* 20 [1], pp. 119–34.

7 See *Briefwechsel zwischen George und Hofmannsthal* (Berlin, 1938). Adorno did not write a 'substantial review', but rather a long essay: 'George und Hofmannsthal: Zum Briefwechsel: 1891–1906', which was published in the mimeographed volume produced by the Institut für Sozialforschung entitled *Walter Benjamin zum Gedächtnis* [In Memoriam Walter Benjamin]; see *GS* 10 [1], pp. 195–237.

167 WALTER BENJAMIN TO THEODOR WIESENGRUND-ADORNO AND GRETEL ADORNO
PARIS, 6.8.1939

Paris XVe
10, rue Dombasle
6 August 1939.

Dear Teddie,

I believe you are on holiday with Felicitas. Presumably these lines will reach you with some delay, and that will give the Baudelaire manuscript, which I sent off to Max a week ago, time to catch them up.

Aside from that, do not be angry with me if these lines should resemble a list of keywords more than a letter. After the weeks of rigorous work that were necessary for the completion of the Baudelaire chapter, and labouring under the effects of the most ghastly climate, I am unusually exhausted. But that will not prevent me from telling you and Felicitas how much I am looking forward to our reunion. (I should not forget that there will still be obstacles to overcome between this prospect and its realization. I have written to Morgenroth regarding the sale of my Klee picture; if you see him, do not forget to ask him about it.)

Though the new Baudelaire cannot be considered a 'reworking' of one of the versions you know, I think you will notice the effects of our correspondence on the Baudelaire of last summer. In particular, I reacted immediately to your statement that you would gladly trade the panoramatic overview of the material complexes for a more precise articulation of the theoretical framework. And that you are prepared to undertake the precipitous ascents that are necessary for an exploration of those parts of the structure which are only to be found higher up.

As far as the aforementioned list of keywords is concerned, it lies in the index of the many and expansive motifs to be found in the new chapter (compared to the corresponding flâneur chapter of last summer). Naturally these motifs cannot be entirely removed from the overall complex of the Baudelaire; instead, I am intending to augment each of them with extensive interpretative developments.

The motifs of the arcade, *noctambulisme* and the feuilleton, as well as the theoretical introduction of the concept of phantasmagoria, are being reserved for the first section of the second part. The motifs of the trace, the type and empathy with the soul of the commodity will be appearing in the third section. The middle section of the second part, in its present state, will present the complete figure of the 'flâneur' only in conjunction with its first and third sections.

I have taken into account the reservations you voiced in your letter of 1 February regarding the Engels and Simmel quotations, though admittedly not by removing them. This time I have indicated why I consider the Engels quotation so important. I found your reservation about the Simmel quotation justified from the start; in the present version of the text it has taken on a less emphatic function through the change in its significance.

I am very pleased about the prospect of seeing the text in the next issue. I wrote to Max about my great efforts to keep anything fragmentary away from the essay while preventing it from exceeding its planned length. I would be glad if no significant changes (pour tout dire: cuts) were implemented.

I am having my Christian Baudelaire borne aloft to heaven by a multitude of Jewish angels. Arrangements have already been made, however, for them to drop him in the last third of the ascension, as if by accident, just before his entrance into glory.

To conclude, dear Teddie, I would like to thank you for inviting my Jochmann article to appear in the forthcoming celebratory issue.

Best wishes to you and Felicitas for enjoyable holidays and a pleasant return home,

Yours,
Walter

A special word of thanks, dear Felizitas, for the book by Dreyfus and the lines[1] announcing and accompanying it. I am thinking of you both a great deal.

Original: typescript and manuscript.

1 Not preserved.

168 GRETEL ADORNO TO WALTER BENJAMIN
NEW YORK, 9.9.1939

Sept 9th, 1939.

My dear Detlef:

to-day I shall try to write you some lines in English and I hope you will understand me although I do not yet know to explain things very well in this language. In any case I have to learn it during the next year.

I shall leave it to the scholars to talk about the war, as I believe that really nobody knows what is going on and all is only tea-table talk. I only wish to tell you how awfully sorry I am about your fate. Couldn't things happen when you were just here for a visit so that you had to stay here. I felt so happy about the possibility seeing you again and now everything is changed.

I am terribly worried that something could happen to you. Please give us some news as soon as possible.

Love yours ever
Felicitas

I am fully enthousiastic about the new version of your Baudelaire, I have to study it much more carefully, but already now I see the marvellous construction.

Original: manuscript. Translator's note: written in English.

169 WALTER BENJAMIN TO GRETEL ADORNO
NEVERS, AFTER 25.9.1939

my very dear friend

you must not be troubled if I am very brief today. I am obliged to be.

As the steadfastness of my morale has proven itself to you on a number of occasions, I must ask you not to worry excessively on my account. Let us hope, above all, that we will live to see the day when we are less distant from one another, a time when the world will have been freed from the Hitlerian nightmare.

I had to leave Paris more than three weeks ago. After an intermediate stage, I am now staying in a hostel. There are a total of 300 people inhabiting the same building as myself. There are other refugees gathered in similar groups in other places of assembly.

I need hardly tell you how important it is for me to receive news from both of you. You probably wrote to me after receiving 'Some Motifs from Baudelaire'. Be that as it may, I have not heard from you since the end of July.[1]

So first of all my address: Centre des travailleurs volontaires groupe VI Clos Saint-Joseph *Nevers* (Nièvre).[2] I would ask you to write to me in French in order to facilitate the work of inspecting the letters.

I have now, after a certain time, regained my footing. What I find irksome is the lack of appropriate equipment (not enough bedding or genuinely warm blankets). Aside from that I am also suffering from the constant lack of news, from my sister as well as my friends in France and Switzerland. In particular, I had written to Mme Favez to ask her to safeguard the money intended for me by the institute. I had asked Max to transfer that money to my bank account. I hope he found out in good time that, as our accounts have been temporarily seized, this option was not practicable.

I am not in need of money for the moment. But it would be extremely important for me to be able to contact Mme Favez[3] if I did require any.

Although there is no one very notorious among the people here, you would be interested to know the names of some of them. I am, for example, in the company of Bruck,[4] an old acquaintance of yours; another one is Hans Sahl,[5] some of whose works Teddie is familiar with; the novelist Hermann Kesten is staying not far from here. So far, we are not at all certain of our fate. It goes without saying that the waiting makes for many a dark hour. Living in a community so large and diverse is not always an easy matter. As a mitigating factor, however, I must say that there is an agreeable spirit of camaraderie in the camp, and that the authorities are showing true loyalty.

At the present time, the fate of letters is a matter of chance. Give me a sign as soon as you have received these lines. Do not be too long; but do not forget to tell me your thoughts on my 'Baudelaire'. Remember that my situation is similar, in several ways, to yours in 1937.

Give my very best regards to Teddie, and my sincere greetings to Max and Friedrich.

I assume Schapiro has returned. We spent a very agreeable evening together.

If either of you have friends in Paris who might be interested in me, do what is necessary without my needing to insist. But perhaps it would be better to wait for now.

All the best   Detlef

PS At the very moment I concluded these lines I received the first message[6] I have had since leaving Paris. It comes from my sister. She informs me of the text of your cable, which I was no longer able to obtain before my departure. I need not tell you how happy I am to know that you are so close to me in your thoughts. What you write about my work on Baudelaire compensates for all the fears I have experienced since the start of the month. So it was not in vain that I spent my summer engrossed in that task.

I assume you are not going to publish the next issue for the moment. It would be extremely useful for me to have some proofs work here. If you could spare a copy, I would be most grateful if you could send it to me. (That is to say: the proofs of the Baudelaire or, if that is not possible, the typed manuscript.)

One of my greatest concerns is my apartment. The rent for three months is around 1400 frcs. I have asked Mme Favez to pay for me. That is all I need for now. – My sister wrote that Mme Favez sent me a letter in which she tells me of Friedrich's great concern for me. Thank you once again!

I will try to remain in contact with Geneva.

Original: manuscript.
On the dating: the card from Dora Benjamin mentioned in the postscript dates from 25 September. Translator's note: written in French.

1 Benjamin would have been able to read Gretel Adorno's short letter of 9 September only after returning to Paris.

2 Benjamin was transferred from the Stade de Colombes, where German emigrants had to go after the outbreak of war, to the Château de Vernuche in Nevers.

3 Juliane Favez wrote the following to Benjamin at the camp on 29 September: 'I was very happy to learn from your letter [lost] that you are well. I had already sent you a postcard to the Stade de Colombe after receiving your first letter. Monsieur Horkheimer has been informed as you requested. I am in contact with Mme. Lévy-Ginsberg. If there is anything you need, write to me. If it is necessary to send money, write to me how much should be sent and by what means. [Paragraph] I hope with all my heart that you are in good health and spirits. Some proofs of the Revue have already arrived and been sent to New York. Very cordially yours.'

4 The little that could be found out about Hans Bruck was gained from a letter he wrote to Adorno on 8 August 1956. It indicates that Bruck was a friend of Ernst Schoen, and conducted numerous concerts in what was then the Südwestdeutscher Rundfunk Frankfurt between 1928 and 1933. He continues: 'Quite by chance, one of the very few things I managed to save was a glowing recommendation by Klemperer written in 1933.' Bruck was able to escape from France to the USA.

5 The writer Hans Sahl (1902–1993) gave an account of his arrival at the camp in his memoirs, *Das Exil im Exil* [The Exile within the Exile] (Frankfurt am Main, 1990), p. 78.

6 Dora Benjamin's postcard of 25 September contains the text [in French] of the telegram sent by the Adornos and Horkheimer: 'Your admirable study on Baudelaire reached us like a ray of light. Our thoughts are with you.' She continues: 'Also, we have had a letter from Mme Favez which I opened together with Mme L. Ginsberg. It is from 9 September. She writes . . . M. Pollock asks me to let you know that he will do everything in his power to help you in these difficult times. I would be most grateful to you if you could keep me informed about everything concerning you. The telegraphic connections between the United States and Switzerland and vice versa are still functioning normally and without delay . . . As Mme L. G. knows about this letter, I am sure she has already responded.'

170 WALTER BENJAMIN TO GRETEL ADORNO
NEVERS, 12.10.1939

my very dear friend

last night, lying in the straw, I had a dream so beautiful that I cannot resist the temptation to share it with you. There are so few beautiful things here for me to tell you about. – It is a dream of the kind that I have perhaps every five years, and which revolve around the motif 'reading'. Teddie will recall the role occupied by this motif in my epistemological reflections. The phrase that I spoke quite distinctly towards the end of this dream happened to be in French. All the more reason to give you this account in the same language. The doctor by the name of Dausse[1] who accompanies me in this dream is a friend who looked after me when I was suffering from malaria.

Dausse and I were in the company of several people whom I do not remember. At a certain point, Dausse and I parted company with this group. After we had left the others, we found ourselves in a pit. I saw that there were some strange beds almost at the bottom of it. They had the shape and the length of coffins; they also seemed to be made of stone. Upon kneeling down halfway, however, I saw that one could sink gently into them as if getting into bed. They were covered with moss and ivy. I saw that these beds were set up in pairs. Just as I was about to stretch out on one of them, next to a bed which seemed to be meant for Dausse, I realized that the head of that one was already occupied by other people. So we resumed our course. The place resembled a forest; but there was something artificial about the distribution of trunks and branches that lent this part of the scenery a vague resemblance to a nautical construction. Walking along some beams and crossing various paths in the forest, we found ourselves on a sort of miniature landing stage, a little terrace made of wooden boards. It was there that we found the women with whom Dausse was living. There were three or four of them, and they seemed to be very beautiful. The first thing that astonished me was that Dausse did not introduce me. That did not disturb me as much as the discovery I made when I set down my hat on a grand piano. It was an old straw hat, a 'Panama' that I had inherited from my father. (It ceased to exist long ago.) Taking it off, I was struck by a large crack in the top of the hat. Furthermore, the edges of this crack showed traces of red. – I was brought a chair. That did not prevent me from fetching a different one myself, which I placed slightly away from the table where everyone was sitting. I did not sit down. In the meantime, one of the ladies had occupied herself with graphology. I saw that she had something in her hand which I had written, and which had been given to her by Dausse. I was slightly unsettled by this examination, fearing that it would disclose some intimate traits of mine. I moved closer. What I saw was a cloth that was covered in pictures; the only graphic elements I could distinguish were the upper parts of the letter D, whose pointed lines revealed an extreme striving towards spirituality. This part of the letter had also been covered with a small piece of fabric with a blue border, and the fabric swelled up on the picture as if it were in the breeze. That was the only thing there which I was able to 'read' – the rest offered indistinct, vague motifs and clouds. For a moment, the conversation turned to this writing. I do not remember the opinions that were put forward; I do know very well, however, that at a certain point I spoke these exact words: 'It is a matter of changing a poem into a scarf.' I had barely spoken these words when something intriguing happened. I saw that among the women there was a very beautiful one who had lain down in a bed. While listening to my explanation, she made a movement as quick as a flash. She lifted a very small corner of the blanket that was covering her in her bed. She performed this action in less than a second. And it was not to show me her body, but rather the pattern on her blanket, which showed a similar image to that which I had had to 'write' many years ago as a present for Dausse. I knew very well that the lady had made this movement. But it was a sort of second sight that had given me this knowledge. For as far my physical eyes were concerned, they were looking somewhere else, and I could not distinguish any of that which had been revealed by the blanket so fleetingly drawn back for me.

After having this dream, I was unable to return to sleep for some hours. I was in a state of joy. And it is for the purpose of sharing these hours with you that I am writing to you.

No news. No decision regarding our matter so far. The arrival of a 'selection committee' has been announced – but we do not know when. My health is mediocre; the rainy weather is not suited to improving it. As for money, I have none; it is not permitted to carry more than twenty francs. Your letters would be a great comfort to me. I am also glad that Mme Favez received Pollock's instructions. Regarding my belongings in Paris, a French friend is taking care of them with the help of my sister.

Apart from your letters, what would offer me the greatest pleasure would be for you to send me the proofs (or the manuscript) of my 'Baudelaire'.

If you find any mistakes in this letter, you must excuse me. It was written amid the constant din that has surrounded me for more than a month.

I need hardly add that I am impatient to make myself more useful to my friends and to the enemies of Hitler than is possible in my present situation. I never stop hoping for a change, and I am sure that you are together with me in your efforts and wishes.

My sincerest regards to all our friends. With love

Detlef

12 October 1939
Camp des travailleurs volontaires
Groupe VI Clos Saint-Joseph
Nevers (Nièvre)

Original: manuscript. Translator's note: written in French.

1 Camille Dausse was a doctor and member of the Comité d'initiative for the 'Internationale Ausstellung über den Faschismus' [International Exhibition on Fascism].

171 GRETEL ADORNO TO WALTER BENJAMIN
NEW YORK, 7.11.1939

November 7, 1939.

My dear Walter,

I cannot tell you how sorry I am that you have to be so far away and cannot stay with us just now. Let us hope that there will be a change very soon. Max and we are doing everything we are able to. –

You are asking me for the proofs of the Baudelaire. Unfortunately there are only two corrected copies which have to stay at the Institute for the future print and therefore I am unable to send you another one. It is not yet clear what will happen to the Zeitschrift, but as soon as I know a little bit more I shall tell you at once. – How is the all-day work for you? Can you do some of your own writing or reading? Did you begin to learn English? You cannot overestimate the knowledge of the language for any stay in this country, we have here the example of Ernst Bloch who is quite desperate being unable to learn English and to understand one word of any serious conversation. –

Teddie is very busy with the Radio Project. For the Institute he wrote three new analyses of song hits[1] and intends to write something about the letters of Stefan George and Hofmannsthal. – Else Herzberger was in New York for three weeks with her marvelous poodle-dog, now she is sailing for Buenos Aires on the same boat as Lix Weil[2] and his new married wife. – If Hans Bruck is still there, please tell him our kindest regards. In former times he knew a lot of extraordinary funnies, perhaps he still remembers and then, at least sometimes, you will have a good time. Elisabeth Wiener, in the meantime, is in Melbourne and continues her life of uninfluenced freedom.

That we all join our wishes in the future destroying of hitlerism[?], you will imagine. – There is no day that we do not think and speak of you. Yours ever

Felicitas

Original: manuscript. Translator's note: written in English.

1 This refers to the texts on the songs 'Especially for you', 'In an eighteenth century drawing room' and 'Penny Serenade', collected as a manuscript entitled *Neue Schlageranalysen* [New Pop Song Analyses], which Adorno later published as the second part of *Musikalische Warenanalysen*; see *GS* 16, pp. 289–94.

2 The economist and social scientist Felix Weil (1898–1975), the son of the institute's founder, and his second wife, Margot.

172 GRETEL ADORNO AND THEODOR WIESENGRUND-ADORNO TO WALTER BENJAMIN NEW YORK, 21.11.1939

21. November 1939.

My dear Detlef:

just this moment we got the news that you are back in Paris.[1] I cannot tell you how glad we are, to know you safe. – In the meantime I got your second letter with the marvellous dream in it, many many thanks. – If you would do me the great favour as to send me a copy of your Kraus,[2] I would be very grateful. As to my health I did not feel so very well and had to go to a new physician Dr. Brenheim, an Endocrinologist, as E thought that my fits of migraine could be connected with the 'Hypophyse' the functions of which I am not so sure about. But only after three or four months I shall know, if he will be able to help me. Otherwise I have to resign and to consider myself an old suffering woman. We hope to hear very soon from you

love

Felicitas

I am happy that you are at home again – happier than I could tell you! And my enthusiasm about the Baudelaire increases steadily! I made the German abstract[3] and the English translation – please, check the

French translation of this resume which does not yet satisfy me. Good luck and à bientôt! Yours ever Teddie

Original: manuscript. Translator's note: written in English.

1 Benjamin's release from the prison camp in Nevers was made possible through the support of Henri Hoppenots (1891–1977), who worked in the Foreign Ministry.

2 Benjamin's essay from 1931; see *GS* 2 [1], pp. 334–67.

3 In the *Zeitschrift für Sozialforschung*, English and French summaries were appended to essays written in German; Adorno had evidently produced one in German first, then translated it into English.

173 WALTER BENJAMIN TO GRETEL ADORNO PARIS, 14.12.1939

my dear Felicitas,

and so you wrote to me in English, and I can read your letters without the slightest difficulty. In fact, I actually find them easier to understand than those written in German. At the moment I am looking for someone to teach me English. I even made some attempts in the camp; but I soon had to give up. So I was unable to do anything there. I sent you the only text I wrote immediately; it was the account of a dream which had filled me with joy. It would be a great shame if the letter had not reached you; but I am almost inclined to assume this, as you do not make any reference to it.

I still often find myself there in my thoughts.[1] It is unclear how things will turn out for those who are still there; for there is not even any certainty for those who are free. I had hoped to see Bruck again here, but he has still not returned, and I am not sure that he will be doing so very soon.

Two weeks ago I received your letter of 7 November. It was sweet for me to read it, and I would have written sooner had I not felt extremely weak. During the first days after my return, I had to devote all my time (and the little strength I had) to taking care of some urgent affairs and carrying out the changes that needed to be made to the proofs of the Baudelaire. (The French exposé was ultimately quite inadequate, at least in terms of its language, and I was glad that I was able to rewrite it.) It is excellent that, at a time when the spiritual activity of German emigration seems to be reaching its lowest point (as much in the exigencies of daily life as the fact of the political situation), the institute can continue its publishing so brilliantly. I have written to

Max, telling him about all the positive qualities I see in his extraordinary essay. This essay, I might add, is written with a magnificent stylistic vigour.

I am curious as to how Teddie will treat the correspondence between George and Hofmannsthal; it seems that there is an entire age between us and the time in which these letters (which I do not yet know) were exchanged. On the other hand, it is not at all wise to be too much up to date. I rather fear that this has been the case with our friend Ernst; and, going on what one hears about him, he strikes me as being a little out of place at the moment – not only geographically, but also in terms of what is going on in the world.

Have you encountered Martin Gumpert over there? He is someone whom I knew well during my internment. Since he is going to publish his autobiography, I asked myself whether I will by any chance appear in it.[2] That would be the first time I would have considered this possible.

Max will show you the copy of a letter from the National Refugee Service[3] which raises a serious problem. I doubt that I would easily find the chance offered in this letter a second time. You will therefore both reflect carefully upon it. (I would ask you anyway if I were not sure.) The question is extremely complex, and it does not seem possible to me to address it without you.

There was an alert on the very first night after my return to my apartment. There have not been any more since then. But the course of life has profoundly changed nonetheless. Since four o'clock in the afternoon, the town has been in darkness. People do not go out in the evening, and solitude constantly lies in wait. Thus work would be a true refuge for me at the moment, and I plan to take it up again soon in spite of everything.

I embrace you warmly and ask you to extend many regards to Teddie. And I must beg forgiveness for the paper; the desire to write to you seized me at a moment when I did not have any other with me.

14 December 1939 Detlef
Paris XV
10 rue Dombasle

Original: manuscript. Translator's note: written in French.

1 Following his release, Benjamin received letters from fellow prisoners – those of Max Aron, Albrecht Neisser and Josef Filzwieser have survived. On 21 November, Albrecht Neisser wrote the following from Nevers: 'I must tell you at once what joy I felt upon hearing the wonderful news, namely that – *hen aggelion* – of your release. Who would have deserved more than you to

be the living proof of this return to the rules of humanity and justice for whose universal application we are all hoping? [Paragraph] Could I ask you – without being indiscreet – to give my fiancée, Mademoiselle Marianne Marcus, 4, rue Edmond Roger, XV (tel. Lecourbe 89-79) a chance to make your acquaintance? I am sure she would be happy to meet you. [Paragraph] The news of your release was welcomed by all those who had the pleasure of knowing you and appreciating your work, and who profited from the comforting legend of Lao Tse through a spontaneous and constant feeling of relief. [Paragraph] Allow me to reiterate this sentiment to you, and [paragraph] You must believe me when I express my most sincere and respectful devotion. Yours, Albrecht Neisser.' A letter from Max Aron and a card from Josef Filzwieser – both dating from 7 December – indicate that Benjamin sent at least two parcels to his former co-prisoners.

2 In his autobiography, *Hölle im Paradies* [Hell in Paradise] (Stockholm, 1939), p. 54, Gumpert writes the following about Benjamin while describing his friends from the time of the youth movement: 'One of us, the most gifted, is an émigré philosopher in Paris and has become a Marxist.'

3 This letter of 27 November to the American consul in Paris was sent to Benjamin's camp address with an accompanying note from Cecilia Razovsky: 'We are pleased to enclose herewith documents for the visa application for Professor Walter Benjamin which have been submitted by Mr. Milton Starr of Nashville, Tennessee. [Paragraph] The following documents are attached: [paragraph] 1. Affidavit of support in duplicate. 2. Friendship letter addressed to the American Consul by Mr. Starr. 3. Statement from the Treasury Department of Nashville, Tenn. [Paragraph] We hope that you will find these papers in good order. We assure you that we are most appreciative for your kind endeavor.'

174 WALTER BENJAMIN TO GRETEL ADORNO
PARIS, 17.1.1940

My little Felicitas,

I have decided to write you a long letter, even though I have not received anything but tiny notes from you – and no letter at all from Teddie in the last six months. Your last sign of life dates from 21 November (though it clearly went out later, since you refer to my return, which was only on the 23rd). I hear that your health is still not satisfactory. And I very much hope that the treatment you are receiving from Brenheim has borne fruit in the meantime. As for my own health, I too have little good news to report. Since the onset of severely cold weather here, I am having extraordinary difficulties walking in the open air. I have to pause every three or four minutes, in the middle of the street. Naturally I have been to see the doctor, who has diagnosed a cardiac infection, which seems to have greatly increased of late. At the moment I am looking for a doctor who can perform a cardiogram; that is no easy matter, since there are only a few specialists with the necessary equipment, and one also has to be on sufficiently good terms with the surgeon. The price of these things is, I believe, fairly high.

The weather, my state of health, and the general state of affairs – the combination of all these factors forces me to lead the most sedentary of lives. My apartment, however, is not sufficiently heated for me to write if it is cold. And so I spend most of the time lying down, as I am doing at this very moment. Though it is true that in the past weeks I have not missed opportunities to go into town in spite of everything. For all the little things to do with civil life are asking to be put in order: I had to have my bank account unfrozen, to reapply for access to the national library, and so on. All that has been demanding many more trips than you would believe. But now it is finally done. I must say that the day on which I went back to the library for the first time was like a little festive occasion at the house. Most of all in the case of the photographic service, where, after making photocopies of some of my notes some years ago, it has been necessary in the last few months to bring quite a number of my personal papers in order to make copies.[1]

The most comforting thing in recent times was a magnificent letter from Max written on 21 December[2] – one in which he asks me to resume my reports on the French letters, at the same time enquiring about my future work plans. I would like, my dear Felicitas, for you to tell him – for now – how precious it was to me to read these lines of his, and at the same time to inform him of this first attempt at a response. By 'first attempt' I mean that I am not yet certain about the essence of the question: namely, whether it would be better for me to write the comparative study on Rousseau and Gide,[3] or rather to begin the continuation of the Baudelaire immediately. The reason for my hesitation is the fear of having to give up my Baudelaire once I have already begun its continuation. It is a work that is conceived on a large scale, and it would be dangerous to resume and interrupt it several times. There, however, lies the risk I shall have to run, and of which I am constantly reminded in my little alcove by the gas mask I recently procured – a disturbing double of those skulls with which studious monks decorated their cells. So that is why I have not yet dared properly to begin this continuation of the Baudelaire, which is much closer to my heart than any other work, but which would suffer badly if neglected – even for the sake of ensuring its author's survival. (It is true, furthermore, that it is very difficult, if not impossible, to think about this subject productively, or even to make suppositions. There is no way for me to leave Paris without previous authorization, which is very difficult to obtain, and which it would perhaps not even be wise to request, since this would, at the same time, not guarantee the possibility of my return.)

Independently of my other work, I will be resuming my analyses of new French publications with pleasure. There is one left, a rather amusing one, that saw the light of day in Argentina. It is there that Caillois followed the famous Vittoria Ocampo, an Argentinian writer, in the course of an amorous affair. He has just published a little volume there, a polemic against Nazism,[4] whose argumentation takes up, without the slightest shadings or modifications, those things affecting the daily lives of people everywhere. It would not have been necessary to travel to the farthest reaches of the intellectual and terrestrial world to report that. It is true, on the other hand, that Caillois is publishing a theory of celebration[5] in the Nouvelle Revue Française, which I will mention in my next letter to Max.[6] I will also be occupying myself with a curious book by Michel Leyris, 'Age d'homme',[7] which was highly noted before the war.

The letter Max wrote to me on 21 December crossed with the one I sent him on 15 December. In the meantime, I have been to the American consulate, where I was told of the questionnaire. It contains the following question as point 14: 'Are you a member of any cult or a teacher at a college, seminary, academy or university?' If I am not mistaken, this question is of decisive importance for me, since, on the one hand, answering in the affirmative will give you the right of passage independently of the quota (non-quota visa), and since, on the other hand, I have been assured at the same consulate that one would have to wait no less than 5 or 6 years to be taken into the quota! It would therefore be absolutely vital to provide a verification of the courses I have taught as a member of staff at the institute in Frankfurt. As I did not want to mention them without the consent of the institute, I have not filled out the questionnaire yet. I will therefore have to interrupt my application until I receive confirmation from your side. (The services of the consulate have been transferred to Bordeaux. It is from there that I would, if things turn out, be given my number; but only once I have handed in the questionnaire.)

I do not think I am speaking merely out of vanity when I tell you that this last issue of the journal strikes me as one of the best the institute has put out in recent years. The article by Max made a profound impression on me, and I have told everyone I could reach to read it. In the course of the frequent conversations I have had about it, which have made it clear just how well founded it is, I had the idea that it would perhaps be both interesting and useful to explore the question of how far the anti-Semitic movement analysed there depends on or rather opposes the medieval anti-Semitism as evoked by Teddie in the context of Wagner (*Der Jude im Dorn*).[8]

I had a favourable impression upon re-reading the Fragments on Wagner.[9] Then I consulted the full manuscript of the text in order to compare the parts which struck me most the first time with those I had underlined in the journal. The result of this comparison was that now, fully convinced by the overall conception, I have become even more attached to particular aspects of the matter than before. One subject we shall have to return to is that of reduction (*Verkleinerung*)[10] as a means of phantasmagoria. This passage brought to mind one of my older projects, which you may remember having heard me mention: I mean the commentary on Goethe's 'The New Melusine'. That could, however, be due more to the fact that Melusine undoubtedly belongs to the species of water-nymphs[11] discussed towards the end. – I was struck by a number of well-chosen formulations in the summaries: the one regarding the virtual opposition of Freud and Jung in Wagner's actual works; also the one where the homogeneity of Wagner's 'style' is denounced as a symptom of inner decay.[12] (One day, Teddie should bring together those passages in his analyses dealing with music as *Einspruch* [protest] and expand the theory of opera contained therein.)

To conclude this long letter I shall add some information regarding certain people that should interest you. Recently I saw Dora, who has returned to London. She gave me news about Stefan – not exactly bad news, but not very good either. I get the impression that the two of them are not on the best of terms. Stefan spends all his time helping his mother with her administrative work. Dora was accompanied by an English friend,[13] who made a very good impression upon me. – I do not think I told you: almost two years ago, Glück moved to Buenos-Aires,[14] where he has found employment – perhaps less brilliant than his previous position, but it seems to be very solid. I have not had any news from him since the war began. – Our friend Klossowski, who is definitely unfit, has left Paris and now found a position at a municipal office in Bordeaux. Kisch,[15] whom you will recall more or less well, has managed to acquire a teaching position in Chile. Our poor friend Bruck, finally, is still in a camp. The prospect of seeing him released soon is not entirely hopeless; but in the meantime he is suffering a great deal. Someone who will pass on my news to you in person, and very soon, is Soma Morgenstern. It seems that he will be leaving for New York before the spring.[16]

As postage rates are extortionately high at the moment, Max will have to excuse me for entrusting you with certain information that perhaps concerns him even more than you. And you must equally excuse me. And I hope that next time you will not be content merely to send me one of your little blue notes, as delightful as they may be. I am counting very strongly on a letter of a few pages' length from you, as also from Teddie. (I would very much like to hear about the latest developments with his work.) With much love from

your old

17 January 1940
Paris XV
10 rue Dombasle

Detlef

PS My English lessons will begin next week.

Original: manuscript. Translator's note: written in French, except for the closing words 'your old' [*Dein alter*].

1 Gisèle Freund had arranged for photocopies to be made of the papers requested by the PEN Club and Henri Hoppenot – including the references – at the Bibliothèque Nationale.

2 The original has not survived; the carbon copy of the typescript is dated 22 December.

3 Benjamin never wrote the essay.

4 Caillois had met the Argentinian writer Victoria Ocampo (1891–1979), founder of the journal *Sur*, during her stay in Paris from late 1938 until June 1939, when he went with her to Argentina, where – having been taken by surprise by the war – he stayed until 1945. Benjamin would have read the French version of the article 'Naturaleza del hitlerismo', which Callois had published in October in issue 61 of *Sur* (pp. 93–107) and sent to Bataille.

5 It appeared in the December 1939 (pp. 863–82) and January 1940 (pp. 49–59) issues of the *Nouvelle Revue Française*; for Benjamin's letter to Horkheimer, see *GB* 6, letter no. 1241.

6 It dates from 23 March 1940; see *GB* 6, letter no. 1352.

7 *L'Age d'homme* by Michel Leiris.

8 Adorno quotes from the fairy tale *Der Jude im Dorn* [The Jew in the Thorn Bush] from the Grimms' collection; see *GS* 13, p. 20.

9 See also letter no. 145, which Benjamin wrote after reading the manuscript of the Wagner book.

10 'The phantasmagoric character of the Venusberg music must be determined in technical categories. It achieves its peculiar sound by means of reduction. A reduced *forte*, the image of distant sounds, is dominant' (*GS* 13, p. 82).

11 See *GS* 13, pp. 140–2.

12 The summaries of the chapters not printed in the journal – 2–5, 7 and 8; see *GS* 13, pp. 497–503. 'Thus Wagner's work becomes profoundly ambiguous in its relationship to the layer of his mythical material. On the one hand, the mythological intention pursues a conscious elucidation of individual

psychology, and presents the seemingly autonomous individual in its dependence on the totality. On the other hand, the myths themselves serve a regression to the age-old and futilely immutable state of being. The opposition of Freud and Jung is virtually present in Wagner's works. This ambiguity is shown using the example of a series of material aspects, and finally in the function of the operatic form' (ibid., p. 502). 'The antithetical right of music in opera, namely to protest against the blind natural context, is forfeited, and music itself becomes an instrument of blind ruin. The ostensibly complete formal immanence of Wagner's music dramas, their 'style', in fact amounts to music's abdication of its specifically musical protest function' (ibid., pp. 501f.).

13 Presumably her second husband, Morser.

14 Gustav Glück had written to Benjamin on 15 July 1939. Towards the end of 1937 Glück had left Berlin for London, where – as a specialist in German foreign transactions – he was unable to find work. He finally took a position at a banking firm in Buenos Aires, and was intending to apply for Argentinian citizenship.

15 Egon Erwin Kisch fled to Mexico.

16 Morgenstern (1890–1976) reached the safe haven of New York only in 1941, following his internment in and spectacular escape from France, via Marseilles, Casablanca and Lisbon. See his posthumously published account *Flucht in Frankreich* [Escape in France] (Lüneburg, 1998).

175 GRETEL ADORNO TO WALTER BENJAMIN
NEW YORK, 20.1.1940

20 Jan. 1940.

My dear Detlef:

I was so happy with your letter of December 1939. As to your English lessons I talked to my English teacher and got the enclosed answer;[1] perhaps it is of some help for you. In the meantime Max told us about that Rasofky affidavit and I hope that the result of it will be that we see each other pretty soon. –

I don't know if Wissing wrote you in the last weeks. He now got a fixed appointment at the Memorial Hospital, and I imagine that Lotte and he will marry during this year. I stopped my objection though I am by no means certain about the procedure. You will be astonished how much they seem to be quite settled petty bourgeois people. All the flère of adventure which I liked most of him has gone.

All of us are very happy about the last issue of the Zeitschrift let us hope that all the next ones may look the same way. –

Since the beginning of 1940 I feel much better, perhaps the new treatment will have any success. – Teddie's work is going on alright, he finished the rough draught [*sic*] of the George–Hofmannsthal. I think it is one of the best things he ever did and I am very anxious to know how you will react. Kindest regards of Teddie

love

yours

Felicitas

Original: manuscript. Translator's note: written in English.

1 'Dear Mrs. Adorno: Mlle Prenez (Blanche) 3 Boulevard Victor Paris 15, is a highly recommended teacher. She was many years at Barnard College and now teaches in Paris, also doing private work. [Paragraph] She has many friends among the intellectual circles of Paris. [Paragraph] With kind greetings. [Paragraph] Most sincerely yours, [paragraph] Florence Warner.'

176 GRETEL ADORNO TO WALTER BENJAMIN NEW YORK, 10.2.1940

GRETEL W. ADORNO
290 RIVERSIDE DRIVE
NEW YORK, N.Y.

Febr. 10, 1940

My dear Detlef:

o, how I hate it to write to you in a foreign language, but nevertheless I think it will be better for an air-mail letter. Did you receive our different messages with the adress [*sic*] of an English teacher in your district, that one where I asked for a copy of your Kraus article and some others? Teddie will write you in German in some of the next days after we have spoken to Max above the things concerning your affairs.

As to your letters to New York I would suggest that you send them air mail on expenses conto of 45 Rue d'Ulm, even if you have to address the Adorno letters also to 429 W 117 Str. – I am very anxious to hear how you feel and if there is really something wrong with your heart. I think that this is a very serious matter and that you have to do everything you are able to for your recovery. If I may give you an advice, I at your place would write quite frankly to Max about the whole situation and I can imagine that he will do something. But I think it much better that you do it alone without any interference neither of Teddie nor of myself.

Of our acquaintances, aside from Else Herzberger, Carl Dreyfuss: Vicente Lopez F.C. C.A. Agouenage [?] 1030 and Peter von Haselberg are also in Buenos Aires; perhaps that will be of interest to Glück. I do not have any address for Peter, but I am sure that will not be so difficult to find out.[1] (I totally forgot to continue in English, if I shall ever get used to it?)

When I was in Paris for the last time in May 1937, I remember a nice supper together with Sohn-Retel [*sic*] and Teddie when you explained us your theory of progress. I would be very grateful if you could send me some notes of it if you have some.

As to my state of health I always feel better when I have much to do. I am not fit at all for the role of a house wife though I think that everybody likes very much to be at our place. If we could only fix already a date for our next meeting. I am terribly longing for you. If you could only feel it when I am thinking of you!

Love yours always
Felicitas

Original: manuscript. Translator's note: written in English.

1 Translator's note: This paragraph was written in German.

177 GRETEL ADORNO TO WALTER BENJAMIN
NEW YORK, 29.2.1940

29 February 1940.

My dear Detlef,

you will be receiving a letter in the next few days from a certain W. Krafft[1] to Max with his response concerning the publication of the Jochmann. What I have heard about this business is completely inexplicable to me. If I can give you some advice, if I were you I would write to Max immediately, and at length if you can, as precisely as you can remember the whole discovery of the Jochmann, so that Max will be completely in the picture. I want to avoid anything that could make you the slightest bit nervous at all costs; but I would also do everything to make the matter as uncomplicated as possible for Max.

At the weekend I spoke to E, who plans to marry in June. (As my stepmother[2] will be most vehemently opposed to this, there is some good in the war after all, for now we will not be hearing anything from her in Germany.) He asks you to send him your x-ray so that he can get an idea of your condition.

The very fondest regards

ever
your
Felicitas

Original: manuscript.

1 Werner Kraft's letter is reproduced in the notes for *GB* 6, letter no. 1354.

2 Amalie Karplus (1878–1956), *née* Jacak.

178 WALTER BENJAMIN TO GRETEL ADORNO
PARIS, LATE APRIL/EARLY MAY 1940

My dear Felizitas,

it is true, I have been silent for a long time; but now prudent hands have prepared a few things for you.[1] I hope they will reach you in good times – the book at the June dawning of a new year; the texts of my own in a moment of well-being and peace. I am very happy that the new treatment is bearing fruit.

I thank you for your last letters. I will not be able to answer them in English very soon, but am not having any trouble reading them. Thank you especially for the letter concerning the Jochmann business. In the meantime, Max has received my in-depth account. I am naturally giving him a completely free hand, so that he can settle the matter as he sees fit without any further correspondence. In the same letter I reported to Max at length about the state of my health. I will send Wissing an x-ray that has been taken of my heart in the next few days.

You will receive the essay on Kraus shortly (I cannot find any requests for other texts of mine, even though your last letter alludes to them). As for your question about my notes, which were probably made following the conversation under the horse-chestnut trees, I wrote these at a time when such things occupied me. The war and the constellation that brought it about led me to take down a few thoughts which I can say that I have kept with me, indeed kept from myself, for nigh on twenty years. This is also why I have barely afforded even you more than fleeting glances at them. The conversation under the horse-chestnut trees was a breach in those twenty years. Even today, I am handing them to you more as a bouquet of whispering grasses, gathered on reflective walks, than a collection of theses.[2] The text you are to receive is, in more ways than one, a reduction. I do not know to what extent reading it will surprise or even disconcert you – which I hope it will not. At any rate, I would like to draw your attention particularly to the 17th reflection; that is the one which should make apparent the hidden, yet conclusive connection between these observations and my previous works by offering concise information about the method of the latter. Furthermore, these reflections, as much as their character is an experimental one, do not methodically serve the sole purpose of paving the way for a sequel to the 'Baudelaire'. They make me suspect that the problem of remembering (and of forgetting), which appears in them on another level, will continue to occupy me for a long time. I need hardly tell you that nothing could be further from my mind than the thought of publishing these notes (let alone in the form I am sending them to you). It would be a perfect recipe for enthusiastic misunderstanding.

The ebbing tide of Surrealism has washed up a strange shell on the desolate shore of literature. I would like to draw your attention quite emphatically to a little work that bears the previously unknown name of Julien Gracq[3] and has been published by Corti. It is entitled Au Château d'Argole. For a while, I thought I was holding a book in my hands that I could have given you with all the gravity I could possibly assign to a present. Subsequently I realized that this Château d'Argole is a thoroughly failed opus. But it is more than just that. And I think that you of all people would recognize that. I must confess that my expectations had been extremely high after the first hundred pages, despite a foreword that already bore the signs of inability and confusion, and that I still consider the description of the castle a text that readers such as ourselves cannot encounter without being painfully touched. Nonetheless, I do not want to send you this of all books (which I unfortunately do not own) as a gift; for that purpose I have decided upon a different, somewhat less weighty one, whose magic you will be able to submit to without regret.

All this should, I hope, reach you in the next few days. We must see to it that we put the best of ourselves in our letters; for there is nothing to suggest that we shall see each other again soon.

Your old, and ageing
Detlef

Yesterday I tried out an English author for the first time. I am reading the wonderful Examples of Antitheta by Bacon.
I will be sending you the manuscript of 'Berliner Kindheit um neunzehnhundert' within the next few days. Please guard it well. And content yourselves with this as far as possible if I still delay the promised theses a little.

Original: typescript with handwritten postscript.

1 Gretel Adorno's words of thanks from 30 May are to be found in a letter from Egon Wissing with additional notes by her, Theodor W. Adorno and Lotte Wissing.

2 These are Benjamin's theses 'On the Concept of History'; see *GS* 1 [2], pp. 691–704.

3 The pseudonym adopted by Louis Poirier (b. 1910). The title of the book is *Au château d'Argol* (Paris, 1938).

179 EGON WISSING, LOTTE WISSING, THEODOR WIESENGRUND-ADORNO AND GRETEL ADORNO TO WALTER BENJAMIN SPRINGFIELD, 30.5.1940

Mon très cher,

Lotte, Gretl, Teddie and I are sitting here peacefully in Springfield, celebrating Lottes and my marriage. – Which took place today in Boston –, we had a remarkably well Lunch at Dr. Levene's[?] (my 'boss') and from there we started our little honeymoon-trip à quatre. That much for today, just to let you know. – I shall write to you in a few days.

All my love yours Egon

My dear Walter, all my thoughts, my anxiety, my hope ist [*sic*] with you! Good luck – and if our fidelity and love *can* attribute to it, it *will!*

Yours ever Teddie

My dear Detlef:

Just before we started to Boston I got your little package with the Maupassant, the Kraus and the lovely present, many many thanks. It's too bad that you are not sitting with us.

Love Yours Felicitas

Very kind regards yours Lotte

N. B. I got the photostatic copy of Prof Abrami's finding through Max, but your X-Ray picture has not arrived as yet. If there is any possibility to put the documents to good usage, we shall most certainly do so. –

À bientôt E.

Original: manuscript. Translator's note: written in English.

180 WALTER BENJAMIN TO GRETEL ADORNO LOURDES, 19.7.1940

my dear Felizitas,

your letter[1] of the 8th reached me within a week. I need hardly tell you how much comfort it gave me. I would indeed say: the joy, but I do not know if I shall be able to experience that feeling in the near future. What weighs on my mind more heavily than anything else is the fate of my manuscripts. I have not yet found time to describe the circumstances of my departure to you. Nonetheless, it will give you some idea if I tell you that I was not able to take anything with me but my gas mask and my toilet bag. I can say that I had foreseen all of this, but that I was powerless to do anything about it. I might add that, if none of the things I cling to are at my disposal now, I can at least entertain a modest hope regarding the manuscripts for my extensive study on the 19th century.

I understand the brevity of your letter; you must also understand the laconic nature of mine. Nothing beyond what is strictly personal is suitable for our correspondence at the moment. To remain within this frame, I shall first of all tell you that your letter of 8 July was the first message from you to reach me since my arrival in Lourdes. I did, on the other hand, receive a cable from Max[2] to inform me that a certificate confirming my work at the institute has been sent. I am counting on you to pass all my thanks on to him (which, on the other hand, must have reached him through Mme Favez). I am sure he will understand how difficult it is for me to write to him in as detailed and precise a fashion as is my custom and my wish.

I hope with all my heart that both his efforts and yours are proving successful. It is possible, even probable, that we have only a limited time at our disposal. I want you all to know how much confidence I have in your combined efforts, and that I am well aware of the difficulties posed by their resolution and the tenacity it demands of you. You can be sure, on the other hand, that I have maintained the only state of mind befitting someone exposed to risks that he should have foreseen, and which he brought upon himself in the knowledge of their causes (or almost).

I will try to obtain permission to go from here to Marseilles for a week or ten days. Mme Favez tells me[3] that Kracauer is staying there, near the American consulate, where he is attempting to arrange his immigration. Having registered a long time ago, he hopes that his case will progress fairly quickly. Regarding your deliveries, I would ask you to address them to Lourdes until further notice.

My sister,[4] who has been released from the camp, is here – in a rather precarious state. – As it is the first time since San Remo that I have been in the mountains, I am realizing all too clearly how weak my heart has become. It is likely that the emotions of the last few months have contributed to this state of affairs. And I am sure you will believe me if I tell you that a situation in which one can be subjected to the most abrupt changes from one hour to the next keeps you on your toes.

I took a single book with me: the memoirs of Cardinal de Retz. And so, alone in my room, I am appealing to the 'Great Century'.

Give all my regards to Teddie, and my devoted thanks to Max and his friend.

Ever your old

Lourdes (Hautes-Pyrénées)   Detlef
8 rue Notre Dame
19 July 1940

Original: manuscript. Translator's note: written in French.

1 Not preserved.

2 Sent on 5 July.

3 The letter in question from Juliane Favez, who was in charge of the institute's Geneva office, has not survived.

4 Dora Benjamin had been a prisoner in the camp at Gurs.

Index